TAKE THE
COLD
OUT OF COLD
CALLING

Web Search Secrets

Know More Than You Ever Thought You Could (or Should) About Your Prospects, Clients and Competition

Sam Richter

3rd Edition

According to a CSO Insight study, if you practice Sales Intelligence—the art of knowing what's important to your prospects and clients—you'll close almost twice as much business versus those who "wing it." If information is power, then Take the Cold is "power on steroids." You'll learn how to use the Web to research companies, industries, and people and use what you find to prepare for great meetings and presentations. You'll amaze your clients, differentiate from the competition, and win!

Includes Sales Intelligence Reference Guides, the CRMT Program with Warm Call Scripts, and access to the Warm Call Resource Center

ISBN 13: 978-1-59298-209-7
ISBN 10: 1-59298-209-3

Library of Congress Catalog Number: 2007943892

Book design and typesetting: Mighty Media, Inc. and SBR Worldwide, LLC

Printed in the United States of America. Third Printing.

11   10   09   5   4   3

Beaver's Pond Press

Adams Business & Professional
an imprint of Beaver's Pond Press, Inc.
7104 Ohms Lane, Suite 101
Edina, Minnesota 55439 USA
(952) 829-8818
www.BeaversPondPress.com

To order, visit www.takethecold.com or e-mail info@sbrworldwide.com. Reseller and special sales discounts available.

The Legal Stuff

For informational purposes only, this book contains the names and Web addresses of Web sites created, maintained, and controlled by other organizations. All materials, images, logos, etc. contained herein are copyright and property of their respective owners. Names of products, services, or organizations mentioned in this book may be protected by trademark and copyright. Other applicable federal and state laws may also protect the sites that are listed, mentioned, and reviewed in this book. SBR Worldwide, LLC has no responsibility and assumes no liability of any nature for the content of any Web Site that is mentioned in this book. The Web addresses were verified prior to the printing of this book edition. The content of these sites may change. The authors and publishers of this book, SBR Worldwide, LLC and Sam Richter, are not connected to these sites other than sites created by and maintained by SBR Worldwide, and do not endorse the present or future content of these sites. These Web sites are provided for your convenience and are not intended as an endorsement by SBR Worldwide, LLC and/or Sam Richter of the organizations operating these sites, a solicitation to contribute to these organizations, nor as a warranty or endorsement of the information the sites contain. A listing or mention of a Web site in this book does not preclude enforcement of those laws by other site owners should a violation of law occur with respect to your use of material on that site. Furthermore, the existence of a mention or review of a Web site in this book does not operate as an indemnification of your misuse of information contained on that site. SBR Worldwide, LLC is not responsible for any loss of business you may incur based on using any information contained in this book, or on any Web site mentioned in this book. By reading this book and/or by visiting any of the Web sites mentioned in this book, you assume any and all risk including any business risk.

Table of Contents

This book is dedicated to ...

Robin, Madeline, and Kameron
– thank you for your patience and
support in helping me help others.

My parents, family, teachers, coaches,
and friends for encouraging me
that anything is possible through
hard work, creativity, and integrity.

Thank you ...

To my many friends, family and colleagues who pushed me to write this book and who have reviewed it and revised it along the way. I couldn't have done it without you.

Special thanks to Robin, Julie, Cathy, Spenser, Wayne, Don, Stuart, Joel, Peggy, Ted, Fran, Walter, Joani, Robb, Sheila, Mom, Dad, and many others for your support and encouragement.

To Harvey Mackay for his support, passion and teachings.

To David Avrin for his coaching and ideas.

To the members and chairs of Vistage for your support and continual education.

To the Edward Lowe Foundation for making its beautiful retreat center in Cassopolis, Michigan available to me so I could spend time writing without distraction (along with a myriad of hotels across the globe, and late-night airplane flights).

To the incredible staff at the James J. Hill Reference Library who understand how the right information can be the key to personal and business success.

To my amazing colleagues at ActiFi for their support and friendship, along with their passion towards a singular focus of serving others and exceeding client expectations.

To Milt Adams, Joe Moses, and Beaver's Pond Press for your guidance.

And finally, to the folks at Dunn Brothers Coffee and Caribou Coffee, both in Minnetonka, MN, for keeping the java hot and the wireless-Internet access working.

What This Book Is, What This Book Is Not

In the past fifteen years, I have had the opportunity to make presentations to thousands of businesspeople across the globe. My topics have ranged from traditional marketing to online marketing, from e-commerce development to leadership development. In 1995, I created a presentation entitled "The Little Engine That Could" and introduced to marketing and public-relations professionals the value of the World Wide Web as a communications and research tool, and how to use popular Internet search engines to find information that could be applied in helping clients manage their business and reputation.

Simultaneously, I was reading a number of books on effective sales and attending numerous sales presentations. All of these training programs and books talked about the importance of preparing for sales meetings by having information about the other person. What they never talked about was HOW to find the information for proper preparation.

Thus, I started writing the outline and brief for a book that combined what I was presenting related to online information, and what I was learning about the importance of research and questioning in the sales process.

Fast forward a few years and in late 2001, I was named president of the James J. Hill Reference Library, the nation's premier non-profit, open-to-the-public source for practical business information (the kinds of information one needs for business plans, marketing proposals, and sales strategies). It was literally my first couple of weeks on the job when I received a phone call from the University of St. Thomas asking me to present to a group of Twin Cities' businesspeople and business students about the Hill Library and how to find information that could be helpful in business.

Not knowing too much about the Hill Library and certainly not skilled at all in the techniques librarians use to find information, I resurrected my "Little Engine That Could" speech and presentation, praying that the information was still relevant. My obvious fear was that four years later, I'd be presenting information that the audience deemed very basic. To my stunned surprise, the presentation went off quite well and teaching people—even students who had "grown up" using the Internet—how to find information was as relevant, and maybe even more important, than four years earlier.

The revelation that the majority of Internet users have little knowledge on how to actually locate relevant, timely, credible, and objective information really shouldn't have been such a shock to me. It's a skill that generally is not taught in schools or universities. It is just assumed that if you know how to use the Internet, you know how to effectively find information via popular search engines like Google and Yahoo. However, when you talk with most people about their ability to find information using online means, millions of search results are commonplace and although most rank themselves fairly high on their ability to use search engines, most also admit they get frustrated trying to locate information they can trust in a timely manner.

I was delivering a presentation in Atlanta when the central importance of searching the Web in improving sales became abundantly clear. Here is how Bud Carter, the leader of the group that invited me to speak, described it to me:

> *What you offer is a way for every sales call to be focused on the identified needs of the prospect. For the salesman to walk in more knowledgeable, in some cases, than existing vendors, with the confidence that credibility creates, can be the key to sales success. The question alluded to in your presentation to my group, but never specifically stated, is 'Who will be more effective, who will be more likely to get the order; the guy who comes in*

and dazzles the prospect with his canned Power-Point presentation, or the guy who walks in and completely understands his prospect's business issues and is able to provide solutions?"

Bud's comments were truly an epiphany for me. I found my old outline and book brief about combining research and online information with the sales process and started revising and updating it. Instead of alluding to, I emphatically stated that the confidence that comes from information is integral to sales and business development success.

Cold calling does not work. Warm calling based on Sales Intelligence does, and it can make a dramatic improvement in your and your company's performance. Knowing what's important to your prospects is imperative for proper meeting preparation. Information is the key to building your credibility, offering customized and relevant solutions, and providing ongoing client value. Understanding your client's world is ultimately what differentiates one company—and one salesperson—from the other.

Knowing what's important to your buyers, and how your solutions can help them achieve their objectives, is the key to winning new business – regardless of economic conditions. When your prospects say "I don't have the budget," what they're really saying is "you don't understand my issues and my objectives and you haven't shown me how your solutions can specifically help me achieve my goals." When you show your knowledge of a prospect's situation and share stories of how you've helped other firms in similar situations, magically budgets appear. Through Sales Intelligence, you have a greater chance of proving a true return on investment.

Take the Cold Out of Cold Calling: Web Search Secrets - Know More Than You Ever Thought You Could (or Should) About Your Prospects, Clients and Competition is not your typical sales or business-related book. It is not designed to motivate you as a salesperson, business development officer, or account manager; although salespeople, business development officers, and account managers who have learned and practiced the techniques discussed in this book have motivated themselves

SAM TIP

In my opinion, the Dale Carnegie classic *How to Win Friends and Influence People*, is one of the best books ever written for those in sales and business, and it should be memorized before reading other sales books.

The book is all about the power of relationships, building trust with people, and becoming an overall better person and leader.

If you master what that book has to teach, you'll naturally become a great salesperson. I have read the book numerous times and try to read it cover to cover at least three times per year.

and their companies to achieve results they could not have achieved before.

This book is also not designed to teach you the art and skill of selling; for that I recommend books like *Customer Centric Selling* from Michael T. Bosworth, *The New Solution Selling* by Keith M. Eades, *Action Selling* by Duane Sparks, *Little Red Book of Selling* by Jeffrey Gitomer, *Beyond Selling Value* by Mark Shonka and Dan Kosch, *Selling to Big Companies*, by Jill Konrath, *The Accidental Salesperson*, by Chris Lytle, and of course *Swim With the Sharks Without Being Eaten Alive* by Harvey Mackay is a must read for anyone involved in sales and business development. I would also recommend attending a Solution Selling presentation, a Miller Heiman training session, an Action Selling program, The Track Selling System Workshop, or a Dale Carnegie sales training course in your area.

Take the Cold Out of Cold Calling is a reference guide for how to practice Sales Intelligence. Use what you learn to prepare for any sales call, sales presentation, client meeting, prospect meeting, for account management, and even for strategic and marketing plan development.

Think of the last sales training book you read or seminar you attended. Most likely, there was at least a chapter in the book or a few minutes at the seminar discussing the value of research prior to a sales call. But what you probably didn't see was step-by-step instructions on *HOW* to conduct research and where to look for relevant and credible information. My aim is to solve the research puzzle for you.

The first few chapters of *Take the Cold Out of Cold Calling* are more theoretical in nature to help form the base for the reference guide portion of the book. The later chapters feature practical online information techniques and sources designed to help you learn more about clients, competitors, industries, and people. The final chapters combine the theoretical and the practical with real-world case studies where I research privately held companies, and then use the information in hypothetical warm calls.

Most of the sales books referenced above, and almost all books related to successful selling considered credible, have chapters related to preparing for meetings and the art of asking your prospects questions, so you can make the relevance of your company's products or services clear. Most good sales books teach how to sell benefits and value, and that proper prospect questioning can ensure that you'll position your solutions in ways that are meaningful to your prospect.

My aim with *Take the Cold Out of Cold Calling* is to take the art of questioning and put it on steroids. It's designed to position YOU as the knowledgeable expert. Contrary to popular belief, buyers are not buying your company or products in the first or even second sales meeting. Rather, they are buying you, your understanding of the buyer's business, their issues, their industry, and their competition. Buyers want to know if they can trust you, and the best and fastest way to establish trust is through a genuine and authentic understanding of the buyer and what he or she cares about by asking relevant and probing questions.

If you practice the techniques discussed in this book, you'll not only do a better job of questioning prospects and existing clients, you'll also be able to start predicting answers prior to even asking questions. You'll be armed with a "crystal ball" showing you what's on the mind of your existing prospects and clients that you can use as a preparation tool prior to meetings and planning sessions.

Take the Cold Out of Cold Calling will help you practice the "Platinum Rule" (more on that later) by providing you tips, tricks, and tools you can easily implement and incorporate into your daily sales life. From personal experience and through talking with thousands of company executives, salespeople, and buyers over my career, I know the process works; practice it and you will succeed.

Take the Cold Out of Cold Calling points you to online reference sources you can use to find valuable information that can be applied in any sales and/or account management process. You'll learn how to quickly find business-related information using popular search engines. You'll learn about the 80 percent of the business-Internet that isn't easily found through commercial search engines, and if you work for a smaller organization (chances are you do as 79 percent of all U.S.-based firms have between two and twenty employees), you'll learn how you can access the same professional business research resources found at Fortune 500 companies.

This book and the corresponding Warm Call Resource Center at **www.warmcallcenter.com** are sure to make you think about selling in a whole new light, and provide you the tools to execute your business development, sales strategies, and account management programs in a more effective, efficient, and ultimately successful manner. Imagine the confidence you'll have knowing that the questions you ask prospects and even current clients, and the solutions you can offer, are relevant to issues and problems you know they have.

I have spent more than twenty years in marketing and sales working on behalf of both small companies and some of the world's most famous brands. I've called on, designed programs for, and sold to executives at organizations throughout North America, so I know what it's like to be in a heated competitive situation related to winning and keeping business. I've also owned my own small company, so I understand the financial and time pressures faced by small businesses and appreciate the skepticism some may have about practicing the techniques discussed in this book for fear it will take time away from an already hectic day.

I wish someone had written a reference guide like *Take the Cold Out of Cold Calling* when I first started in business; although that would have been impossible as back then there was no such thing as the World Wide Web as we know it. With a reference tool like this, I could have provided so much more value to my clients beyond the task I was hired to do. I could have done a much better job preparing for meetings, and differentiating my company, my employers, and myself, from the competition.

In addition, my teams would have saved our employers thousands of hours, and untold dollars, because we would have had the information to make sound decisions based on facts, rather than "gut feelings," and hunches. Not that "gut feelings" and hunches are bad—successful business leaders count on them all of the time—however "gut feel" decisions based on objective and relevant facts are much more likely to deliver positive results.

There is an incredible world of information out there, most of it available for free, that when applied correctly can have a major positive impact on your business, on your career, and on your bottom line. In this book, you will learn how to quickly find relevant, credible information that can play a significant role in the planning process, the sales process, and most importantly, in your ability to provide client value.

Don't try and read *Take the Cold Out of Cold Calling* in one sitting. Rather, read the first few chapters so you understand the theory. Then like any reference book, use it when needed for a specific piece of information. Know that I've also sprinkled the book with resources that admittedly are less relevant to sales and more for your curiosity and enjoyment (or, as attendees to my presentations have told me, "you want to scare me with all of the personal stuff you can find online").

Finally, remember that you have access to the Warm Call Resource Center Web site at **www.warmcallcenter.com**, featuring direct links to all of the sites profiled in this book plus other valuable resources. Make sure to sign up for the Warm Call Newsletter so you can receive search tips and new sites as I discover them. And absolutely make sure to download the **Warm Call Toolbar** so you can access the best online business sites directly from your browser. I will automatically update your Toolbar with new sources for a very selfish reason: I use the Toolbar at least a half-dozen times every day.

My hope is that this book and its companion Web site and Toolbar become resources you rely upon prior to every sales call, every business planning session, every meeting with a new prospect, and every review session with an existing client. I know that if you practice the concepts outlined in this book that you will increase your sales call success rates. In addition, you'll also enjoy making sales calls more because with each prospect interaction, you're providing real value.

I hope you enjoy reading *Take the Cold Out of Cold Calling* and applying what you learn as much as I enjoyed writing it. I look forward to your feedback.

Sam Richter
sam@sbrworldwide.com

Foreword

During the past fifteen years, the World Wide Web has dramatically changed business as we know it. Just as dramatically, the Web has changed the world for anyone involved in sales and business development. Although there are literally thousands of books and training programs designed to help people improve their sales effectiveness, very few if any show how to take advantage of Web-based information tools to improve sales performance. *Take the Cold Out of Cold Calling* is the first such book.

In 1988 when I wrote *Swim With the Sharks Without Being Eaten Alive*, the World Wide Web was just a curiosity for most businesses, and it certainly was not a tool relied upon by sales and business development professionals. In the B2B space in particular, most business was done as it had been done for decades: Companies produced products or delivered services, marketing people tailored messages, and sales people were largely successful (or not) based on their personal networks and their ability to negotiate a fair price.

Exceptional sales people understood the lessons in Dale Carnegie's breakthrough book *How to Win Friends and Influence People*, a business and personal success "bible" written in 1936. Top sales people succeeded because they were able to build meaningful relationships based on getting to know clients and their concerns, and providing relevant solutions and value.

To help more sales people reach the "exceptional level," I wrote *Swim With the Sharks* and established the *Mackay 66 Customer Profile*—a tool for asking questions and organizing information—to help sales people learn about and document their customers inside and out. Get to know your clients, their needs, their industry, their customers, and learn how you and your company can provide value by solving real business issues, and you can quickly differentiate your company.

Fast forward to 2007, and while the rules for sales success are still the same, the techniques are much more sophisticated and difficult to execute. Why? Because in today's hyper-information world, it is not as easy to get an executive's attention and even have the opportunity to practice Carnegie's techniques. Unless an e-mail message or voice mail "breaks through the clutter" in the first few seconds, it gets prioritized to the bottom of the pile, or often, prioritized to the digital wasteland via the one-click action of a delete key.

If I had to name the single characteristic shared by all the truly successful people I've met over a lifetime, I'd say it is the ability to create and nurture a network of contacts. Your network is your secret weapon for getting in doors and establishing relationships with important people and business decisions makers.

However, in today's world of information overload, dropping a name or getting a referral might help get you a meeting, but it certainly won't help you establish credibility or make a great first impression. Your network might get you in the door, but when you have the opportunity to meet with a decision maker, you had better make sure you have done your homework.

No longer can you "wing it" during your first communication with a new contact. The precious time you have with a busy executive should not be wasted asking questions like "what's going on in your industry?" and "where do you see your company going in the next year?" You're expected to know that information. Unfortunately, knowing how to get that information before walking in the door is not taught in business schools, and not even in three-day sales training workshops costing thousands of dollars.

What Sam Richter has captured in *Take the Cold Out of Cold Calling* is not only the theory of why having credible and objective information is imperative, but unlike any sales training book or program, Sam also tells you how to gather the data. Sam's "Fourth R – Research" techniques opens up the incredible world of online information in a way that's easy to understand, and more important, easy to implement.

In 2006, Sam visited MackayMitchell Envelope Company and unveiled his unique program to our staff. To say our team was amazed is an understatement. Even our sales people who grew up using the Internet walked away shocked at what they didn't know, and stunned at the amount of information available online and accessible with a few mouse clicks.

Sam's system for organizing and applying information using his "Client Research Management System" perfectly complements the *Mackay 66*. Using Sam's techniques, we're now able to answer many of the questions in the "*66*" before we even walk through our prospect's door. By having a good understanding of our prospects, their companies, their industries, and the issues they face, we are able to make a great first impression and immediately establish our credibility. Our people are able to ask highly relevant questions, and we're able to get right to the heart of how our custom direct-mail solutions can solve what can sometimes be complex business and marketing issues.

If you wish others to believe in you, you must first convince them that you believe in them. If you believe that your growth is predicated on your ability to help others achieve their goals, then what Sam provides in the following pages is the jump-start to helping you achieve your own.

Harvey Mackay
www.harveymackay.com

CHAPTER ONE

The Emotional Ride of the Sales Call

"If you want others to like you, if you want to develop real friendships, if you want to help others at the same time you help yourself, keep this principle in mind: Principle No. 1 is 'Become genuinely interested in other people'."
– Dale Carnegie, *How to Win Friends and Influence People*, New York: Simon and Schuster, 1936.

Before we begin, let's set the record straight and make sure we're on the same page. I want you to ask yourself this question: Do you cold call? When I give presentations to any group other than a sales meeting and ask this question, very few hands in the room go up. So it's likely that you answered "no" to this question.

Now ask yourself these questions: As part of your job, do you ever meet with new clients? Has a friend ever invited you out to coffee to meet with someone who could become a client? Have you ever been paired in a golfing event with someone who could be beneficial to you or your business? Have you ever attended a networking event where you know a potential client will also be? Do you ever meet with people as part of your job?

If you still answered no, please return this book or give it to a co-worker. If you answered "yes" to any of the questions, congratulations, you're now officially a salesperson. In fact, any person in your company who encounters clients and prospective clients is a salesperson to some degree, but that's another book altogether. And unless you're already practicing the techniques outlined in this book meaning you know a lot of information about the other person and their issues prior to every prospect meeting, you're officially a cold call salesperson. **Everybody at one time or another cold calls!**

Now let me also be blunt—**COLD CALLING DOES NOT WORK.** That probably sounds odd from someone who wrote a book about the topic. But I don't believe in cold calling. Rather, I'm a huge believer of **"warm calling"** based on Sales Intelligence. The "how" of warm calling is what you're about to learn, and what this book and its corresponding resources are designed to help you practice.

From an emotional perspective, a "cold" sales call where you meet with a prospect and you're not prepared, is uncomfortable at best, and downright scary for most people. Whether your job is making phone calls off of prepared lists or calling on prospects following referrals, if you don't have a good understanding of the prospect, the prospect's issues, and the value your company's solutions can provide, cold sales calls just aren't very much fun (for you or the prospect).

Yet for most companies, calling on prospects without an existing relationship is as important to the firm's survival as quality products and/or services. It's typically the only way to ensure a consistent pipeline of potential new business, an imperative in challenging economic times where future revenue from existing clients is unknown. Revenue forecasting is done in the executive offices with fancy financial software. Yet the success of almost any business comes down to those responsible for hitting the sales numbers. Let's look at a hypothetical scenario using the traditional roles of inside and outside sales:

- **CEO:** "Our first quarter budget is $10 million in *new* sales." (No one is really sure how this number came to be, but it's a nice round number and an increase over the year before.)

- **Sales VP:** "Okay, if the number is $10 million and our average sale is a little more than $15,000, we must close 666 new sales." (My devilish sales figure is pure coincidence, but it is no wonder that so many in sales often consider their jobs some form of eternal damnation for past sins.)

- **General Sales Manager:** "That's more than we've ever sold before, but we have new products and a 12 percent growth rate over last quarter isn't impossible." (The Minnesota Vikings winning the Super Bowl during my lifetime isn't technically impossible either.)

- **Outside Sales Manager:** "Well, we have ten outside sales reps, the people who actually make the physical presentations to the customer. We typically close 30 percent of all sales calls where we make a formal presentation; therefore we need to make 2,222 presentations during the quarter or 740 per month. That comes out to about four in-depth phone or in-person sales calls per day per sales rep." (Where's my résumé?)

- **Inside Sales Manager:** "When my team makes prospecting calls over the phone, we typically can get a follow-up appointment with a customer 6 percent of the time. I have twenty-five inside telephone-sales representatives, the folks who qualify the prospects and set up the appointments, so we need to make a total of 12,333 phone calls per month or actually talk to twenty-five customers per representative per day. (Where's my résumé?)

- **Outside Sales Rep:** "Four in-person calls per day? Plus e-mail, plus proposal writing, plus travel?" (I hope my kids don't 911 when I come home at night because they see a strange person in the house.)

- **Inside Sales Rep:** "Twenty-five prospect conversations per day? Okay." (Can I still join the Army?)

Take a few minutes and breathe. If you're in any form of sales, you've most likely been a part of a similar example, your heart is beating faster, and your blood pressure has increased just by reading and visualizing your own experiences or worse, your current reality. My chest is tight just after writing it because I've been there and have lived "the impossible sales goal." Granted, the above example is representative of a mid- to large-sized company, but the example occurs every year, every quarter, and every month by many organizations.

In smaller companies, although the numbers might be in the hundreds of thousands of dollars versus the tens of millions, the pressure is just the same, if not higher. In smaller organizations, typically the inside sales rep, the outside sales rep, and sometimes even the sales manager are all the same person wearing multiple hats throughout the day.

In smaller organizations, the salesperson is usually the one setting the appointment, meeting with the customer/client, and reporting to executive management. Often, the salesperson in a smaller firm *is* executive management and often is the owner. Meaning that "hitting the numbers" is more than keeping the boss happy. In smaller organizations, you have to hit the numbers to keep the lights on, keep employees paid, and sometimes to keep the house.

Now for the good news: impossible sales goals are only impossible if you continue to sell the same old way. Sales should be more than hitting the numbers. Sales should be providing a client a valued product or service that solves a real problem; do that and the money will follow.

The Webster Dictionary defines sales as "the act of selling; *specifically*: the transfer of ownership of and title to property from one person to another for a price." Those in selling, those passionate about providing benefits to clients and also receiving the rewards of providing that benefit, believe selling is so much more.

My dear friend, Don Craighead, believes selling, or as he terms it, "being a peddler," is one of the more honorable professions one can undertake. When done right, selling not only solves a client's problem but in small and sometimes even in big ways, selling improves the client's life. (Many times, what I've sold has helped my client achieve their personal business objectives allowing them to receive their annual bonus.)

It is this overall mindset that differentiates the great salespeople from the average ones. The average salesperson wants to hit quotas; he/she wants to "hit the numbers." The great salesperson wants to hit quotas but also knows what problems the client faces and how the product or service he or she is selling can be a solution to that problem.

Def. of selling

The great salesperson wants to be prepared to provide value with every interaction. The great salesperson knows that by providing valued solutions, "hitting the impossible sales numbers" becomes possible. The goal is not the numbers. Rather, the goal is providing value, differentiating oneself from the competition, creating loyalty, and ultimately making the life of the buyer better. Accomplish that and the numbers take care of themselves.

Learning to become a great salesperson, business development officer, or account manager who provides value brings with it an additional, very personal benefit, one that extends beyond increased bonuses and commissions. The fact is that a great salesperson providing value to clients is a salesperson that is going to have fun.

The average salesperson's life can be one of drudgery dealing with constant rejection and clients insisting on lower prices. The great salesperson, however, is one who provides solutions, has the client's respect, and is a valuable member of a client's team. The great salesperson is determining more ways to provide relevant solutions, high value, thus resulting in greater margins (and greater commissions).

What are the day-to-day emotions that an average salesperson has to deal with? Imagine every day going to work, staring at a list of companies or names that you know nothing about, and then having to make phone or in-person calls hawking products that you have no clue whether your prospect needs or desires.

Every call is prefaced with a fear of rejection. Once you hear "no" repeatedly, it is natural that you would begin to feel depressed. Frustration probably sets in regularly. You believe you have to manipulate to close a deal. Friday afternoon is your favorite time of the week. You dread Mondays. You long ago forgot the meaning of positive self-confidence.

Contrast these emotions with the emotions of the great salesperson who sells value with each interaction. Imagine what you would feel like knowing that every sales call you make provides a relevant and important solution to a problem you know your prospect is probably facing.

When you prepare, how much fun are you having each time you meet with a prospect? How good do you feel about your company and yourself knowing that what you offer will provide value to the person across the table? How much confidence do you think you exude? You'll probably still look forward to Fridays. But every Monday you'll wake up excited to go to work and provide value to clients.

If you're in sales, you like people (if you don't like people, save yourself a life of frustration and introduce yourself to a new career opportunity). As I'll mention numerous times throughout this book, people buy from people. People buy from people they like. People like people they trust. People trust people who genuinely care for the well-being of others. If you genuinely care about the well-being of your clients, then you want to provide them with solutions to problems you know they're experiencing.

When you're providing real value and helping clients solve a mission-critical need, another benefit happens: the typical rejection statement of "I like what you offer but I don't have any budget" starts to disappear. It's amazing how most companies can find money for a solution that helps them achieve their objectives faster, cheaper, and/or better than they could do on their own. When you provide real, meaningful value and return on investment, you can succeed in any economic environment. In fact, in challenging environments, you can thrive versus your competition.

As a salesperson—and to emphasize again, all of us in business who come in contact with customers/clients are to some degree involved in sales—there is truly no greater feeling than knowing you helped your clients overcome an issue they were facing, and receiving fair compensation for solving that problem. A truly wonderful sales experience is one where there is an exchange of true value: you exchange a solution to a client problem and in return, they return the exchange by signing an invoice and processing a check. A salesperson who consistently provides and receives value is one who is recognized by peers and superiors as one of the best, will receive the top compensation, and will go to work each day expecting to have fun.

CHAPTER TWO

Sales Intelligence: Turning Cold Into Warm

"If there is any one secret to success, it lies in the ability to get the other person's point of view and see things from that person's angle as well as from your own."

– Henry Ford

In the July/Aug. 2006 issue of Harvard Business Review, an article by Thomas Stewart noted that a major shift was occurring in the world of selling, primarily, the change in buying behavior. Stewart's article discusses how the Internet has changed the buying process. Prospects and clients have ready access to a wealth of product information, service reviews, and company data via vendor Web sites, blogs, social networks, etc.

When prospects meet with a salesperson, they are frequently already up to speed at least on the basics (if not the details) of what a salesperson is selling. Stated another way, because of the Internet and company Web sites, your prospects have "Buyer Intelligence."

With prospects already informed about the solutions offered by the salesperson's company, during the initial meeting, if the salesperson is unable to prove that their solutions meet a defined need and solve a real problem, there most likely won't be a second meeting. Yet what Stewart noted was that while buying processes have evolved in our world of instant communication, for most companies, selling processes have in general have remained the same.

If your prospects have Buyer Intelligence, what is the process for turning cold sales calls into warm ones? The answer is Sales Intelligence.

According to a 2007 study by CSO Insights, Sales Intelligence is one of the most effective tools for improving a salesperson's and a company's sales effectiveness. When a salesperson understands the prospect – the company, the industry focus, the issues the prospect is facing, and even details about the individual with whom the salesperson is meeting – the salesperson is able to customize the presentation and conduct a meaningful warm sales call – and get results that crush the competition who conduct standard cold sales calls.

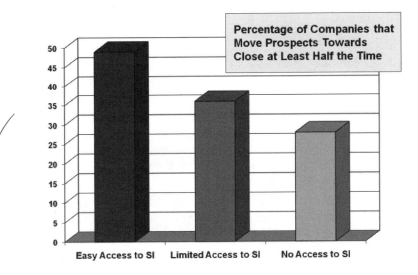

Percentage of Companies that Move Prospects Towards Close at Least Half the Time

The following chart from the CSO Insights study shows the improvement in close ratios when a company's sales team embraces Sales Intelligence (SI):

The above chart shows that more than 48% of the companies that make Sales Intelligence easily accessible are able to move prospects further down the buying path at least half the time, compared to only 28% of sales organizations with difficult or no access to this type of knowledge.

The data is clear: if you have access to information about your prospect and what your prospect cares about, you're more likely to make a great first impression, connect on a personal level, and provide relevant solutions. You're more likely to turn cold sales calls into warm ones. **Most important, the data shows that you're more likely to close the deal!**

Yet, according to the CSO Insight study, fewer than 10% of companies provide their sales reps the training and resources necessary to conduct Sales Intelligence. If you understand the concepts of Sales Intelligence, and more importantly, if you understand how and where to find information, and then how to apply what you've found, you will have a considerable advantage over the competition. You'll turn your cold sales calls into warm ones where the buyer is actually excited to meet with the seller (especially after the first meeting) because the buyer knows he or she is going to receive real value and solutions that solve real and immediate issues.

Let's look back at our example. Instead of an unprepared "cold sales call" where the discussion invariably quickly turns to product features and price, what if the inside and outside sales representatives practiced Sales Intelligence? What if they knew what problems the prospect faced and knew how they could solve the prospect's problems? For example:

- **Standard Telephone Cold Call:** "Hi ... I'm Sue from Acme Corporation and I was hoping I could set up a time for one of our representatives to stop by and show you the specs and PowerPoint presentation for our new Widget Robotic Manufacturing System."

- **Value-Based Telephone Warm Call:** "Hi, Mr. Jones. My name is Sue Smith and I'm calling from Acme Corporation. I read the recent article in *Widget Digest* where your CEO, Ed Anderson, was quoted saying one of the biggest issues you're facing is your competition outsourcing to Asia. I found that comment interesting because my firm has a new Widget Robotic Manufacturing System that we've implemented at companies just like yours and we've virtually eliminated low-cost outsourcing as an issue while simultaneously adding more than 10 percent to our clients' bottom line. I'd like to show you how we might help you achieve similar results."

Then, when the outside sales representative makes the in-person sales call, instead of showing product catalogs and discussing product features, a value-based, Sales Intelligence-based "warm" conversation takes place. For example:

- **Standard In-Person Cold Call:** "Hi ... I'm Joe from Acme Corporation. I really appreciate your taking thirty minutes out of your busy schedule to meet with me. I brought our product catalogs and I was hoping we could spend the next few minutes going through my PowerPoint presentation and talking about all of the new features of our Widget Robotic Manufacturing System and what makes Acme such a great company."

- **Value-Based, In-Person Warm Call:** "Hi ... I'm Joe from Acme Corporation. I really appreciate your taking thirty minutes out of your busy schedule to meet with me. First off, congratulations on your new promotion; I'm hoping what I'm going to show you today will help you "hit a home run" with your new supervisor right out of the gate. I did a little homework on your company; it seems like you're not experiencing the growth you're used to, and your CEO attributes that to overseas manufacturing competition. We work with a number of companies facing the same issues. I'd like to show you how our Widget Robotic Manufacturing System has solved our clients' problems and added on average 10 percent to their bottom line. Then I'd like to discuss how we might be able to do the same thing for your company."

In both scenarios, the inside and outside sales rep making the standard cold sales calls did what the majority of salespeople unfortunately do: They spent the limited time they have with a client talking about products/services. Showing catalogs and discussing features is nothing more than an egotistical exercise that ultimately leads to a sale only when the product or service offered is cheaper than the competition's.

For the inside and outside sales representative using the Sales Intelligence-based warm call approach, the interaction is more engaging. By taking time on the front end to learn about the client's problems, the sales rep was able to customize the pitch and tailor the solution to the client's specific needs.

A warm call is one that excites the client – you're solving problems and making lives easier. A warm call leads to company differentiation, even salesperson differentiation, which ultimately leads to more loyalty and more orders. Over the long term, the salesperson who consistently provides client value with every interaction becomes a valued business partner instead of just a product vendor. This is incredibly important because in challenging times, valued partners continue to receive orders while vendors contend in a battle of proposals against competitors, ultimately leading to price lowering.

In his book How to Win Friends and Influence People, Dale Carnegie perfectly sums up the warm call and providing exceptional value, and the benefit it has to the salesperson and the client. Carnegie states:

> *Thousands of salespeople are pounding the pavement today tired, discouraged, and underpaid. Why? Because they are always thinking only of what they want. They don't realize that neither you nor I want to buy anything. If we did, we would go out and buy it. But both of us are eternally interested in solving our problems. And if salespeople can show us how their services or merchandise will help us solve our problems, they won't need to sell us. We'll buy. And customers like to believe that they are buying, not being sold.*

Think in ways that benefit the client: think of what the client wants and solve the client's problems and issues. If you lay out the needs and wants of the client and how your product or service solves those problems, you'll sell more. It's a very simple process yet one that 90 percent of all salespeople ignore. Paraphrasing Carnegie, when you are "selling" it's a cold interaction where you're trying to convince your client to do something that he or she wasn't thinking of doing – purchasing something from you. However, when you solve problems, you are providing something that the client does want – you're making life easier for the client and you're solving a real need. Let's review the numbers from the earlier scenario:

To hit $10 million in new quarterly sales, there has to be 666 new sales per quarter. To accomplish this task, the twenty-five inside sales representatives must average twenty-five prospect contacts per day and get 6 percent of those calls to agree to see an outside sales representative. The outside sales force then must close 30 percent of those calls at an average sale of a little more than $15,000 per client.

What would happen if the inside sales rep consistently used a Sales Intelligence-based warm call approach and increased meeting rate percentages to 7 percent – a 1 percent increase? Using Sales Intelligence, what if the outside sales reps' close ratios jumped just 5 percent to 35 percent? The result: How about quarterly new sales revenue of $13,800,000 or a 38 percent improvement over the CEO's already incredibly aggressive goals! Too big of a jump, you say? Inside sales reps won't talk to that many prospects, and outside reps can't have that many meetings?

Using a warm-call sales approach with a 7 percent inside sales and 35 percent outside sales success rate, to hit the CEO's goal of $10,000,000 in new quarterly sales, the outside sales team only needs to conduct a realistic three sales meetings per day. To generate those meetings, the inside rep has to connect with approximately 18 prospects per day. So worst case, by employing a warm-call process, the company hits its goals and keeps the sales team from updating their résumés.

CHAPTER THREE

The Platinum Rule

SAM TIP ⬆
Platinum Rule:

"Do unto others as they would have done unto themselves."

What's going on in the other person's world, and how can you provide value? The Platinum Rule will change the way you sell, lead, and act towards other people. When you take the time to prepare and learn about the other person, you will build mutually beneficial and valuable relationships.

There is a great book and an entire suite of products and assessments, developed by Dr. Tony Alessandra, devoted to the Platinum Rule. You can find them online at www.platinumrule.com.

Dr. Alessandra has a process you can use to embed the Platinum Rule into all areas of your life. When you implement the Platinum Rule, you will be amazed at the great relationships you'll be able to build with other people. To learn more, visit www.alessandra.com.

In an initial sales meeting, whether it's with a new prospect or an existing account, why do buyers buy? If we assume that the goal of that first meeting is a second meeting or an opportunity to present a formal proposal, what causes a buyer to say, "I'd like to learn more about this company"?

You might be surprised at the answer. Most people think that buyers buy because of the product or service being sold, and the company selling it. That's why most salespeople during an initial sales meeting spend the majority of time selling their company and their company's solutions.

Remember, however, that most buyers already have "Buyer Intelligence." Most likely, your prospect already knows something about your company and its products or services or you wouldn't have even been invited to the discussion.

So while your marketing teams have developed fancy brochures and PowerPoint presentations and you've spent countless hours perfecting your company pitch and sales script, the reality is that during the initial sales call, those items are not what's most important to your buyer. Rather, what your prospect is really interested in is YOU.

While you're pitching your company, your buyer is asking himself or herself questions like: "Can I trust this person?" "Does this person have an understanding of my business?" "Does this person understand my issues?" "Can I relate to this person...are we connecting on a personal level?" "Do I like this person and can I see myself doing business with him or her on a long-term basis?"

This is even true in challenging economic conditions. As sellers, we often automatically think the major barrier to a sale is price. Although price is important, in most business-to-business sales opportunities, it is not the determining factor in moving the sales process forward.

A recent study by The Sales Board, creators of the Action Selling program, showed that the number one reason why customers actually choose to buy is NOT because of price; rather, it is because of a high-quality relationship with a salesperson. According to the study, the customer's relationship with the salesperson was cited SIX TIMES more often than price as the major factor determining buying decisions. The more the salesperson knows about his or her prospect, the more likely they are to develop a relationship that the buyer considers "high-quality."

Buyers want solutions to their immediate issues. They want you to solve a need faster, more efficiently, and with higher quality than they could do on their own. Remember Buyer Intelligence—you wouldn't even be there if the buyer didn't believe that your company had a beneficial solution.

To provide value, however, you need to have a complete understanding of what's important to the other person. What does your prospect or client care about? What's going on in his or her world? What are his or her issues? What would create a high degree of loyalty and help you develop a deep and meaningful business relationship?

If you want to provide value in every interaction every time, there is only one surefire way to accomplish that goal: **It's by practicing the Platinum Rule.**

Because it's been drilled into our heads by our parents, teachers, and clergy most of our lives, we all understand the Golden Rule, *"Do unto others as you would have them do unto you."* It's applicable in many areas of our lives, specifically in our relationships and interactions with others. For example, if you don't want to be lied to, do not lie to other people.

Now, close your eyes and slowly repeat the Golden Rule, and really think about its meaning specifically how it relates to sales: ***"Do unto others as you would have them do unto you."***

From a sales perspective, isn't that an exceptionally selfish statement? Why in the world should I think that what I want to sell is what you want to buy? What gives me the right to dictate to you your likes and dislikes? When it comes to relationships—and sales is all about relationships—I like to practice the Platinum Rule.

The Platinum Rule is higher than the Golden Rule. The Platinum Rule simply states: ***"Do unto others as they would have done unto themselves."*** Treat people like ***they*** would like to be treated, not how you would like to be treated. Sell what the other person wants to buy and needs, not what you need to sell to make your commission. Find out what is important to the other person and deliver!

Let me tell you a story that will probably help you remember the Platinum Rule. When I was in college, I played football and had to overeat just to maintain my weight. So almost every day after practice, I would stop at the grocery store on the University of Minnesota campus and purchase a Sara Lee cherry cheesecake. I would then eat the entire cheesecake, 30,000 calories and all. Needless to say, I LOVE cherry cheesecake and still can't pass up a slice when it's offered.

If you were coming over to my house for dinner, I would practice the Golden Rule. I like cherry cheesecake, so you must too. Guess what we're having for dessert?

Thank goodness my wife, Robin, practices the Platinum Rule. If you were a new friend and I invited you to my home for dinner, Robin would ask me for your phone number, call you, and see what you like to eat. She would "do unto others as they would have done unto themselves." A simple analogy? Yes. But what if you were allergic to dairy and I served cherry cheesecake? The Platinum Rule rules again.

How do you practice the Platinum Rule? Easy. You ask questions. How do you ask great questions as part of the sales process? Easy. You prepare. You gather and study information about the other person, their company and their industry. When you meet with your prospect or client, you ask questions about areas you know are important to them. Because you have Sales Intelligence, you already have a good idea about how your prospect or client is going to respond, and thus you are prepared for the next question. You stop talking about your company, and you start talking about topics you're 95 percent sure are important to the other person.

"Do unto others as they would have done unto themselves."
You build your credibility as you share your knowledge and experiences, you differentiate yourself from other sales people, and you share solutions and ideas that you know will provide value to the other person.

In a 2002 Cahners Research study of 23,000 purchasers of business-to-business products, 76 percent reported being "sick and tired" of salespeople who don't understand their client's business needs (I'm trying to figure out who the other 24 percent are; talk about easy sales). Buyers want salespeople to present unique solutions. Buyers want sellers who diligently practice the Platinum Rule. A "one size fits all" approach no longer cuts it, especially because the buyer knows that a comparable solution is a phone call or mouse click away.

A company cannot afford to employ a sales force whose sole talent is to send catalogs and make solicitation phone calls to general lists. A company can no longer afford to employ salespeople who don't see things from the other's point of view. Take a careful look at your sales force and sales process. If your company's sales calls, solicitation letters, and sales presentations are the same from prospect to prospect, if you sales team is not customizing your firm's communication in a way that is relevant to each prospect and each prospect's specific issues, you may need to make changes.

The Platinum Rule in the Account Management Process

Do you want to be a vendor that always competes on lowest price or a valued business partner that clients come to rely upon for solutions? A vendor is a company that can quickly be discarded: *"Your competition is 10 percent less expensive, so you'd better meet the price or I'll have to do business with them."* A valued partner, on the other hand, is a firm relied upon for solutions. A partner is very difficult to replace: *"I know their competition is 10 percent cheaper, but I can't put a price on the ideas I keep receiving, many of them having nothing to do with their business but a lot to do with growing mine."*

If providing value is integral to the sales process, it is critical in the account management process. Prospects become clients for many reasons, but the only reason clients become former clients is that they believe they are no longer receiving full value for the price they're paying. Okay, there are other reasons like your competitor marrying your client's daughter, but for the most part, losing a client means that somewhere along the line, you stopped providing value. Somewhere along the line, you screwed up.

Too many companies believe that once the contract is signed, they can stop paying attention to the clients' ever-changing world. **Too many stop practicing the Platinum Rule.** Think about your own vendors. Remember those initial sales calls where they seemed to genuinely care about you? You felt great receiving all of their personal attention.

Then what happened? Not too long after you paid your first invoice, the questions stopped. You signed the contract and the care they showed during the sales process magically disappeared. Within a year, you started noticing the competitor's ads. You started taking sales calls because you were interested in what their competition had to offer. You shopped around because you wanted to be well informed about all of your options. Ultimately, you might even switch.

Imagine after you sign your contract and pay your first invoice that the care shown to you in the sales process actually increased. How would you feel about your existing vendors if they consistently practiced one or more of these activities:

- Every time you or your company is mentioned in the press, they send you an e-mail congratulating you.

- About once a month, you receive a letter highlighting something that your competitor is doing, or a study related to recent trends in your industry, or some information about a potential piece of new business for you.

- When you get together, you're asked about your company goals and your personal objectives. Then the next morning you receive an e-mail referencing a piece of information or article relevant to what you discussed.

- On your birthday, you come to work and there's a hot cup of coffee and a slice of cherry cheesecake waiting on your desk (okay...I admit, this one's a bit selfish).

Forget the "Information Age" or the "Internet Age." We live in the "Value Age" where the difference between organizations and individuals that thrive and those that fail will be the ability to provide value in every interaction. What would you think about a company that consistently provides information and value as described above? My guess is that company would be considered a valued business partner, and when it has a program that it wants to sell, you'll listen.

In his best-selling book, *The Accidental Salesperson*, Chris Lytle has a chart that shows the various levels of prospect and client relationships (you can download Chris' chart at **www. apexperformancesystems.com/resources.aspx**).

Most salespeople "wing it." They don't know the client, and thus buying decisions are often based solely on cost. Great salespeople know their clients and their issues. They are trusted industry experts clients rely on for information. These great salespeople also command top dollar.

In today's "What have you done for me lately?" world, it is imperative that you continue to differentiate your company and yourself long after the sale is complete. Providing ongoing value above and beyond your clients' expectations is the way to turn cold client relationships into consistently warm client partnerships.

Being a reliable source of relevant, timely, credible, and objective information is one way of being a valued business partner. Knowing what is important to your clients and helping them meet their objectives is how you will remain a valued business partner with your clients long into the future.

Dedicate time each week to finding information that has everything to do with your clients achieving their goals, and little to do with you achieving yours. Send them a piece of research on their customer's industry. Locate information on one of their competitors. E-mail your client an article about a possible new business lead for him or her. Practice the Platinum Rule on a regular basis and become a true partner.

CHAPTER FOUR

"The Fourth R" – Research

"The real key to successful selling is finding out what people do. If you understand what they do, how they do it, when they do it, where they do it, who they do it with, why they've chosen to do it that way, and whether your product could help them to do it better, you're going to be successful."

– Stephan Schiffman, *Cold Calling Techniques*,
Holbrook MA: Adams Media Corp., 1999

Historically, students of business and sales are taught that success comes from mastering the traditional "Three Rs" of reading, writing, and arithmetic. If you learn to communicate effectively, write a good proposal, understand a financial spreadsheet, and manage a realistic budget, the chances are good you'll succeed in business.

In today's value-oriented business marketplace, the "Fourth R" – research – is the tool that truly differentiates one business from the next and one salesperson from the next. You need to understand the value of Sales Intelligence and how to quickly and ethically conduct research if you're going to effectively practice the Platinum Rule.

The "Fourth R" separates the traditional salesperson or account manager—who uses a cookie-cutter approach to serving client needs and thus consistently competes on lowest price—from today's successful client-centric, Sales Intelligence-based salesperson or manager who knows how to find relevant, credible, and objective information and apply it in ways that solve client problems in unique ways.

For most companies, the marketing and sales departments' performance determines the bottom line. Let's look a bit deeper at the value of research in sales by using a hypothetical case study.

Assume two companies are going to make a sales call to the VP of Marketing for a medium-sized financial institution. Both salespeople are selling a proprietary version of Customer Relationship Management (CRM) software. Both CRM systems have similar features, price points, and both companies are respected in the CRM space. Because the VP of Marketing has Buyer Intelligence, in the mind of the VP, when comparing the two companies, CRM software is a commodity.

Salesperson One meets with the VP and immediately launches into his PowerPoint presentation. He adeptly shows off his CRM system's bells and whistles and closes with a detailed listing of optional components price options. He leaves the VP a generic chart comparing the cost of the CRM system with the return on investment the VP could expect.

By all accounts, Salesperson One has done a nice job. He showed why his CRM system is different, offered a variety of price options, and produced a general analysis on how purchasing his CRM system will ultimately increase profits.

However, Salesperson One failed to provide his client any value; he did not differentiate his CRM company from competitors, and as a salesperson, he did nothing to differentiate himself from the next salesperson. He didn't show how his CRM system could solve his prospect's unique issues because he had little information on the prospect and what issues the VP is most likely facing. Instead of customizing his presentation, Salesperson One did a standard presentation, the same one he's given to hundreds of prospects. In the mind of the VP, Salesperson One and his CRM is still a commodity.

Salesperson Two practices Sales Intelligence and has embedded the Platinum Rule into her sales process. She meets with the VP and before even turning on her laptop, mentions that she really liked the recent article in the *Business Journal* featuring a profile of the VP. She was most impressed that he not only led a division of a large company, but that he had time to coach his daughter's soccer team and he was leader of his son's Boy Scout troop. She remarked that his time spent with family is impressive considering that the VP's company is doing 12 percent quarter over quarter growth, while the industry average is only 3 percent.

After additional small talk, Salesperson Two starts her official presentation. Instead of just showing her CRM system's features, she shares the benefits of her system and how it will directly impact the VP's business. They discuss how the flexibility of the CRM system is perfect for the VP who is looking to expand his sales force in the southeast. They discuss how the CRM system will seamlessly integrate into the VP's back office accounting package. She demos how her CRM system will work with the VP's largest client. At the end of the presentation, she discusses how her system can directly increase the VP's return on investment, and her charts use examples of how different divisions within the VP's company will use the system.

Salesperson Two used information to provide value; she practiced the "Fourth R." She researched and read articles about the company. She searched databases and found information on competitors and customers. She used proprietary content sources from her local library to search for additional information on the company's divisions and leaders. Salesperson Two differentiated herself from the competition.

At the end of the day, people still buy from people. When faced with two similar firms with two similar products priced approximately the same, the VP will choose Salesperson Two. She did her homework, she showed she understood what was important to the VP, and she provided value beyond what one would expect from a CRM software vendor. Salesperson Two showed how her product could solve the VP's unique issues. She got in the door and closed the deal by making exceptional use of Sales Intelligence and the "Fourth R."

Talk with anyone who is an expert at influencing people, from a minister to a politician to a great salesperson, and they all practice the "Fourth R." If you understand what interests the people you meet with, if you know what they genuinely care about, you can ask relevant questions and engage people to share what they most likely don't share with others.

In *How to Win Friends and Influence People*, Dale Carnegie shares a story about President Theodore Roosevelt and his adherence to practicing the "Fourth R" prior to meeting with people. Carnegie writes about Roosevelt:

> *Everyone who was ever a guest of Theodore Roosevelt was astonished at the range and diversity of his knowledge. Whether his visitor was a cowboy or a Rough Rider, a New York politician or a diplomat, Roosevelt knew what to say. And how was it done? The answer was simple. Whenever Roosevelt expected a visitor, he sat up late the night before, reading up on the subject in which he knew his guest was particularly interested. For Roosevelt knew, as all leaders know, that the royal road to a person's heart is to talk about things he or she treasures most.*

If the president of the United States can practice the "Fourth R," you certainly can. If you say that you don't have the time to conduct research on your prospects, I would challenge you to look at your daily calendar and imagine comparing it to the calendar of Roosevelt. The question you need to ask yourself is "do you want to be good at what you do, or do you want to be known as one of the best?"

Sales Intelligence through the "Fourth R," when applied correctly, is incredibly powerful. In a sense, the "Fourth R" can act as a crystal ball into the mind of your prospect and provide accurate insight into the core issues they most likely are facing. This crystal ball ensures that your conversation, and your offering, is relevant to your prospect's needs and it helps you craft engaging questions.

Companies spend tens of thousands of dollars sending salespeople to training seminars designed to teach how to ask better questions. The "Fourth R" is the complimentary "silver bullet" to any sales technique where the key success component is asking questions so the prospect shares key issues. Why? Because the "Fourth R" takes the guesswork out of knowing what kinds of questions you should ask.

Instead of generic questions, the "Fourth R" helps you tailor questions and establish your credibility in ways that are more likely to solicit a response. By having an informed understanding of the issues your prospect is most likely facing before you begin a meeting, you are able to ask relevant questions that are more likely to generate a meaningful response.

Imagine the dialogue you could engage in if you knew your prospect's annual revenue growth, the trends in your prospect's industry, how your prospect's competitors were performing, new products your prospect or its competitors were introducing into the marketplace, and even how your prospect's customers were doing and the issues they were facing.

When you're armed with relevant data, you're able to not only ask better questions, but you also massively increase your credibility. Remember, people buy from people. People buy from people they trust. And people trust people who can intelligently engage in dialogue that is relevant.

Asking a generic question like: "What are the key barriers to you achieving your objectives?" shows your prospect that you're a trained salesperson. Asking a prospect a question like: "I see that your biggest competitor, Widget Corporation, is coming out with a new product and I was wondering how you plan to differentiate yourself" shows your prospect that you're a sales professional who understands the market.

The "Fourth R" is a powerful tool that, once applied in every sales interaction, will elevate you to the top one percent of all salespeople. You'll elevate your value in the minds of your prospects from a vendor to a valued business partner. It is a critical component of practicing the Platinum Rule. You can't guess what is important to your clients. Rather, you must have accurate information if you're going to help clients in ways they want to be helped. The "Fourth R" techniques taught in this book to locate information will help you practice the Platinum Rule every time, for every meeting.

The good news is that virtually anyone can learn to master the "Fourth R." You don't have to attend library school. You don't need a private investigator's license. You too can learn to take the cold out of cold calling, and turn every sales call into a warm one.

Practicing the "Fourth R"

With the explosion of information resources available on the Internet, the answer to any question is seemingly "out there somewhere." Modern technology has brought access to information to an unprecedented level. Many good search engines are able to locate mass quantities of potentially valuable and usable data. Anyone with a computer and an Internet hook-up can freely access the information resources available via the World Wide Web.

Yet while the key to success in business may be sitting literally in your lap, it does not mean that you automatically have access to the complete world of business information resources available online. The most pertinent information is often either held under cyber-lock-and-key, buried in layers of citations, or available only to those with the financial means and expertise to find it. Knowing where to look and how to search is the key to tapping into targeted, relevant information.

Searching for information online can be very frustrating. Popular search engines like Google, Yahoo, MSN, and Ask continue to make amazing strides in their ability to gather information, adding tens of millions of Web pages to their databases and introducing new search features that make finding information easier and more personal. New search engines seem to launch every week, each with a new way to locate and display search results.

With all of the advances made in search technology, finding relevant, credible, and timely information online is challenging and time-consuming for most people. A 2004 study by research firm Find/SVP found that when it comes to businesspeople trying to locate business information online:

- 45 percent encounter broken links that do not work.

- 39 percent believe that information found online is out-dated and 21 percent are not confident that their search results come from credible sources.

- 55 percent said that they receive search results that are unfocused and provide irrelevant information.

The GUV 10th WWW Survey reported similar results with 42 percent of respondents reporting they often find "junk" when searching for information online and 45 percent reporting having to pay for the information they desire (of-tentimes being asked to pay for information that previously was available for free).

A 2006 Pew Internet Foundation study found that 75 per-cent of people who locate health information online don't bother to check the source of the information meaning it could be completely false! One can only assume that if people are not checking the source of information on something as important as health, they probably aren't checking to see whether the source of their business information is credible and objective either.

These studies and many others come to the same conclu-sion: people are often frustrated with what they find online, they're frustrated with how long it takes to find information, and they don't bother to check the validity of what they do find.

Yet at the same time where people say they are excep-tionally frustrated with locating information online, the Find/SVP study reported that 67 percent of businesspeople find it difficult or impossible to do their job without Inter-net research. Meaning that even though businesspeople are discouraged with searching and many don't even trust what they find, the large majority of businesspeople believe they couldn't do their jobs without regularly going online to find business-related information.

While the "free Internet" is an amazing resource with search engines providing an incredible window into the world of information, they actually cover a small percentage of the information available on the Internet via the World Wide Web*. In addition, anyone today with a computer can be a content publisher for very little cost, rendering a large proportion of the business-related content on the Internet biased and unreliable for those lacking the skills to differentiate one site from another.

In their 2000 book, *The Social Life of Information*, published by the Harvard Business School Press, John Seely Brown and Paul Duguid discuss the growing concern about coping with the amount of information to which we have access. They cite the Internet as a major information resource, but go on to equate the time spent looking for information on the Web with the daily experience of astronomers at the University of California, Berkley, "searching through an unstoppable flood of meaningless information from outer space for signs of intelligent life."

Knowing how to find information online can be very difficult and time consuming. Many people, even young people who have grown up using the Internet, have little knowledge of how to conduct efficient searches and, thus, waste an incredible amount of time searching the World Wide Web for business information.

According to a Gallup poll, the typical employee with Internet access spends approximately one-and-a-half hours per day online looking for business information (not including e-mail). Let's assume that the average employee generates $50 per hour for an employer:

This means that the average employee with Internet access is costing employers $19,500 per year in lost opportunity cost trying to find information online.

Or as a study produced by the information firm Factiva cited: U.S. companies waste approximately $107 billion per year having employees look for free information online, typically limiting their "online toolkit" to popular search engines like Yahoo and Google.

Adding to the "information gap" is the fact that much of the best business information available in electronic form is "cyber-locked up" in subscription databases typically affordable to only larger organizations or those who know how to locate similar information elsewhere. The perception is that "it's all out there for free" and "I can find anything using my favorite search engine" when the reality is completely the opposite.

In the Factiva study, 62 percent of businesspeople surveyed said that 100 percent of the business information they need is available on the "free" Internet. Those same businesspeople were then asked to list the sources they think are credible for their industry (e.g., *Wall Street Journal*, industry trade magazines). After reviewing the list, only 34 percent of the information sources even had free, searchable articles online. The data these businesspeople need is available online, yet ironically, in the "age of the free Internet and information," they just might have to pay for it.

Make no mistake, the Internet holds a wealth of data accessible via popular search engines if you know what questions to ask and how to ask them. There are thousands of valuable "hidden" data sources free to use if you know where to look. There are no-cost and affordable public and privately funded resources that provide access to proprietary subscription databases. And if you know where and how to look, you can even find online business information resources featuring experts to help you find the data you need (online and offline), often for free or at a reasonable cost.

By using the resources cited in the Resource Guide portion of this book, you will learn how to locate information that will help you take the cold out of cold calling, provide for a more effective sales process, practice the Platinum Rule, and create better business, marketing, and sales strategies and plans. Whether you're an entrepreneur starting your first business or the experienced sales manager of a mid-sized company, when you and your teams apply the practical knowledge contained in the pages hereafter, you're virtually guaranteed of saving time, saving money, and providing ongoing value to your clients thus ensuring long-term, mutually beneficial relationships.

Take the Cold
Out of Cold Calling

"Fourth R"
Resource Guide

Practical online searching tips you can immediately use to practice the "Fourth R" for effective Sales Intelligence

CHAPTER SIX

Is Your Sales Assistant Some Yahoo Named Google?

> "Nolan Ryan, the baseball great, once said, 'Pitching is easy. Preparation is hard,' This baseball truth is also true in the sales profession. 'Selling is easy. Preparing to sell is hard work.'"
>
> – Barbara Gerahaughty, *Visionary Selling*,
> New York: Simon and Schuster, 1998.

The original title for this book was going to be *Is Your Business Consultant Some Yahoo Named Google?* However, even though I'm going to share the reasons I think Yahoo and Google are so great from a salesperson's perspective, I didn't want to face the legal departments of either organization. In addition, Bud Carter's statement "you help take the cold out of cold calling" makes for a much better book title geared towards assisting sales teams.

Regardless, as the title of this chapter implies, there are a number of businesspeople and salespeople whose primary information consultant or assistant is a search engine like Yahoo or Google. As you'll learn in later chapters, there is much more to online information than Yahoo and Google and in fact, popular search engines actually "search" a very small portion of the business information available online.

However, Yahoo, Google, MSN, Ask, and other popular search engines are still very powerful business information tools when used properly. "Used properly" is the key phrase.

In a recent Find/SVP study, 72 percent of those surveyed felt that they would be more efficient at work if there were better Internet search tools. After presenting and training thousands of businesspeople, I can emphatically report that it's not better Internet search tools that are needed. Rather, what the majority of businesspeople need is better search education. Here are some startling results, and some editorial, from the Find/SVP study:

- **84 percent of online American adults have used search engines. That amounts to 210 million people. On any given day, 56 percent of those online use search engines.** [Based on my presentations to thousands of business people across the country, I believe that more than 90 percent of business people and salespeople use search engines each business day.]

- **92 percent of those who use search engines say they are confident about their searching abilities, with over half of them, 52 percent, saying they are "very confident."** [Scary. I guarantee you that the majority of people who are confident about their searching abilities know very little of what we're going to discuss in upcoming chapters. The good news for you is if you study and practice the ideas discussed in *Take the Cold Out of Cold Calling* you'll be way ahead of your competition.]

- **87 percent of online searchers say they have successful search experiences most of the time, including 17 percent of users who say they always find the information for which they are looking.** [I can only conclude that they're searching for some basic information. Ask any salesperson if they're able to find detailed financial information on a private company using search engines and the success rates will be in the single digits.]

Popular search engines are incredibly powerful and when used correctly can return credible and relevant search results usually within the first 40 result listings. You must, however, think of a search engine like Yahoo or Google as a big filter: if you put junk in at the top of filter, regardless of how powerful the filter, you're still going to get junk out. Put "good stuff" in the top and you're going to get good results out.

The next few chapters are designed to help you learn how to input better information into "search engine filters" so you can start to get the search results you're looking for the first time, every time. I guarantee you that when used, the following tips and tricks will cut your searching time by a third, maybe even by half. For anyone in business development and sales whose time is money, these tips represent significant savings of both. Just as importantly, the results you'll receive will be timely, more relevant, and more credible than ever.

As this book is not meant to be the epitome of a "become a better salesperson" book, the next few chapters are not meant to be the ultimate guide to using search engines like Google and Yahoo either. For that, I recommend *Google Hacks: 100 Industrial-Strength Tips & Tools* by Tara Calishain; *Google: The Missing Manual* by Rael Dornfest; *Google and Other Search Engines: Visual QuickStart Guide* by Alfred Glossbrenner; and *Yahoo! The Ultimate Desk Reference to the Web* by HP Newquist. One of my favorite search engine experts is Chris Sherman and his book *Google Power: Unleash the Full Potential of Google.* I would highly recommend Sherman's book to anyone who wants to learn the full power that Google offers to the casual and serious searcher.

For those involved in the sales process, however, the next few chapters will provide a quick Sales Intelligence guide you can count on to help find information you can use to practice value-based/solution-based warm call selling. I've used these techniques on a regular basis to cut my searching time dramatically. I can personally attest to how I've been able to find information on companies, industries, and individuals that not only impress others in a sales call, but allow me to tailor my sales pitch and provide value during the cold call.

CHAPTER SEVEN

Types of Search Engines

Not all search engines are built alike. Search engine companies typically earn revenue by "capturing eyeballs," meaning the more people who use a particular search engine, the more that engine can charge for banner advertising and pay-for-placement search listings. Therefore, each search engine offers and markets unique features that can make a difference in the time it takes to find good information, and in the types of results you see. Knowing which type of search engine to use for a particular search is the first place to start before conducting your search.

Directory Engines

There are two primary types of search engines: directory engines and index engines. A directory engine really isn't a search engine at all in the truest definition. Rather, a directory engine is a list of Web site links organized into categories and subcategories by human beings. Yahoo was one of the first commercially popular directory engines.

A directory engine is somewhat like a traditional library in that a human reviews an information source and the source is then placed in a category/subcategory that is logical and intuitive to find. So imagine, in the basement of Yahoo, they have hundreds of employees looking at Web sites all day and placing those sites into very logical categories and subcategories, making it easy and intuitive to locate information.

For example, let's say you're making a sales call on a plastics manufacturer and you quickly want to learn a bit about key companies in that space. You log into Yahoo and click on the More tab and then the Directory link on the pull-down menu.

SAM TIP ➤
Yahoo Directory:

A directory is the online equivalent of a library where information sources are reviewed and placed in logical categories and subcategories.

1. Go to: **www.search.yahoo. com/dir**

2. Type in a very broad search term (e.g., medical).

3. You'll see a list of related categories; click on one for results under that category.

4. Or directly underneath each search result you'll see the category that result was assigned to.

5. Click on a category for a listing of subcategories and related Web sites.

Or you can access the Yahoo Directory by going directly to **www.search.yahoo.com/dir**. Enter the world "plastics" and click "search." At the top of the results page, you find five main categories related to plastics.

By clicking on the fourth category/subcategory "B2B > Materials > Plastics," you're presented with seven subcategories. By clicking on the Manufacturing subcategory, you instantly see a listing of hundreds of plastics manufacturers.

So literally, within two clicks of entering the broad search term "plastics," you can get to exactly what you're looking for; a list of plastics manufacturers. The Directory search on Yahoo and other search engines is an easy and logical way of finding information on a broad subject topic.

Once you're in a particular category, you can restrict your searching to within that specific category. On the top of the search form box, there are three radio buttons. Choose the "this category" button and search for results only within that category. Using our plastics example, if you were to enter *California* into the search box and restricted your search to "this category," the results that appear are related to plastics in California.

SAM TIP
Directory Engines:

Remember that human beings build directory engines, so the number of information sources you're searching is going to be limited.

Use a directory engine to get overviews on a particular topic.

Using our plastics example where the subcategory listed a few hundred plastic manufacturers, it's safe to say that these are probably *some* of the key firms in the plastics industry, but for certain they are not every plastics manufacturer in the world or even in the U.S.

Index Engines

An index engine is really a true search engine as we know it, meaning it searches the World Wide Web for a list of results most closely matching what the searcher entered into the search form. If you discount the paid search listing inclusions, an index engine has no human involvement at all in its results listings and the results are only as good as the quality of the words or groups of words originally entered into the search form.

Google is the world's most popular index engine, although most popular search engines today use an index engine as the primary method for displaying results. Even Yahoo, when you first conduct a search, shows index engine results.

Think of an index engine as a big vacuum cleaner that scours the World Wide Web looking for Web sites with words on them. Once an index engine finds words, it "vacuums" them up and dumps them in a massive database. When you enter a word or words into the search form, all the index engine is basically doing is saying "Okay ... someone is searching for this word or words; where do those words appear most often in our database of 'vacuumed' Web pages?" Then the index engine delivers the list of results.

So, for example, when you go to Google and type in the word "plastic," all Google is doing is saying "Okay ... this person wants to know every Web site we have with the word 'plastic' in it, so here you go."

We told Google that we want every Web page that Google found with the word "plastic" in it, so Google will display almost two hundred million search results! In addition, the search results cover all topics related to plastic, from "plastic surgery" to "plastic products."

There are business rules and mathematical algorithms that determine how index engine results are ranked; however, the model above basically describes how most index engines work. Unlike directory engines where humans logically list categories and subcategories of Web sites, index engines are entirely dependant upon the information the user enters into the search form. Therefore, if you do a poor job of entering information into the search form, the search engine is going to do a poor job of delivering search results.

So Remember ... "Garbage In, Garbage Out." The better job you do entering information into the search form, the better results you'll get.

You probably just had one of those "A-ha" moments. Finally, you have the answer to why you get millions of search results every time you use your favorite search engine. That still begs the question: When doing research for the sales process, when should you use a directory engine vs. an index engine? The good news is that the answer is really quite simple:

- **Directory engine:** Use a directory engine when you want information on a broad subject (e.g., key topics related to a particular industry).

  BROAD TOPIC

- **Index Engine:** Use an index engine when you're searching for something specific (e.g., company name, person, specific product).

  SPECIFIC INFO

SAM TIP ⚲
Search Engines:

Directory: Yahoo (make sure to choose the directory link under the More tab) – use when you're searching for a broad topic.

Index: Google – use when you're searching for a specific word or phrase.

Using a directory engine is self-explanatory. You type in the broad subject of interest and then choose from the various offered categories and subcategories. The broader the subject, the more likely you'll get meaningful categories and subcategories.

Using an index engine is more difficult than a directory engine. Remember, "Garbage In, Garbage Out." The next chapter discusses how to get better results out of index engines primarily using Google as our example, but it also discusses some search tips in Yahoo and introduces you to a few other powerful Index engines.

CHAPTER EIGHT

Search Right the First Time, Every Time

"Your chances of success will be improved by using a 'rifle' rather than a 'shotgun' approach, one that is specific to a particular title, business issue, and industry segment."
> – Michael Bosworth and John R. Holland, *Customer Centric Selling*, New York: McGraw-Hill, 2003.

As previously mentioned, this book is not designed to be the ultimate guide to using search engines. However, some basic tips you should know would dramatically decrease the amount of time you spend trying to locate relevant and credible information.

Imagine spending ten minutes or less searching for and gathering the information for Sales Intelligence to practice warm calling and spending the rest of the time actually going on sales calls. Consistently use these tips and you'll likely cut your searching time by a third, if not more.

The following tips work in just about every search engine. Whether you're using a popular search engine like Google or Yahoo, or premium subscription databases that we'll discuss later, use these tips and you'll say goodbye to millions of search results and say hello to finding exactly what you need the first time, every time.

+ AND
− NOT
| OR

General Tip #1: Boolean Searching – Better Info In, Better Info Out

Boolean is a mathematical system devised by George Boole that combines propositions with logical operators. When you conduct a search using Boolean terms, what you're doing is giving the search engine specific instructions on what exactly you want found on a particular Web page. You're putting better information in, so you get better results out.

Professional librarians use several Boolean tricks, but the following are the easiest to remember and provide the most benefit to salespeople looking to quickly find information on companies, individuals, and industries:

- **+ (the plus sign):** When you type + between two words (some search engines use an all uppercase AND), you're telling the search engine that *all of the words must appear* on the page. For example, by entering "medical + diabetes + trends" into the search engine, you're telling the engine that all three of those words must appear somewhere on the page in no particular order; but all three must be there. The good news is that most search engines already

🔲 Live Search   medical + diabetes + trends

JAMA-NUS 2008
... diagnosis, and treatment of these diseases. Recent **Trends** in **Diabetes**, Obesity, and Syndrome —a conference presented by JAMA, the Journal of the American **Medical** ...
www.jama-nus.com · Cached page

A Decade of Inpatient Diabetes Management: Trends at an Academic ...
A Decade of Inpatient **Diabetes** Management: **Trends** at an Academic **Medical** Center: Abstract Number: 432-P Authors: JANIS E. BOZZO, ZHENQUI ...
professional.**diabetes**.org/Abstracts_Display.aspx?TYP=1&CID=62565 · Cached page

Type 2 Diabetes Complications and trends
Learn the type 2 **diabetes** complications and **trends** of recent years. ... and renal hypope often in the setting of multiple concomitant **medical** ...
www.januvia.com/sitagliptin/januvia/hcp/janumet/science_behind_diabetes/diabetes_tr
· Cached page

assume you mean + or AND when you type in multiple words (this is important to remember for the next tip). Some specialized search engines still require you to enter the + or AND, however.

- **OR:** When you type in OR in all uppercase between two words, you're telling the search engine that *either one or the other* of the words you entered, or all, must appear somewhere on the page. For example, by entering "advertising OR marketing" in the search form, I'm telling the search engine that at least one of those words must appear.

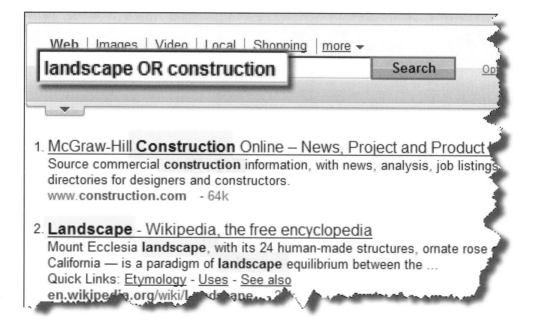

- **- (the minus sign):** Using the minus sign (or some search engines use an all uppercase NOT) is an often overlooked yet extremely powerful search tip. When you use minus, you actually *remove search results* from a page. For example, let's say I want to search for information on the Vikings, not the soon-to-be world champion football team (in the history of the world, a span of sometime in the next 200 years can be considered "soon to be"), rather, I want information on the Norwegians with the big boats and swords. If I search for "Vikings," I receive millions of results, the majority being about football. However, by using the minus sign, I can remove the word football from the results, e.g. "Vikings –football." **NOTE: the minus sign must be "touching" the word you want to remove.**

Before

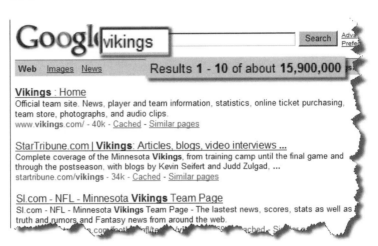

After (using the minus sign)

General Tip #2: Quotes – Search for an Exact Phrase

This next tip is one that will save you an amazing amount of time. It's called Quotation Marks and it is an incredibly important search tip when you're looking for proper nouns like the name of a company or individual or if you're looking for an exact phrase like "annual revenue," "vice president of sales," or "marketing strategy."

When you put multiple words within *quotation marks*, what you're telling the search engine is that your chosen words must be on the Web page found in *the EXACT order entered*. Remember that most search engines, when you type in multiple words, assume you mean AND; the words must appear somewhere on the page but not necessarily next to each other. When you put multiple words in quotation marks, the search engine treats those words as a phrase and the results will appear with those words in the exact order entered.

Here's a before and after example of searching for a person's name, William Scott Johnson.

Notice that in the "Before" example all three words—William, Scott, and Johnson—appear on the page, but in no particular order. Meaning William can be in the first paragraph, Scott in the fifth paragraph, and Johnson in the ninth. Because the search engine is providing results with those three words somewhere on a Web page, we receive millions of search results.

However, in the "After" example, every result shows "William Scott Johnson" in that exact order. More important, instead of millions of search results we have a few dozen.

> **SAM TIP** ➤
> **Quotation Marks:**
>
> If you type words into a search engine, it will automatically think you mean AND, meaning the words you type in will appear somewhere on the page, but in no particular order.
>
> By surrounding your words or phrase with quotation marks, you're telling the search engine that those words must be found in that exact order.

Before (No Quotation Marks – 41 million results)

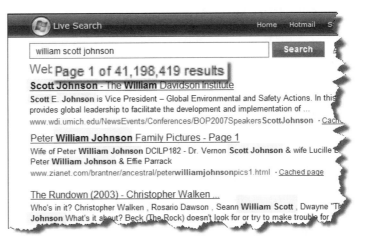

After (With Quotation Marks – 117 results)

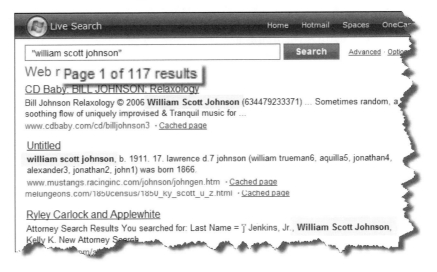

General Tip #3: Combo Search – Start Searching Like a Pro

The real trick for getting excellent search results is when you start combining Boolean terms and quotation marks. Remember: good stuff in, good results out. When you combine search terms, you tell the search engine exactly what you're looking for, reducing your search results from millions to thousands or hundreds (or even dozens).

In General Search Tip #7, I'll show you a way to make combining search terms intuitive and easy. However, I recommend trying some combo searches on your own using your favorite search engine so you can see the types of results that you can achieve.

Let's try a hypothetical sales example and see what kind of results we can get conducting a combo search. Let's pretend we're looking for the vice president of marketing at Lawson Software (a St. Paul-based company where I can see the corporate headquarters by looking out my office window). Now, let's also pretend that we don't know if "vice president of marketing" is the exact title, so we'll separate "vice president" from marketing.

So, in our combo search example let's use: "vice president" + "Lawson Software" -marketing (we're telling the search engine that we're looking for the exact phrase "vice president" with the exact phrase "Lawson Software" but we don't want any results with the word "marketing"). Note that I am including the plus sign even though I really don't need to, because the search engine already assumes I mean AND when I type in multiple words:

Web | Images | Video | Local | Shopping | more ▾

"vice president" + "lawson software" -marketing   Custo

LWSN **LAWSON SOFTWARE: Lawson Software** Names Balmforth Seni
Vice ...
TradingMarkets News for LWSN - **LAWSON SOFTWARE: Lawson Software** Names Ba
Senior **Vice President** of Support and Delivery
www.**tradingmarkets.com**/.site/news/Stock News/863564 - 57k - Cached

SCM Directory - Supply Chain Management Software Community - **Lawso**
SCM Directory - Supply Chain Management Software buyers guide, SCM news, SCM art
more., **Lawson Software** Names Osborne **Vice President** of Managed Services
scmdirectory.com/People-in-the-News/**Lawson-Software**-Names-Osborne-Vice-Presid
Managed-Service... - Cached

Lawson Software Names Osborne **Vice President** of Managed Service
ST. PAUL, Minn.–(BUSINESS WIRE)–**Lawson Software** (Nasdaq:LWSN) today anno
appoint   of Osborne as   of managed senior Osborne ...

Look what we were able to find in the first few results; a number of Web sites listing the names of vice presidents at Lawson Software. By doing a combo search, in less than ten seconds we found exactly the information we needed.

On another note, yes, we did return more than 20,000 search results, which admittedly will take some time to get through. However, just for comparison purposes, when I took out the Boolean and just searched the words vice president lawson software, I received more than 480,000 results. By doing the combo search, I reduced the results by almost 96 percent!

General Tip #4: Word Order Matters

SAM TIP
Word Order:

Search engines read left to right, meaning they place emphasis on the first word and less on the last word. Therefore, the order in which you enter words does matter.

If you're not getting the results you expect, try changing the word order around in your search to see if you return better results.

A simple search tip that works on all search engines is "Word Order Matters." Search engines read left to right and therefore put more emphasis on the first word or phrase versus the last word or phrase entered into the search form. So sometimes if you're not getting the search results you expect, just changing the word order can shift the ranking of results in a way that gets you what you want in the first few listings.

Let's conduct an industry search related to pharmaceuticals; in particular, we want to find key trends in the industry related to diabetes research as we're going to be calling on a company that specializes in this area and we want to appear somewhat knowledgeable.

We'll search for pharmaceutical + diabetes + research. We'll try the search two times and change the word order. Notice how the number of results stays about the same, but the result rankings change because the emphasis has changed.

Search One

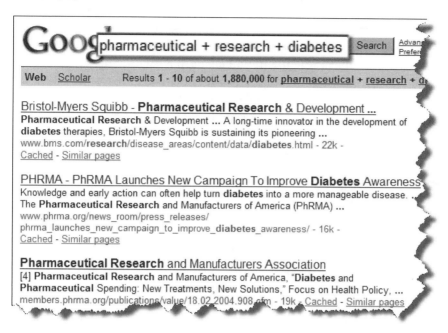

Search Two

General Tip #5: Cached – The Solution to "Site No Longer Appears"

One of the bigger issues I come across when giving presentations is the frustration people have with "Sorry, Site No Longer Appears." If you do any searching online, you know what I'm talking about. You conduct a search using your favorite search engine, find a result you think you're interested in, but when you click on the link, the site doesn't appear.

I'm happy to announce that there is a solution! Remember how index engines work. They're like big vacuum cleaners that search for Web sites with words on them and if the index search engine finds a Web site it likes, it "sucks up" the words and throws those words in a big database that you can search.

Well, a few years back, Google mounted a Polaroid camera on its vacuum cleaner and started taking pictures of Web sites that it indexed. In other words, Google has a virtual picture library of almost all of the Web sites it has in its database. Other search engines like Yahoo and MSN also now take pictures of visited Web sites and all of these pictures can be accessed with a mouse click.

How? Next time you conduct a search, look to see if there's a grayed-out underlined item under your search result called "Cached." This is a rotten name for the link and what it does. In my opinion, more people would use it if they called it "Polaroid Picture" or something like that. When you click on the Cached link, you'll get a picture of what the Web site looked like the last time the search engine indexed the page. (How often a search engine indexes a page depends on how popular the page is; some sites and pages are indexed daily while others are only indexed every few months.)

Below is a Google search of "Sam Richter" and "University of Minnesota." One of the results that appears is an article from the University of Minnesota Alumni Magazine. When you click on the Cached link, you'll see the full article or a picture of what the Web site looked like when Google indexed the page.

There's an added benefit to the Cached Link when using Google: When you click on the Cached link in Google,

all of the words that you're searching for are automatically highlighted.

Have you ever clicked on a search result and the page that appears is filled with pages after pages of text? You can use your browser's "Find" tool to find the search terms that appear on the long page of text. Or, you can click the browser's BACK button, return to the search result page, and click on the Cached Link instead.

On the Cached Link result, all of the words or phrases you're searching for will appear highlighted, each word and phrase in a different color. To find your terms, just scroll through the page, and look for the highlighted text. I use this trick a lot and can tell you that it is a huge time-saver.

Clicking on the Cached Link

The Cached (or Polaroid Picture) Results Highlighting Requested Words/Phrases

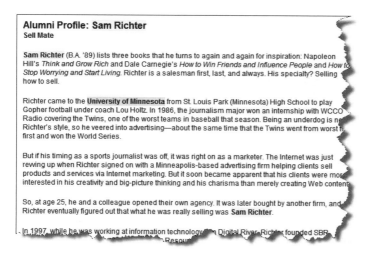

General Tip #6: Conduct a Database or "List of ..." Search

SAM TIP ▸
Searching for Lists:

When searching for lists of names or companies, type in terms like "library of links," "list of links," "database," or "membership list" followed by the type of information you want.

There's a decent chance that somebody has already created the list that you want and posted it online.

If you're looking for a specific type of information, think like the person who created the Web site and ask, what would you have titled the Web page?

When conducting research prior to a sales call, what you're often looking for is a list of companies, names, or general industry information. Good news: there's a decent chance that the list you're looking to build already exists and may be posted online ready for you to download.

The trick in locating existing lists is to think how Web site developers would title a list that they were going to post online, and then enter the appropriate search terms into an Index engine to locate the list.

For example, let's say you create a Web page featuring a list of medical device companies. You might title the name of the Web page "List of Medical Device Companies." Or maybe you've built a search tool that allows you to search the various companies. In this case, you might name the page "Database of Medical Device Companies." Even if you don't name the page something that specific, you probably have some text on the page saying something like "Click Here for a list of my favorite medical device companies."

By searching using those types of list terms followed by the type of list you're looking for, you might get lucky and find that someone has already done the work of compiling this valuable information for you.

General Tip #7: "Cheat Sheet" – The Advanced or Power Search

If you remember nothing else from this section, *remember this tip*. It's really the "Cheat Sheet" for much of what was discussed with some of the earlier tips.

> *Use your favorite search engine's "Advanced Search" capabilities.*

Almost every good search engine allows you to conduct an Advanced Search. If you're like most people, you've probably seen the link (some search engines call it "Power Search") but have been afraid to click on it. You've probably said something to yourself like "That Advanced Search ... that must be for an advanced searcher. I don't need that." Like the Cached link name, "Advanced Search" is a bad name as it seems intimidating. They should call it "Searching for Simple People" or some other friendly name like that so more people like me would use it.

The reality is that yes, advanced searchers, like professional librarians, do use the Advanced Search link. However, they use it because it's fast and it quickly helps them think more critically about search terms so they put great information into the search form and get great results back.

One of the challenges of online searching is that, although the tips I shared with you earlier work for most search engines, they don't work for all, and each search engine has its own peculiarities. For example, some search engines use AND while some use +. Some use NOT and some use -. Some use quotation marks, some use parentheses, some brackets, and so on.

If you're like me, you don't have time to remember all of this stuff. The good news is you don't have to. Just click on the Advanced Search form and let the search engine do the work for you. When you click on the Advanced Search form, you'll see a page similar to ...

SAM TIP ➤
Advanced Search:

All good search engines have an "Advanced Search" or "Power Search" link, typically situated next to the search form or button.

When you click on the link, you get a form asking you to fill out the types of information you desire. By following the form, you're putting good information in, the search engine will automatically craft the Boolean search, and you're more likely to get good information out.

Ask™ **Advanced Search**

Find results with	all of the words	
	the exact phrase	
	at least one of the words	
	none of the words	

| Location of words | Anywhere on the page ▼ |

Domain

Notice how you can search *"all of the words,"* this is like searching with the plus sign or AND; *"this exact phrase"* is like searching using quotation marks; *"at least one of the words"* is like searching with OR; and *"none of the words"* is like searching with the minus sign or NOT. You can of course enter different combinations of words in each field and thus perform a Combo Search as described earlier.

The Advanced Search feature will vary from search engine to search engine. And the visual above shows just a portion of the available options when using Advanced Search (for example, some of the search techniques I discuss in the next chapter can also be done via Advanced Search).

I guarantee that if you train yourself to start using the Advanced Search of your favorite search engine, you will decrease the amount of time you spend searching and increase the relevance of your search results.

NOTE: make sure to read about Google's Advanced Search in the next section and you will see how easy it is to quickly learn Boolean and proper search techniques.

CHAPTER NINE

The Power of Google

http://www.google.com

In my presentations, when I ask what search engine people use, 90 percent of those in the audience raise their hands when I mention "Google." For business people, Google seems to be the general search engine of choice, and the good news is that Google is a very powerful search engine for locating information that can be used during a sales call. However, very few salespeople truly understand the power of Google.

The following tips will help you get the most out of your Google search. What's discussed is only a portion of what Google has to offer (for the definitive guide to Google searching, check out *Google Power: Unleash the Full Potential of Google* by Chris Sherman), but it's the most relevant to the types of information needed by salespeople for Sales Intelligence.

Also note that many of the following tips work in Yahoo and MSN, along with other search engines. The search engine world is constantly evolving and the "search wars" are as fierce as ever, with the three major search engines battling for eyeballs by constantly introducing new tools.

However, because Google seems to be the search engine of choice for salespeople (and because I personally think that the folks at Google are brilliant), the following tips are ones I've learned over the past few years that make my Google searching much more powerful and get me the information I need to practice warm calling, usually within the first 20 or so search results.

NOTE: All Google screenshots in this book are reproduced with permission 2007 by Google Inc. Google and the Google logo with permission of Google Inc. are trademarks of Google Inc.

Google Tip #1: Search within Results

SAM TIP
Search Within:

If your Google search returns a high number of search results, <u>scroll down to the bottom of the page and click the "Search within Results" link.</u>

Enter a new term into the new search form that appears and instead of searching the Web, you'll now only search for the new term within your original result list.

You can "Search within Results" as many times as you wish to narrow your search.

Sometimes you can do all of the right things when searching and still get thousands, if not tens of thousands of results. Google has a tool you can use to narrow those results further. It's called "Search within Results."

What "Search within Results" does is let you type in additional search terms but limit your search to just the original results that appeared. So, for example, let's say you were looking for information on medical devices and you correctly typed in **"medical device industry"** using quotes in the search form. Unfortunately, you would have returned hundreds of thousands of results.

Instead of getting frustrated, just scroll to the bottom of your Google search results and locate the "Search within Results" link. Click on it, type more information into the search form, and your search results will now be limited to the new terms found within your original search results.

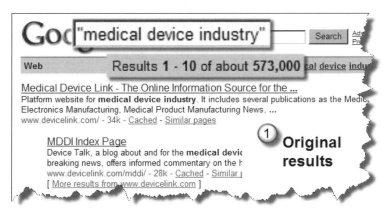

Using our example, let's now type in the word **diabetes** and choose "Search within Results." My search will be limited to only the results that originally appeared related to medical devices, and the new results will only be sites that include information related to the "medical device industry" AND diabetes.

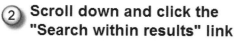

**Scroll down and click the
"Search within results" link**

**Enter in a new search term, then click
the "Search within results" button**

Get a new result list

If you are paying attention, you probably just said to yourself "Hey, why didn't we do a Boolean Combo Search to begin with using **"medical device industry" + diabetes"**?

You are correct; we could have done that. However, what often happens during a search is we just type in the words we think we're looking for, and then based on the results, we come up with additional ideas. The "Search within Results" technique allows you to continually "drill down" in a search and think of new ideas as you see results.

Google Tip #2: Search for Historical Information

Sometimes when you're calling on a prospect, it's nice to have some historical knowledge of what the company was doing during a particular time frame. This is especially useful if you want to locate old product manuals or sales material.

Google lets you do a neat trick that can limit your search results to pages that contain a date range. When filling out the Google search form, just enter the words and/or phrases you're interested in, and then end with a date range separated by two periods.

So for example, if I want to learn about IBM and network security but limit the information to 1997 through 2002, I would enter the search query: **IBM "network security" 1997..2002.**

Below is a view of what that search query returns. You'll note that every search result had the word "IBM," the phrase

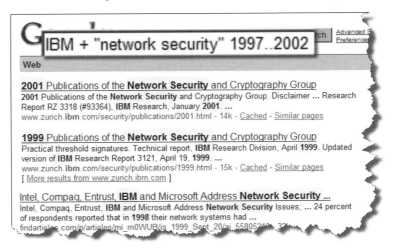

"network security" and the Web pages feature dates between 1997 and 2002.

Google Tip #3: Amnesia Assistance – When You're Not Quite Sure

Have you ever been at a trade show or networking event where you meet someone and then when you get back to your computer and want to search for information, you can't remember the person's name or company name? This is assuming of course that you misplaced a business card and I'm assuming I'm not the only person in the world who does so. Thank goodness Google has a cure for people like me who suffer from "temporary amnesia."

When you can't remember a word or number of words when doing your Google search, just replace the missing word with an asterisk (in the library world, the asterisk is known as a wildcard) and Google will fill in the blank(s) with words that complete your search.

If you know the exact number of words you're missing, enclose the entire search in quotation marks and enter one asterisk for each missing word. Google will replace each asterisk with a word.

So for example, let's say I was at a trade show and I met someone from Anderson XXXXX, XXXXX Associates, and we're going to get together for coffee tomorrow morning. I'm now in my hotel room and find that I left my collected business cards back at the trade show, and I'd like to do some research on the company prior to my morning meeting.

Instead of getting frustrated, I open up Google and enter **"Anderson ∗ ∗ Associates"**, enclosing the entire phrase in quotation marks. I use two asterisks because I know I'm missing exactly two words.

If I don't know exactly how many words are between Anderson and Associates, I'd just enter one asterisk and not enclose the phrase in quotation marks (e.g., Anderson ∗ Associates). Google will then return all results where a phrase starts with Anderson and ends with Associates.

SAM TIP ⬉
Asterisk:

If you can only remember part of what you're looking for, enter an asterisk in your search and let Google fill in the blanks.

For example, enter **"3M" + "vice president of ∗"** and your results will return Web pages featuring the word 3M and listing the names of vice presidents from various divisions of 3M, or organizations that work with 3M.

However, in this example, I know there are exactly two missing words so I use two asterisks, enclose the search in quotes, hit the search button, and see what appears (note how Google is smart enough to know that Assoc. is an abbreviation of Associates):

Goo "anderson * * associates"

Web   Books

Anderson, Niebuhr & Associates, Inc.
Anderson Niebuhr & Associates, Inc. is a full-service, custom-design, market
company specializing in questionnaire design, sample design, ...
www.ana-inc.com/ - 5k - Cached - Similar pages

Welcome to **Anderson-Perry and Associates**, inc
Services and Solutions | About Us | Careers | Awards Copyright 2007 **Anderson,
Associates**, Inc. | Design and Coding by Paul J. Weinert.
www.andersonperry.com/ - 13k - Cached - Similar pages

Welcome to **Anderson, Randles & Associates**
It will provide you with Information about how **Anderson, Randles & Associates**
Tradition of Excellence in Circulation Consulting, Training and ...
www. andles com 9k Cached Sim pages

For salespeople, another way to use the Google asterisk trick is when you're searching for various job titles at a company. For example, if you're looking for the various vice presidents at a company, you can enter the name of the company into the Google search form (remember to use quotation marks), then enter the partial title followed by an asterisk (again, enclose the title within quotations). Using our Lawson Software example, I enter **"Lawson Software"** + **"vice president of ∗"** and return some great results.

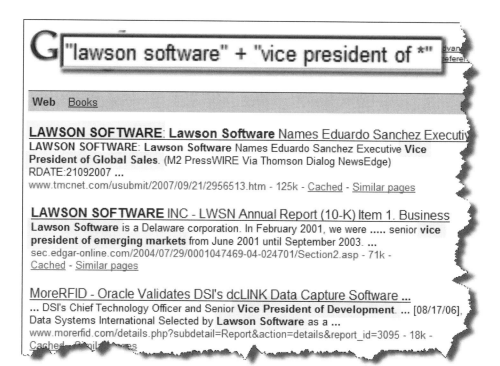

Google Tip #3.5: Locating E-mail Addresses

You can use the Google asterisk trick in another way that answers a question I receive from salespeople quite often: how do I get e-mail addresses for my prospects?

Most e-mail addresses end the same way as the company Web site address. For example, one of my Web site addresses is **www.sbrworldwide.com**, thus all of the e-mail addresses associated with that site end in xxxxxx@sbrworldwide.com.

To locate e-mail addresses, just use the asterisk as a replacement for the first part of the e-mail address. For best results, but your search between quotation marks. For example, if you wanted to find e-mail addresses for some of the people at SBR Worldwide, you would enter "*@sbrworldwide.com".

Often times, by clicking on the link, you can see the title or job responsibilities of the person whose e-mail address you found.

SAM TIP
E-mail Locator:

Use the Google asterisk trick to locate e-mail addresses by entering an asterisk in front of the @ symbol, followed by the company's Web site extension. Put between quote marks for better results.

For example, **"*@mmm.com"** will return e-mail addresses from people at 3M.

Goo **"*@sbrworldwide.com"**

Web Video

Put the Develop Back Into Development
Sam Richter. CEO. SBR Worldwide. **sam@sbrworldwide.com**. www.
takethecold.com .... Contact:. Sam Richter. **sam@sbrworldwide.com** ...
www.mncn.org/EventMaterial/2008Tech/DevelopIntoDvlpmt_Richter.pdf - Si

Business Expert Webinars
... Marketing; Small Business; Sales - General; Sales Management; Sale
Development; Sales - Telesales. **julie@sbrworldwide.com**
www.businessexpertwebinars.com/component/option,com_comprofiler/
task,userProfile/user,136/Itemid,29/ - 25k - Cached - Similar pages

Take the Cold Out of Cold Calling
reading, email info**@sbrworldwide.com**. TITLE. Take the Cold Out of Co
Secrets for the Inside Info ...
www.takethecold.com/press-room/media-kit/take_the_cold_fact_sheet.pdf

If you do get a lot of results, and you may when you're trying this for larger companies, you can also add search terms
to the query. For example, you can add job titles (e.g.,"vice
president"—remember to use the quotation marks) or even
add a name. This may help you better identify prospects or
even a specific person's e-mail address.

It's important to note that there is no guarantee that the
e-mail addresses will be correct, or that the person even works
at the organization any longer. But this is a quick and easy way
to identify e-mail addresses and address naming conventions
(e.g., if you find psmith@widget.com, janderson@widget.
com, etc., it's highly likely that Julie Jones' e-mail address at
Widget Corp. is first initial, last name, jjones@widget.com).

Also, don't get frustrated if this doesn't work for you; I've
tried this and periodically no results appear, or you get some
very strange results that don't have anything at all to do with
an e-mail address.

Remember, what you're doing is searching for information on a Web page, meaning that the e-mail address has to
be in virtual print somewhere. It could be a bylined article or

a listing on an internal Web page, for example. However, you are not searching a company's e-mail directory; the information has to be in the public domain for you to find it.

Finally, it's incredibly important to remember to not use this trick to blindly gather e-mail addresses and then use them to send unsolicited e-mail.

Spamming is not only unethical, it is also the quickest way to create a negative reputation for you and your company. It can cause all future e-mails from you to get blocked and/or end up in your recipients' junk mail box, and instead of gaining new business, you'll lose it. Only use this trick when you know the person and/or company you want to contact and you know they want to receive your e-mail.

Google Tip #4: Company Site Search

A great way to eliminate thousands, if not millions, of search results, while ensuring you get relevant information related to your search, is to limit your search to a specific site. This can be very helpful for the salesperson looking to get specific information on a company or trying to locate a person by title or name at a company.

The trick to a Site Search is to end your search with *Site:* (site colon) and then the name of the Web site for the company you're interested in. When entering in the Web site name, do not enter the *http://.* Rather, just enter *Site:www.xxxxxx* and replace "xxxxx" with the name of the Web site including .com, .org., etc.

For example, let's say I'm interested in learning the names of marketing managers at General Mills. I could enter "marketing manager" AND "General Mills" in Google and get some good results; 27,800 in all. Another way would be to restrict my search to only Web sites operated by General Mills by entering the following search query:

"marketing manager" site:www.generalmills.com

As you'll see, entering this query returns results only from the General Mills Web site, 152 results in all, and the re-

You can limit your search results to a specific Web site by using the Google site search tip.

Just enter the information you desire, followed by Site: and then the company's Web site address.

sales site:www.3m.com will only search 3M Web sites for pages with the word sales.

sults include press releases and news articles with the names of various marketing managers at General Mills.

You can also use this type of query when looking for phrases like "annual revenue" or "marketing strategy." Just enter the phrase using quotation marks followed by "site:"

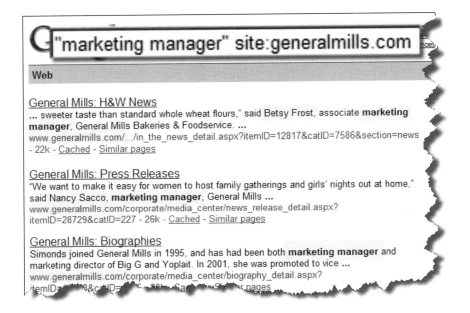

and then the address of the specific Web site (e.g., "marketing strategy" site:www.widget.com). Obviously, the phrase you're looking for must be somewhere on the site you're interested in or you will not receive results.

Another good use of the Site: search is when you quickly want to learn about a company's history prior to a sales call. You could just go directly to a company's Web site and see if they have an "About Us" or "Company History" page directly off the main Web site navigation.

Or you could save yourself a lot of time by instead going to Google and in the search form entering this query: "about us" OR history OR biography site:www.widget.com. The search results will deliver pages with the phrase "about us," or the words *history* or *biography* thus getting you the information you need, instantly, versus spending time searching the company's site.

Google Tip #5: File and Document Search

Have you ever tried to e-mail a file to someone only to have it bounce back because the attachment was too large? To solve the problem, you posted the file to a Web page (or had your IT department post the file), created a link to the file, and e-mailed the link to the intended recipient. You figured that because the only two people who knew the link and page existed were you and the recipients, the file was private. You forgot about the Google "vacuum cleaner."

When you upload a document of any kind to the Web, unless you've put it behind a secure area requiring a username and password to access it, there's a decent chance Google can find it and index it. All too often companies upload files not knowing that prying eyes can find the file if they know where and how to look.

The kinds of files people and companies post online include: company directories, client lists, budgets, vendor programs, sales presentations, manuals, and other sensitive information, just to name a few. A salesperson trying to develop leads and research prospects may find this kind of information to be quite valuable (we'll talk later about whether you have the moral right to use this information).

The Google file type search allows you to check to see if a company has posted different types of documents online. Conducting a file type search is relatively easy. On the Google search form, just type in the name of the company or individual you're interested in (or any search term or phrase), and then type in filetype:XXX. Where I have XXX, replace it with the type of file you're interested in finding.

For example: **"Lawson Software" filetype: pdf** will search for any PDF files that exist online that contain the term "Lawson Software" (there are more than 17,000 PDF files featuring that phrase).

SAM TIP
Filetype Search:

You can find files that have been posted online by using this Google search trick. In the Google search form …

1. Enter the information you want and/or the company name. Use quotes around phrases.

2. Enter filetype: (filetype colon) and then choose a file extension (pdf, xls, ppt, doc).

3. Your search results will be limited to the information you searched for contained within a specific file.

4. Note that with Office '07, filetypes have an x added to the end, e.g. pptx.

Here is a chart with a list of common file types that can be found online:

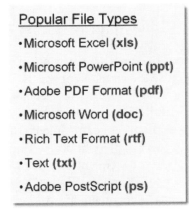

Popular File Types

- Microsoft Excel **(xls)**
- Microsoft PowerPoint **(ppt)**
- Adobe PDF Format **(pdf)**
- Microsoft Word **(doc)**
- Rich Text Format **(rtf)**
- Text **(txt)**
- Adobe PostScript **(ps)**

NOTE: If the document was saved in the latest Office 2007 version, the filetype will have an additional X at the end. Thus, if searching for Excel documents, you may want to conduct a search for filetype:xls and a filetype:xlsx search; PowerPoint ppt would be pptx; and Word doc would be docx.

What might you find related to a particular file type? Excel spreadsheets might contain client lists and budgets. A PowerPoint document might be a sales proposal or a copy of a presentation given at an industry conference. Same for a PDF file. A Word document could be a copy of a speech, a résumé, or grant proposal. There is a lot of valuable information "floating" in cyberspace that you can use to provide value during the cold calling process and to help better serve accounts.

Let's take a look using our neighbors at Lawson Software again. We'll specifically search for a presentation by doing a PowerPoint search using **"Lawson Software" filetype:ppt**.

The first result that appears is a presentation from Lawson's chairman related to the company's merger. Do you think that might be important information to have if you're conducting a sales call? How impressive will you be as a salesperson calling on Lawson if you can tailor your solutions to what the chairman said will occur in the future, rather than what occurred in the past.

Go| "lawson software" filetype:ppt | Search

Web News

[PPT] **Lawson Software**
File Format: Micro... owerpoint - View as HTML
Lawson Busi... elligence Getting the Most from Your Investment Kern Eaker Sr.
Solutions... nt. Page 1. LBI...
www.dig... urse.com/dropzo...
200216... imilar pages

[PPT] La... Tem...
File Form... int
Copyright ©...
Lawson Softwa... ghts...
lglug.org/absence%20ma... gemen...

[PPT] Exploring Organizational...
File Format: Microsoft PowerPoint...

Lawson Business Intelligence
Getting the Most from Your Investment

Kern Eaker
Sr. Solutions Consultant

Go| "university of minnesota" filetype:xls | Search

Web

[XLS] 1-500
File Format: Microsoft Excel
30, 24, **UNIVERSITY OF MINNESOTA**, 575, $22...
INVOICE INSIGHT, LLC, 1, $277883, 0, $0, 0, $0...
grants.nih.gov/grants/award/trends/Rnk_05_All.x...

[XLS] careergenled titles...
File Format: Microsoft E...
1577, 10044306, Idea E... ea Group Inc. Wo...
Changing Paradigms... versity of Minne...
www.lib.tsinghua.edu... me/pro... ssion.x...

[XLS] NIH...

	A	B	C	D	E	F
1	NIH Awards to All Institutions by Rank					
2	Rank 1 to 500					
3				All Awards		Research Grants
4	Rank*	Organization	Number	Amount	Number	Amount
5	1	JOHNS HOPKINS UNIVERSITY	1,299	$607,222,589	1,113	$537,02...
6	2	UNIVERSITY OF PENNSYLVANIA	1,153	$471,350,481	1,000	$433,26...
7	3	UNIVERSITY OF WASHINGTON	997	$462,021,658	849	$408,269...
8	4	UNIVERSITY OF CALIFORNIA SAN FRANCISCO	988	$452,165,301	843	$392,62...
9	5	WASHINGTON UNIVERSITY	855	$394,788,334	773	$370,202...
10	6	DUKE UNIVERSITY	795	$391,196,272	685	$351,399...
11	7	UNIVERSITY OF MICHIGAN	975	$386,027,410	848	$353,344...
12	8	UNIVERSITY OF CALIFORNIA LOS ANGELES	914	$385,788,286	782	$360,017...
13	9	UNIVERSITY OF PITTSBURGH	969	$385,680,084	865	$354,525...
14	10	YALE UNIVERSITY	868	$336,742,948	734	$308,44...
15	11	COLUMBIA UNIVERSITY	763	$330,754,949	670	$307,420...
16	12	SAIC-FREDERICK, INC.	1	$328,152,023	0	
17	13	HARVARD UNIVERSITY	682	$321,223,983	521	$290,257
18	14	UNIVERSITY OF CALIFORNIA SAN DIEGO	681	$309,416,840	598	$286,571...
19	15	STANFORD UNIVERSITY	763	$305,561,055	634	$282,13...
20	16	UNIVERSITY OF NORTH CAROLINA CHAPEL HILL	782	$296,566,365	646	$272,779
21	17	MASSACHUSETTS GENERAL HOSPITAL	694	$286,968,597	637	$271,551
22	18	CASE WESTERN RESERVE UNIVERSITY	673	$278,820,079	614	$240,754
23	19	VANDERBILT UNIVERSITY	668	$266,236,625	586	$245,942...
24	20	UNIVERSITY OF WISCONSIN MADISON	670	$257,144,598	564	$225,606
25	21	BAYLOR COLLEGE OF MEDICINE	585	$256,809,346	504	$233,41...
26	22	BRIGHAM AND WOMEN'S HOSPITAL	566	$253,333,482	518	$241,57...
27	23	UNIVERSITY OF ALABAMA AT BIRMINGHAM	518	$228,687,941	460	$195,874...
28	24	UNIVERSITY OF MINNESOTA	575	$227,338,684	510	$206,94...
29	25	EMORY UNIVERSITY	574	$221,790,571	490	$207,8...

Let's do a more generic search. Let's see if we can find business information related to my state university by searching for **"University of Minnesota" filetype:xls**.

I found a spreadsheet listing grant awards from the National Institute of Health. If you know someone who attends John Hopkins University, congratulate them as their school received more than $607 million in award grants! My school didn't do too bad, I suppose, receiving a little more than $227 million.

Over the past couple of years since I've learned the Google file type trick, I've found an incredible amount of information on a wide variety of public companies, private companies, and non-profit organizations. It's stunning to see the types of information people post online. Here's a real example that happened to me a couple of years ago.

I was giving a presentation on how to use the Web to find information and the audience was made up of executives from a major hotel chain. I did an Excel file type search in Google using the name of the hotel chain and filetype:xls. You will not believe what appeared.

With a mouse click I was able to pull up an Excel spreadsheet containing the complete listing of the global employees of this hotel chain, including full contact information with job titles and e-mail addresses. In addition, next to each name was the employees' salary and benefit package; from the maid to the company's CEO.

Apparently, what happened was this hotel chain had contracted with a human resources benefits consultant to analyze the hotel chain's employee compensation package. Upon creating the final report and spreadsheet, the HR firm posted the information online, presumably for the HR people at the hotel chain to download. I'm guessing that the HR firm and the hotel chain both thought the link was private because it wasn't being shared with anyone else.

I'm sure you can imagine the surprise of the people in the room during my presentation when I showed them the information I found. To save you some time (in case you wanted to try the search on your own), the hotel chain had the file pulled within minutes of my presentation, and something

SAM TIP ➤
Government Docs:

When you conduct a file-type search, you're likely to find information from government Web sites including proposals and vendor lists.

That's because much of the information submitted to or created by a government agency is publicly available via the Freedom of Information Act.

If your prospect or your competition does business with the government, this is a great way to locate interesting information, everything from RFP responses to government vendor spending figures.

tells me the person who posted the information online is now looking for a new career opportunity.

The Google file type search also begs a very important question: *"Just because you know how to find information, does that give you the ethical and moral right to use it?"* The discussion related to that question could probably be a book all its own.

In my opinion, the answer is "no." The analogy I would use is "just because I know you have a garbage dumpster at the back of your office, does that give me the right to start searching through your trash trying to find old sales presentations?" In my opinion, "dumpster diving" is outright unethical and wrong. Carry that through to the online world and the answer is "just because I can find information online doesn't mean that I should use it."

You'll need to make your own judgment about what's right for you. My baseline is if it was a document that was originally intended to be made available to the public (the Lawson chairman's report or the county's vendor list), then it is okay to use. If it's a document I wouldn't want someone to see if it was coming from my company, then it's not okay to use.

You might ask then, "Why are you teaching me how to find this sort of information if you think it's wrong?" Again, I don't think it's wrong to use it if the author's intent was for it to be a public document. In addition, I wanted you to learn about the file type search so you can try it on your own company and make sure you don't find anything you don't want others to see.

Google Tip #6: Local Business Search (with photos)

As a salesperson, you're always looking to maximize your time when making sales calls. Google Maps Search is a great way to find out where types of companies are located within a specific geographic area.

You can access Google Maps in one of two ways. The first way is to visit **http://maps.google.com**. The second way is by clicking on the Maps tab/link on the top of the main Google page.

SAM TIP
Street Views:

Have you seen the Google car driving around your neighborhood? Google has a fleet of cars with roof-mounted cameras driving the country taking 360 degree photos.

If you're involved in real estate, interested in moving your office to a new area, or just want to spy on your colleagues, you'll find Google Street Views valuable (and if you're not careful, a huge time waster as it is addicting). To use...

1. On the Google home page, click the Maps link.

2. Enter the name of a company, or an address.

3. On the results page, click and hold the "person icon" and then drag it to a spot on the map.

4. The streets outlined in blue have Street View photos.

5. Use the arrows to rotate and/or "drive" the street.

To use, just enter the type of information or company you want to find. So for example, you could enter "advertising agency" (or you could enter "Asian restaurants" if you're hungry), then enter the city name and/or state. If you're looking for a specific company, you can just enter in the name—make sure to put the name within quotation marks if it's a multi-word name. If you receive too many results, then go back and enter the city and/or state name.

Click the Search button and you'll see a map of your desired companies along with a listing of those companies. Each company listed corresponds to an identified spot on the map. Click the spot on the map or choose a listing and a window will pop up with the full address and links for directions to and from the location.

Another neat feature is the ability to switch between a graphical map and an actual satellite photo, or in some locations, a street view photo.

Besides being cool, this feature is helpful to the salesperson who is visiting prospects in a new town and who prefers pictures to maps. In addition, looking at a satellite or street view photo of a company can give you a "picture" of the company's size, how many cars are in the parking lot, surrounding business, and more.

To access the satellite view, click the Satellite tab. Use the + or – icons to zoom in or out. If Street View is available, click and hold the "person icon" and drag it to a spot on the map.

When you click and drag the icon, you'll notice that some streets outline in blue. Place the "person icon" on a blue street and you'll see a street-level photo of the location.

You can use the arrows above the zoom lever to pan right, left, up, or down. You can even click the arrows within the Street View map to "drive" the street, neighborhood and city.

Here's a satellite and street level view of the General Mills Corporate headquarters in Minnesota.

Google Tip #7: Google People Search

Try Google if you need an address or phone number for a person. Just enter the name of the person you're interested in (remember, put quotes around the name so Google treats it as a phrase) and the state where the person is located. Most of the time Google returns credible results complete with direction links.

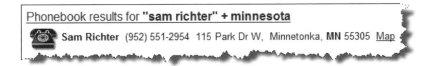

Phonebook results for **"sam richter" + minnesota**

Sam Richter (952) 551-2954 115 Park Dr W, Minnetonka, **MN** 55305 Map

Google Tip #7.5: Reverse Phone Directory

Got a phone number but don't know the name or the company of the person you're calling? Just enter the phone number,

Phonebook results for **952-551-2954**

Sam Richter (952) 551-2954 115 Park Dr W, Minnetonka, **MN** 55305 Map

including area code and dashes, into Google. A good majority of the time Google returns solid results.

Remember that with any online phone directory, the information can be out of date.

Google Tip #8: Google Alerts

www.google.com/alerts

If you ask most people, especially salespeople, what they could use more of (besides money), the answer would be time. Google Alerts can help.

With Google Alerts, you set up a search query and anytime the Google "vacuum cleaner" indexes a Web page that contains the words or phrases for which you're searching,

Google Alerts sends you an e-mail with a link to the page. If it finds 10 new items, you don't get 10 e-mails; rather, you get one e-mail with the 10 links.

Google Alerts is completely free. Just go to **www.google. com/alerts**, enter your search query, and select how often you'd like Google to email you new results. You may want to test your search query in Google first to ensure you receive good information. You can sign up for as many alerts as you want, but you have to do it one at a time. Even if you have many Alerts, they are very easy to manage.

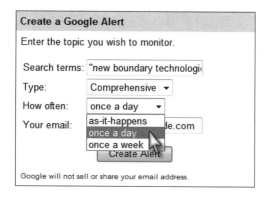

Imagine what you could do as a salesperson if you received up-to-date information on news your prospects have released. As an account manager, how could you practice the Platinum Rule?

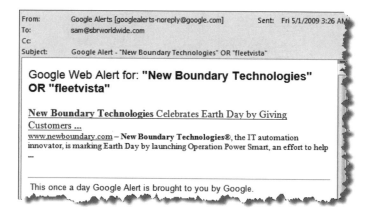

SAM TIP
E-mail Results:

Let Google do the work for you and e-mail you new results with Google Alerts.

1. Visit **www.google.com/alerts**

2. Enter a company name, person's name, or any other search query.

3. Make sure to use Boolean, when setting up your search.

4. To ensure you get helpful results, first try your query in Google. If you receive good information, just copy the query from Google and paste it into Google Alerts.

5. Choose how often you'd like Google to e-mail you new search results.

6. Set up Alerts to keep track of your key prospects and clients, to track industry trends, etc.

For example, when I receive an alert that links to a news story where my client is featured, I send a congratulatory e-mail with some personal comments. I've received alerts when one of my prospects has added a new hire, which was a great opportunity to call and discuss how my business could help the new hire make a great impression. I even use Alerts to track what people are saying about me and my business.

Google Alerts helps me stay on top of what's important to my clients and prospects, helps me build better relationships, and best of all, it's a semi-automated way of practicing Sales Intelligence.

Google Tip #9: "Cheat Sheet" – Google Advanced (revisited)

Another "cheat sheet" that is a superb search learning tool is the **"Google Advanced Search"** feature. In the General Tip section, we discussed how the Advanced Search feature helps you more intuitively put better information into search engines so you get better information out. The Google Advanced Search feature offers this and a whole lot more.

To access Google's Advanced Search, just click on the **"Advanced search"** link to the right of the standard search form:

Once inside Google's Advanced Search, you can easily conduct a search by entering words or phrases into the various search forms. Easily conduct OR searches, and eliminate words from results as well. You can limit your results by file format (e.g., PowerPoint, Excel document, PDF file), and if you click the + button, you'll see additional options.

Google Advanced Search

research "plastics industry" trends OR issues –marketing

Find web pages that have...

all these words:	research
this exact wording or phrase:	"plastics industry"
one or more of these words:	trends OR issues

But don't show pages that have...

| any of these unwanted words: | marketing |

Need more tools?

| Results per page: | 10 results |

SAM TIP
Google Advanced:

Take the guesswork out of searching and learn Boolean with Google Advanced.

1. Go to **www.google.com**

2. Click the Advanced Search link to the right of the main search button.

3. As you enter words and phrases into the various fields, and/or use the various pull-down menus, watch as Google automatically builds the Boolean search query.

4. Use Google Advanced for one week, study the auto query that Google creates, and you'll soon have advanced Boolean searching memorized.

My favorite part of Google Advanced is as you type in words, you can watch Google automatically create the Boolean query. **My promise to you:** Use the Google Advanced Search for one week. Watch as Google creates the query and within a few days, you'll have Boolean searching memorized. You'll never search the same way again!

Google Tip #10: Google Options

After a Google search, wouldn't it be great if you could sort your results by date range, product/company review, chat forums, type of result, or even visually see how your results are related? You can, with Google Options.

Google "plastics industry"

Web   Show options...

On the Google results page, click the "Show Options" link located under the Google logo. On the left side of the results page, you'll notice numerous links that when clicked, allow you to sort your results in a number of ways including...

By Type. Choose "All Results" to see a standard Google results list. Choose "Forums" to see what people are saying about your searched topic. For example, enter an industry (e.g., "plastics industry") and you'll find results where people are discussing industry issues. Choose "Reviews" and if your search is on a company, product, or person, you'll find articles and sites providing both formal reviews and general opinions. Choose "Videos" and your results will feature videos about your topic.

By Date. Click on any of the "Date" links to sort your results by most recent, past day, past week, or past year. This is obviously very helpful when researching a company, industry, or person as you can quickly find the latest information.

By Text or Image. Click on the "Images From the Page" link and your results list will include both a site abstract and images that appear on the indexed Web page. Click the "More

Text" link and the results list will provide longer abstracts than found in a standard Google results list.

Three additional options offer new search results based on your original query. Clicking on the "Related Searches" link delivers a list of categories above the main results list, with each category offering new ways to find information related to your original search.

Related searches for **"medical device industry"**:		
medical device industry **profile**	medical device industry **report**	**bc** medical device industry
medical device industry **china**	medical device industry **coalition**	medical device industry **definition**
medical device industry **israel**	medical device industry **issues**	medical device industry **japan**
medical device industry **research**	medical device industry **taiwan**	medical device **manufacturing** industry
minnesota medical device industry	**recruiters** medical device industry	**salaries** medical device industry

For example, do a search on a company, and on the Related Search categories you'll find options related to the company's location, products, customers, and more. Conduct a search for industry information and you'll find helpful categories that lead you toward industry profiles, research reports, etc.

The "Wonder Wheel" option is interesting in that when clicked, you see an image of related searches and how they relate to your original search. Entering a company name or person's name delivers mixed and sometimes confusing results. Wonder Wheel is most helpful with broad industry searches, as it delivers relevant concepts that you can click for additional results and information.

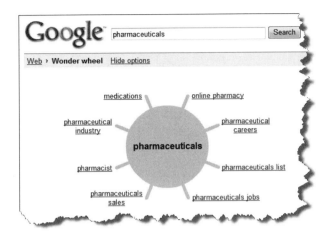

One of my favorite Google Options is the "Timeline." When you click on the link, Google delivers a graphical and interactive news/events timeline related to your search.

Conduct a company search and on the timeline graphic, you can click on a date range to see the information Google has on the company during that time period. This also works great on industry searches where you can see key moments plotted on a timeline, and with a click, pull up the details.

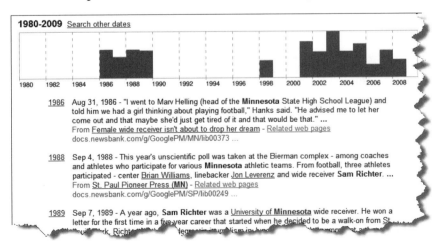

Where I've really found some interesting information is on people searches. For example, when I type in the names of executives, it shows a chronologically ordered list of press releases and news articles featuring the searched person. This is wonderful material when preparing for a meeting and you quickly want to learn the history of the person with whom you're going to meet. What was scary was when I ran a search on my name, the articles it found from 20+ years ago!

Google Tip #11: Google Search Assistant

Need help with your search? Not sure what to type? Just start entering letters in Google and let the Search Assistant take over.

As you start typing your search, after a few letters, Google will start making suggestions underneath the search form. The suggestions come from words and terms that Google has indexed or "vacuumed up." The more you type, the more refined Google's suggestions become.

For example, as I typed in the word "medical," Google's suggestions were not very relevant. But by the time I got to the letter "v" in my search, the suggestions became highly relevant and helped guide my search. Just click on any of the suggested phrases in the pick list and instantly receive Google's relevant results.

$$Google^{TM}$$

medical dev	
medical device companies	3,670,000 results
medical devices	14,700,000 results
medical device sales	768,000 results
medical device jobs	387,000 results
medical device directive	198,000 results
medical device industry	1,360,000 results
medical device recruiters	523,000 results
medical device company	1,390,000 results
medical device daily	411,000 results
medical device link	439,000 results
	close

CHAPTER TEN

Yahoo Search Tips

http://www.search.yahoo.com
or
http://www.yahoo.com

SAM TIP 🖑
Yahoo Assistant:

Yahoo will make suggestions to you as you enter a search query.

1. Go to **http://search.yahoo. com**

2. As you start typing into the search form, Yahoo will start making suggestions on what kind of information it has indexed related to your search.

3. Choose a suggestion via the automatic pull-down menu.

4. Under the search form on the results page, there is an inverted triangle. Click on it.

5. Yahoo will present additional terms and concepts related to your search. Choose one for results related to those terms.

A s described earlier, the "search wars" are really heating up, and although I find Google to be the engine that seems to launch new search technologies first, Yahoo also has some brilliant developers on staff who have introduced some nice features.

Following are a few Yahoo search tips perfect for the salesperson, account manager, or business executive needing to quickly find information on companies, industries, or people.

Yahoo Tip #1: Yahoo Search Assistant

http://search.yahoo.com

Yahoo was the first popular search engine to come out with a Search Assistant. Just like Google's Search Assistant, Yahoo will present search result options as you type letters into the Yahoo search form. As you type, if you see a search query that interests you, just click on it and a list of results will appear.

Yahoo's Search Assistant not only helps out in the initial query, it also provides additional options once you've conducted your search. On the Yahoo search results page, make

NOTE: All Yahoo! screenshots in this book are reproduced with permission 2007 by Yahoo! Inc. YAHOO! and the YAHOO! logo with permission of Yahoo! Inc. are trademarks of Yahoo! Inc.

sure to click the inverted triangle directly underneath the search form. The Yahoo Assistant will provide additional related search terms and phrases along with concepts related to your original search. Using the scroll triangles, you can view the complete list of suggested phrases and concepts.

Just click any of the suggestions for a result list containing those terms or phrases. Once on that result page, make sure to click the inverted triangle again to see additional related phrases and concepts.

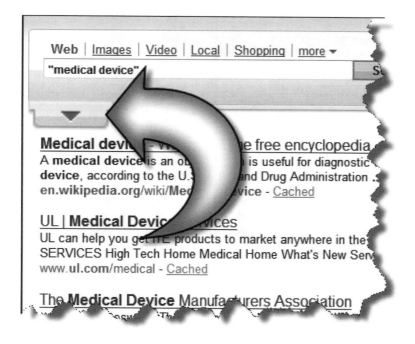

This feature works very well when searching for information related to an industry. For example, I can start with a very broad search term like "medical device," and when I click on the inverted triangle, I'm presented with additional search terms: "medical device manufacturer," "medical device companies," "medical device sales," and more. Yahoo also presents me with concepts related to the medical device industry including regulatory, FDA, implants, and more.

The Yahoo Search Assistant works equally well for information on companies and people. As you type in the name of a company or person, let the Yahoo Assistant help guide you to the information it has related to your search. On the result list, click the inverted triangle to see what other kinds of information Yahoo has related to your company or person.

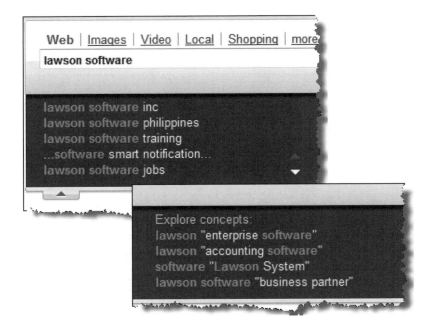

For example, a search on Lawson Software delivers millions of search results. When I click on the inverted triangle under the result list search form, I see suggested search terms related to the company including information on Lawson Software in the Philippines, their training programs, and jobs at the company.

On the "Explore Concepts" area related to Lawson Software, I'm presented with options like "enterprise software," "accounting software," and more. Instead of searching through the millions of results or spending hours on Lawson's Web site, these suggestions help guide my search to information about the company that can be very helpful in preparing for a meeting or presentation.

Yahoo Tip #2: "Free-to-Use" Articles

http://search.yahoo.com/cc
(Note: no www in URL)

Creative Commons features articles that you can link to and sometimes modify for your own personal or business usage. Looking to write a company newsletter? Want to update your site with topic-specific articles? Search Creative Commons for an article you can immediately use without copyright worries.

We've discussed the Platinum Rule and how important it is to communicate with your clients about aspects of their business that you know they care about, regardless of how it impacts your business. So, for example, let's assume that you have multiple clients in the same industry. You can use Creative Commons articles to create e-mail newsletters featuring information you know your clients will care about. By using Creative Commons articles in your newsletter, you don't need to worry about permissions or copyright violations.

Searching Creative Commons is very easy. Go to the Creative Commons site at **http://search.yahoo.com/cc** (note that there is no www).

Enter words or phrases using Boolean logic in the Creative Commons search form. Then choose one or both of the other check boxes to limit your search to content that you can use for commercial purposes, and/or content that you can actually modify.

Click the "Search CC" button and you'll receive a list of results/articles that you can use or modify.

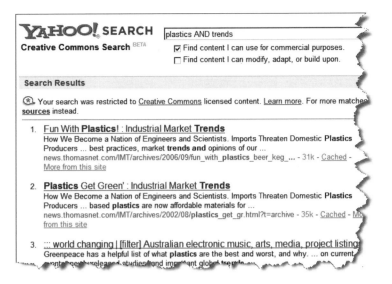

You can also use Creative Commons to search for articles related to a specific company. Just enter the company name in the search field, using quotation marks if the company name is multiple words. Check one or both of the boxes, and click the "Search CC" button. Your result list will include copyright-free articles that others have written about the company, articles actually produced by the company, or articles that reference the company. Here's an example of a Creative Commons search on Lawson Software.

Yahoo Tip #3: Company "Friend Search"

Why would one company link to another company's Web site? Typically, it's a company's "friends," meaning, it is customers, suppliers, employee Blogs, or associations. Or sometimes it could be a company's "enemies," or Web sites that publish negative information such as negative customer reviews. If the company has separate products with unique Web sites, those sites most likely also link to the "parent" site.

If you're researching a company prior to a sales call, this type of information can provide some solid business intelligence. Yahoo makes it easy to find this information with its **"Link To"** search.

There are two ways to conduct a "Link To" search in Yahoo. Go to **http://search.Yahoo.com**. Then type Link: (link, colon) and then the Web address of the company you're interested in researching.

Or you can go directly to the Web site **http://siteexplorer. search.yahoo.com** and once there, just enter in the name of the Web site you're interested in exploring.

SAM TIP
Yahoo Link To:

Learn who is linking to a Web site by doing a Link To search.

1. Go to the **http://search. yahoo.com**

2. Enter Link:, and then a Web site address.

3. Choose the Inlinks tab to see other Web sites that have linked to your chosen site.

4. On the "From All Pages" pull-down menu, select "Except From This Domain" and you'll only see other sites linking to your chosen site.

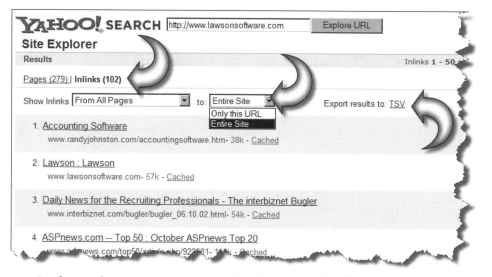

On the results page, there are two tabs. The Pages tab will show you a list of Web pages that Yahoo has indexed for your chosen domain. For the "Company Friend" search, choose the

Inlinks tab and you will see a list of all of the Web sites that have linked to your chosen site.

Use the "From All Pages" pull-down menu and select "Except from this domain" or "Except from this subdomain" to limit your results to only external Web sites that have linked to your chosen site. Use the "Only this URL" pull-down menu to limit your search to sites linking specifically to your chosen Web page. Or choose "Entire Site" to find Web sites that are linking to any page within your chosen Web site.

A nice feature is on the right side of the results page, where you'll see a link that says "Export Results to TSV" or Tab Separated Values. If you click the link, you can export the results to a file by saving the file to your desktop that you can then open in a spreadsheet or other data management tool. You can download up to 1,000 results at a time.

For those in marketing, this is very important as part of a search engine optimization program. Having relevant external links to your Web site is critical if you want to show up in the top natural search results for words and phrases related to your company. Here is the TSV list of Web sites linking to my Web site, www.takethecold.com.

	A	B
1	List of inlinks to the URL http://www.takethecold.com	
2	TITLE	URL
3	Hidden Internet Tips For Sales And Bus	http://www.hiddenbusinesst
4	Marketing Interactions: Warm Calls are	http://marketinginteractions.ty
5	startups	http://www.startupbizcast.com
6	entrepreneurs	http://www.startupbizcast.cor
7	First-of-Its-Kind Sales Success Book Lau	http://www.prweb.com/relea
8	Marketing Interactions: Are You Living	http://marketinginteractions
9	The Selling Power without the Search I	http://hiddenbusinesstreasu
10	Warm Call Resource Center - Improve	http://www.warmcallcenter.co
11	Sales Shebang Conference Speakers		http://www.salesshebang.cor
12	Sam Richter - LinkedIn	http://www.linkedin.com/in/s
13	Contact - Harvey Mackay	http://www.harveymackay.cor
14	You Can Kiss Your Competitors Goodby	http://goldencompass.com/b
15	Selling to Big Companies Blog: Sales Sh	http://sellingtobigcompanies
16	Marketing Interactions: Books	http://marketinginteractions

CHAPTER ELEVEN

Not All Engines Are Equal: Other Cool Engines

I n my experience meeting with business people and sales-people, the majority have their favorite search engine and they stay pretty loyal to it. In fact, most people think that all search engines are equal, that all pretty much deliver the same results. Nothing could be further from the truth. In fact, the search engines themselves all claim they offer better, or more, results than the competition.

When you conduct a search and you don't find the results you're looking for in the top twenty listings, it can sometimes be a good idea to check a different search engine.

Here's an example of the exact same search; **"metal stamping" AND industry AND trends** in Yahoo, Google, and MSN. Notice the massive difference in the number of results and, at least in Yahoo and Google's case, the top results.

Yahoo Search – www.yahoo.com – 15,800 results

YAHOO! SEARCH "metal stamping" AND industry AND trends

Search 1 – 10 of about 15,800 ng" AND industry AND trends –

1. IBISWorld US Motor Vehicle **Metal Stamping Industry** Market Research Re
   Industry Research Report: Motor Vehicle **Metal Stamping Industry**. In depth analysis,
   trends, market share, forecasts. Latest Oct 2006. Download instantly. ...
   www.ibisworld.com/**industry**/definition.asp?**industry**_id=836 - 40k - Cached - More from t

2. IBISWorld US Forging & Stamping **Industry** Market Research Report
   In depth analysis, data, **trends**, market share, forecasts. Latest ... Establishments making
   forgings, **metal stamping**, and metal spun products and further ...
   www.ibisworld.com/**industry**/definition.asp?**industry**_id=609 - 40k - Cached - More from th

3. **Industry** Report: Motor Vehicle **Metal Stamping** in the US
   Motor Vehicle **Metal Stamping** in the US - Price: $544.50. Available as a downloadable P
   ibisworld.ecnext.com/comsite5/bin/comsite5.pl?page=description&... - More from this si

Google Search – www.google.com – 65,600 results

MSN Search – www.msn.com – 3,205 results

Google/Yahoo Search Comparisons

www.googleguy.de/google-yahoo/

Googleguy.de is a search engine that simultaneously searches both Google and Yahoo and displays the results side by side. Use this search engine to see what results Google has that Yahoo doesn't and vice versa. It's also interesting to see which sites get ranked higher. Here's a Googleguy search comparison for **"metal stamping industry."**

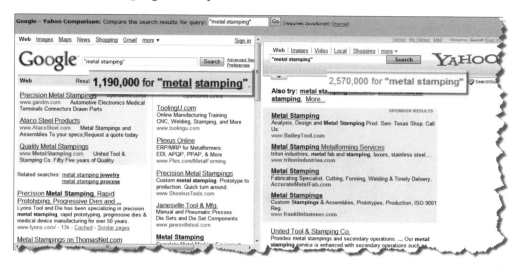

Notice how the number of results are different, by quite a bit. Yahoo claims to have indexed a larger number of sites than Google, and the results when doing comparison searching seem to back up that claim.

In addition to the "Big Three" of Yahoo, Google, and MSN, a number of other general search engines can be helpful when searching for information that can be used in the cold calling and sales process. Here are some of my favorites:

Meta-Search Engines – Search Multiple Engines Simultaneously

http://www.mamma.com
http://www.dogpile.com

As I have discussed, different search engines "vacuum up" or index different Web pages, and they all rank the relevance of results differently. Wouldn't it be nice if there was a "central vacuum cleaner" that showed you the index results from multiple search engines? There are such central vacuum cleaners and they're call meta-search engines.

Use a meta-search engine if you're having difficulty finding results with your favorite search engine. Some meta-search engines even search directory engines and index engines simultaneously.

Here's a look at a search result for trends in the financial services industry. Note how the results from this meta-search engine, Dogpile.com, are listed as coming from a number of different index search engines.

MSN – Industry Related Search

http://www.msn.com

The Microsoft search engine, MSN, has a nice feature that quickly allows you to search various industry topics. It's called "Related Searches" and it can be a good time-saver for locating multiple information sources related to an industry.

For example, if I'm looking for information on the pharmaceutical industry, I enter the broad search term *pharmaceutical* into the main MSN search form. Because MSN is an index engine, the results page for such a broad topic returns more than

14 million listings. However, on the right side of the results page is a list of related searches to the pharmaceutical industry.

By clicking on any of the related results, I go to a new search that is specific to that topic. So for example, by clicking on the "pharmaceutical companies" list, I receive more than one million search results related to companies in the pharmaceutical industry, which is still more than I want. But notice on the right hand side that I have a new set of related search results, all related to pharmaceutical companies.

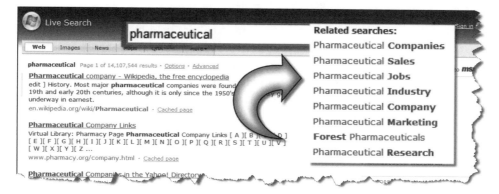

Clicking on the link "top pharmaceutical companies" delivers sites with listing of the top companies in the field. I can even click on the next set of related results and narrow my search to the top 100 companies, or even top ten.

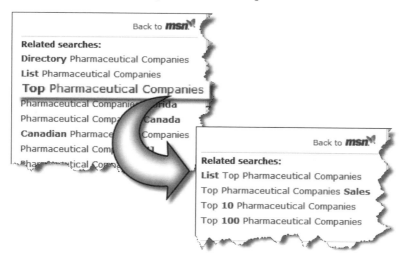

This drill-down method allows me to start with a very broad industry search term and narrow my focus by clicking on results related to my original search. In a sense, this is an automated version of a directory engine with its categories and subcategories.

Mool – News Search

http://www.mool.com/media

SAM TIP
Mool News:

Use Mool media search to locate current and some archived news stories on companies, people, and industries.

1. Go to **www.mool.com/ media**

2. Enter search terms as you would with any search engine.

3. Use Boolean to expand or narrow your search.

4. Instead of searching billions of Web sites, Mool limits its search to about 4,500 key news sources.

Search engines are an excellent way to search for news on companies, people, and industries. Unfortunately, news stories get mixed in with Web sites which can cause you to spend time sorting through results trying to find relevant articles.

Most popular search engines now feature a news-specific search, and Google even lets you search for news archives where you can purchase older articles on an individual basis (http://news.google.com). A great choice, however, for free news articles is Mool.com (http://www.mool.com/media), which is a meta-search engine that takes advantage of Google's Custom Search technology.

Use the Mool Media Search Engine just like you would any search engine, being careful to use Boolean to narrow or expand your search. Instead of searching the entire Web and its billions of indexed Web sites, Mool limits its search to about 4,500 key newspaper, magazine, newswires, and broadcast news Web sites.

A friend of mine is president of a company that helps match franchise owners with people who want to own a franchise. If I were going to meet with Lori and wanted to learn what was going on at her company so I could ask intelligent questions during our conversation, I would use Mool and I'd get some great results.

Mool does not come close to accessing the news articles featured in premium news sources discussed later in this book. However, for a quick search of publicly available and free news articles, Mool does a good job of delivering results.

Mool

Media Search Engine | franchoice | Search

Google
Custom Sea...

Finding the Perfect Franchise Fit
Franchise consulting services, such as FranNet and **FranChoice**, are another free resource available to entrepreneurs. Working on a commission-based
www.businessweek.com/sb20060728_328561.htm

Today's franchises run the gamut: tried-and-true, odd and new - US ...
That's why **FranChoice**, an Eden Prairie, Minn., company that helps entrepreneurs find the ...ers to take a thorough ...
www.usnews.com/cles/040802/2franchise_3.htm

Should You Consider Franchising? - Small Business News Story ...
Franchisors prefer working with people who can follow the rules, rather than true ...Jeff Elgin, CEO of **FranChoice**, an Eden Prairie, Minn., ...
nbc5.com/ness/8037645/detail.html

Franchises: How much can you earn? - Jul. 1, 2004
A good broker -- Bond named **FranChoice** as one -- can also help. ... Many franchise buyer...hoice spokeswoman) obtain ...
money.cnn.com/wmuchfranchise/

Should You Consider Franchising? (Small Business) | SmartMoney.com

Clusty – Clustering Search Engine Results

http://clusty.com
(Note: no www in URL)

Clusty.com is a search engine that acts like an index engine/ directory engine combination. Clusty's index engine is actually a meta-search engine, meaning the results appear from a number of other search engines.

What makes Clusty special is that it uses a search technique called "clustering" in which the engine scans for common words in a list of results and "clusters" them in folders, or categories, much like a directory engine. Unlike a directory engine, Clusty does its clustering instantly and automatically, without any human review.

Clusty is a good search engine for industry information because the clustered results often help you drill down into the essence of what you really need. By reviewing the clusters, you can quickly identify which topics will be most help-

SAM TIP
Clusty.com:

Clusty.com (**http://clusty. com**) delivers index engine results in its main results page and "clusters" information on the results page left-hand side.

- **Industry Search:** Reviewing the clustered results can help you focus your search to specific industry topics.

- **Company Search:** Limit your search by using the Site Colon search; e.g., entering **site:acme.com** will deliver only results from the Acme Web site, and the clustering will quickly let you see different areas of the site.

ful in your search, and by clicking on the corresponding link, you can get the results related to just that topic.

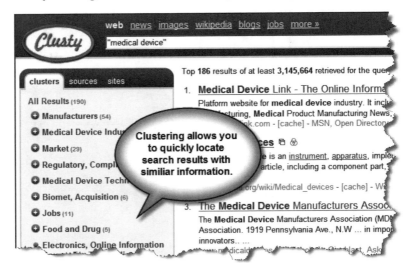

Notice the clusters on the left side of the Clusty search result page and how they nicely separate into easily searchable categories.

Clusty.com is also a great site for company searching. Use the Site Colon search and limit your search to a specific Web site. For example, **site:lawsonsoftware.com** in Clusty limits the search to just the Lawson Software company Web site. The clustered results then help you "break down" the company into manageable areas to research.

Cuil – Relevancy Engine

http://www.cuil.com

Cuil has received a lot of press lately as a search engine that compiles and displays its results in ways supposedly quite different than the more popular search engines.

Cuil (pronounced "cool"), an old Irish word for knowledge, was developed by a group of ex-Google executives and PhD research scientists. Rather than rely on popularity metrics, Cuil searches for and ranks pages based on their content and relevance. When Cuil finds a page with your keywords, the engine instantly analyzes the page's content and inter-relationships to deliver categorized search results.

Cuil claims to be the world's largest search engine in terms of the number of sites it has indexed (or vacuumed up). The company claims to have indexed three times as many Web pages as Google and ten times as many as Microsoft When I did some comparison searching, I found that Cuil indeed listed many more results than both Google and Yahoo, although I'm not really sure that's a good thing as the number is not as important as the quality.

That's where Cuil offers some neat technologies. The engines allows you to start with a very broad search and using the Cuil tools, you can quickly drill down into results that are relevant to what you want.

For example, a very broad search on the word "automotive" delivered 1.4 billion results! Glancing at the results page, like the same search in Google or Yahoo would show, the top results are all related to sites that want to sell me automotive products. However, what Cuil does is that—similar to

SAM TIP
Cuil.com:

Cuil claims to be the world's largest search engine, having indexed more pages than Google and Yahoo. Where Cuil delivers is in its clustering of results into relevant categories.

1. Go to **www.cuil.com**

2. Conduct a standard search however, use a broad search term for the best results.

3. On the results page under the search form, look for tabs of higher level result categories. Click on a tab to review the results within that category.

4. Or, on the Explore By Category drop-down menu, choose a category, click on a sub-category within the main category, and review those results.

5. Continue to "drill down" using the category/sub-category menus until you start finding results relevant to the information you desire.

Clusty—it clusters related results, in Cuil's instance along the top as tabs, and as expandable menu items. Where it goes beyond Clusty is that as you click to expand a tab or topic, Cuil clusters the new results as well, allowing you to continue to search for topics and providing you ideas for new searches.

Another Cuil feature (sorry, I couldn't help the double entendre) is the various ways you can identify a category/sub-category structure. Both the top-level tab menu and the drop-down menu have "More" buttons that when clicked on, provide numerous new categories related to your original search. You can continue to click on the various menus until the search results get to a number where Cuil no longer has category listings. I also like how Cuil displays the results in columns, with logos and other information attached to each result.

Where I find Cuil falling short is when I do want do conduct a more specific search, Cuil delivers me too many results. In addition, on the more detailed searches, often, there are no related categories/subcategories or if there are, they are not very relevant to my original search. For example, in Cuil, when I search for a person's name, the results aren't nearly as relevant as with other search engines. Cuil also does not offer an Advanced Search or Boolean option.

Exalead – Searching Made Easy

http://www.exalead.com/search

One of the problems with writing a book like this is that Web sites constantly change, and new search technologies enter the market on a regular basis. (To stay on top of the changes, make sure to register for my monthly Warm Call Newsletter at **www.takethecold.com**).

A new search engine I recently found, Exalead, does a nice job of combining some of my favorite advanced search techniques from other engines into their main search results page. Exalead (**www.exalead.com/search**), created by a technology firm in Paris, France, is quite simply, along with Cuil, one of the better search technologies I've come across in some time. Although it does not yet index enough of the Web to bring back results that I know exist (for example, a Google search on my name delivers 6,510 results, Cuil delivers 8.7 million, while Exalead delivers just 341), Exalead has bundled many of the best search "bells and whistles" into one easy-to-use engine.

I recommend skipping the main search engine and going directly to Exalead's advanced search feature, the link located directly to the main search button. When using Exalead's Advanced Search, you're presented with a number of different searching options, all with easy-to-understand examples. Click on any of the options and the search form will direct you; all you have to do is type. You can choose any option

SAM TIP ↖
Exalead.com/ search:

Exalead offers a search engine with the features to make searching the Web easy.

1. Go to **www.exalead.com/ search**

2. Conduct a standard search or ...

3. Use Exalead's Advanced Search link, located directly next to the main search button.

4. In Advanced Search, follow the prompts and narrow or expand your search. No need to know Boolean as Exalead does the work for you.

5. Click the "preview" button on the search results for a preview of what the selected site looks like, complete with highlighted search terms.

6. Narrow your search by choosing one of the links on the right side.

7. Make sure to click the More Choices button on the right side for additional narrowing options, including a "Search Within Results" form.

combination to narrow or expand your search, and you don't need to know or even understand Boolean terms, as Exalead takes the guesswork out of advanced searching.

When conducting a search for recent information relat-

Advanced search   Close ☒

`"medical device industry" after:01/01/2007`   [**Web Search**]

What?

- exact phrase *e.g. "to be or not to be"*
- forbidden terms *e.g. cow -mad*
- words starting with *e.g. messag**
- phonetic spelling *e.g. soundslike:exallead*
- approximate spelling *e.g. spellslike:exlaead*
- adjacent words *e.g. (stock NEAR exchange)*
- logical expression *e.g. ((fast OR speed) AND NOT light)*
- regular expression *e.g. /a.c/*

Where?

- [Choose a country ▼] *e.g. country:USA*
- [Choose a language ▼] *e.g. language:en*
- on a given site *e.g. site:wikipedia.org*
- in files of a given format *e.g. filetype:pdf*
- in the title of the page *e.g. intitle:(official website)*
- in the address of the page *e.g. inurl:music*
- on pages that contain a given link *e.g. link:http://www.exalead.com*

When?

- modified after a given date *e.g. after:31/12/1999*
- modified before a given date *e.g. before:31/12/1999*

---

ed to the medical device industry, I chose "exact phrase" and "modified after a given date." Exalead made it easy for me to enter my information and conduct my search.

Exalead's results page offers some intriguing ways to view your search results. You can click directly on a result link to visit a specific Web page. Or, next to each search result is a miniature screen shot of the indexed Web site.

Click on the Preview button and the Web site opens up in a new window. In the window, all of the search terms that

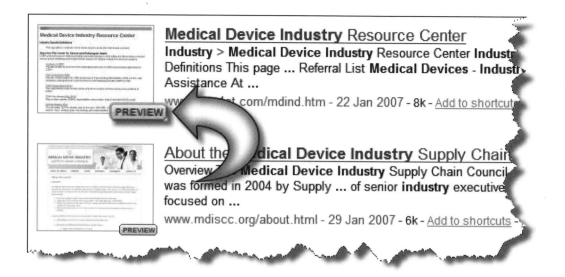

you're looking for are highlighted. Much like the Cached link in Google and other search engines, the Exalead preview feature allows you to quickly locate information in a long page of text.

Back on the main search results page, Exalead offers a number of different options to narrow your search. Make

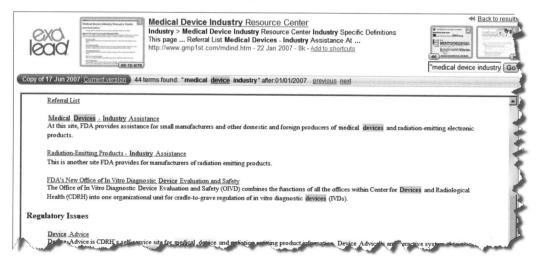

sure to click the More Choices button to view all of the different options.

"Related terms" allow you to add or remove words and/or phrases suggested by Exalead. You can choose to add or delete specific site type searches, like Blogs, with the "Site type" limiter. You can even choose to include or exclude multimedia formats, languages, and specific file types.

You can also limit or include specific geographic regions to your search, allowing you to narrow or expand your search by where the Web site is located. You can even limit your search results to sites that have been included in Exalead's Directory.

Another nice feature is the Search Within Results form. Just add additional terms, but instead of searching the entire Web for those terms, you will limit your search to just your original result set. This allows you to start your search using a very broad topic, and then continually narrow down by adding additional terms.

Narrow your search

Related terms
- Medical device industry   exclude
- Device industries   exclude
- Medical device company   exclude
- Medical device manufacturer   exclude

Site type
- Blog   exclude

Multimedia
- Video   exclude
- RSS   exclude

Languages
- English (532)   exclude
- French (9)   exclude
- German (3)   exclude
- Italian (2)   exclude

Directory
- Business and Economy   exclude

File types
- Acrobat (.pdf) (16)   exclude

Geographic location
- North America (407)   exclude
  - United States   exclude
  - Canada   exclude
- Europe (116)   exclude
  - United Kingdom   exclude

Search within results
[   ] Go

« Less choice

Once Exalead indexes more search results it might become your search engine of choice. That's of course if they remain independent and don't get purchased by one of the Web search behemoths, Google, Yahoo, or MSN.

CHAPTER TWELVE

The "Invisible Web"

"The time spent doing research and preparing questions can give you a compelling competitive advantage."
– Chris Lytle, *The Accidental Salesperson*,
New York: AMACOM, 2000.

In my presentation, when I ask people what percentage of Web pages that can be accessed by search engines like Google and Yahoo, the typical response I receive is 75 percent or higher. Would it surprise you that at best, combined, popular search engines probably index less than 20 percent of publicly accessible Web pages?

I've read some estimates that put the number of Web pages that exist on the Internet at more than 500 billion, and that number is growing by the millions each week! In Google's marketing, I've seen the number of pages they index at around 15 billion, meaning that the most popular search engine in the world, Google, indexes a little more than 3 percent of Web pages online (to be fair to Google, studies do show that Google indexes about 70 percent of the sites that are possible to index).

So where are all of these Web pages that popular search engines miss? How come Google, Yahoo, MSN, and the rest can't find them? These billions upon billions of Web pages reside on what's called the "Invisible Web."

I first heard of the "Invisible Web" after reading a book of the same name by Chris Sherman and Gary Price, two of the most knowledgeable individuals around when it comes to finding information on the Internet. I highly recommend reading their book as it provides an exceptional overview of what the Web is, isn't, what it contains and how to find in-

SAM TIP
Invisible Web:

The term "Invisible Web" was coined by search gurus Chris Sherman and Gary Price. It refers to the billions of Web sites that cannot be indexed or "vacuumed up" by search engines like Google, Yahoo, and MSN.

The "Invisible Web" makes up the majority of online information. The good news is it is accessible and the content is often free; you just have to know where to look.

A quick way to access the "Invisible Business Web" is via the Warm Call Center at **www.warmcallcenter.com**.

formation. Chris and Gary are truly Web search gurus and you can also sign up for their newsletters and blogs (just do a Google search on "Chris Sherman" or "Gary Price" and you'll easily find a lot of their material).

I've also heard of the Invisible Web referred to as the "Deep Web" or the "Hidden Web" but basically, these terms are referring to Web sites and pages that can't be indexed by a typical search engine.

Why can't a search engine index a Web page? Remember how an index engine like Google works: it's basically a big vacuum cleaner that runs around looking for Web pages with words on them. When Google finds a page with words, it "sucks up" the words, goes back to Google headquarters, and dumps the words into a big database.

What happens when Google finds a Web page but there are no words to "suck up?" Google just goes away.

What kinds of Web pages don't have words on them? What kind of Web sites can't Google and other popular search engines access?

Have you ever gone to a Web site that requires you to register to get access to the information? Once registered, you have access to a library of information. Until you register, that content sits behind a secure wall.

Google can't register. Google can tell you what's on that Web site's home page, but unless the Webmaster has opened up a "back door" for the Google vacuum cleaner to enter, that entire library of information—although free for you to use after registration—is missed by Google; the entire article library resides on the Invisible Web.

Other examples of Web pages that are on the Invisible Web include Web pages that are built using "dynamically driven content." What this fancy term means is the words on the Web page never really exist because the content is displayed differently for each site viewer. How could that be?

Have you ever gone to a Web site where you're asked a series of questions and then based on your answers, information appears? The information never really sits in a format for Google or other search engines to vacuum. The information that you're seeing emanates from a secure database. It only resides temporarily on your Web browser screen and appears only based on your answers the initial questions. Google, in particular, is getting much better at indexing dynamically generated Web pages like online catalogs, but data-rich Web pages are still often missed by popular search engines.

Another more practical way to look at the Invisible Web is as Web pages that are indexed by popular search engines but that appear in search results 1,000–100 million. Meaning, even if the Web page can be indexed by a search engine, they are typically featured far down on the results list so in effect, they are "invisible" to most searchers as most people don't bother to look past the first few hundred search results.

The good news is the majority of the Invisible Web is publicly accessible and most of the content is free; if you know where to look. (Hint: because you have this book and access to the Warm Call Center at **www.warmcallcenter.com**, you now know where and how to look.)

For a salesperson, account manager, or for anyone involved in business development, business planning, strategic planning or marketing, the Invisible Web has an amazing amount of information. The following chapters are a review of my favorite Invisible Web sites that will help you prepare for any sales presentation, account meeting and help you consistently practice the Platinum Rule. I've divided the sites into three categories.

1. **Invisible Web – Company Information:** This chapter features reviews of Web sites you can use to practice the "Fourth R" and get information related to a company's activities. These sites are superb when researching prospects, competitors, your clients' competitors, and your client's current customers.

2. **Invisible Web – Industry Information:** Remember the Cahners Research study in Chapter II that showed the vast majority of purchasers of business-to-business products expect salespeople to have a good understanding of their clients' industry? Using Invisible Web sites prior to any sales call can be the key between "winging it" and knowing what issues your prospect is facing and

how your products/services are relevant to solving your prospect's problems.

3. **Invisible Web – Personal Information:** Where can you get information on people? Whether it's finding individuals at a company, the demographics of a community, or the lifestyles of those in a zip code, these Invisible Web sites provide a wealth of information for the salesperson, account manager, and business or marketing planner.

Find the sites that are most helpful to you and you'll begin to get the information you need to practice the "Fourth R," the Platinum Rule, and value-based/solution-based selling and account management. These sites will ultimately help you take the cold out of cold calling and turn client/vendor relationships into long-term, value-added partnerships.

CHAPTER THIRTEEN

The "Invisible Web" – Company Information

> "Make sure you've done absolutely all your homework on the client company, the client marketplace, and the client individual, and that it's absolutely up to the minute. Even if you know them and their business cold, there is a likelihood that there will be some news clip about your client that will have been published that very day."
> – David H. Maiser, Charles H. Green, and Robert M. Galford, *The Trusted Advisor*, New York: The Free Press, 2000.

In the sales process, think how valuable it would be to, during your cold call, have in-depth information about the company you're calling on, including a good understanding of their current offerings and possible needs. As an account manager, imagine having solid information on your client's competitors. How much more value could you provide?

The following "Invisible Web" sites are ones that business information experts use to research prospects, customers, and competitors. The sites work for finding information on public and private companies, and non-profit organizations.

Company Data – Manta

http://www.manta.com

At one time or another, you've probably heard about Dun & Bradstreet and its numerous company information databases and lists that you can purchase. We'll discuss D&B in detail

SAM TIP 🖈
Manta:

Get free basic D&B information on virtually every U.S. public and private company.

1. Go to **www.manta.com**

2. Register for free or log in with your username and password.

3. Enter the company name on the main page search form.

4. Locate the company you want in the results listing; click on the link to see basic D&B data.

5. On the top of the company detail page, click on links that will then list additional companies in the industry and/or geographic region.

later; however, there is a free service from the Web site Manta (**www.manta.com**) that, with registration, provides basic D&B data.

Manta actually is a gateway to company and industry reports from numerous research organizations that you can purchase. To generate interest and users, they offer the free D&B data. In my opinion, it's the best company information search engine on the Web, as it is the best at finding information on private companies.

You can get very basic company information including location and industry via Manta without registering. However, if you register, you can access additional company data including the number of employees, revenue figures, year started, where incorporated (important if you want to look at government documents related to the company), company Web site(s), the key executive(s), and more.

To begin your search following registration, just type in the name of the company you want in the main Manta search form. Note that, unlike other search engines, you don't have to use quotation marks around a company name to generate the best results.

After your search, you'll need to scroll down the page a bit to locate your result list. Because Manta/D&B will list all companies with the name that you want, don't be surprised if there are many results. Unfortunately, when I add a location in my search (e.g., lawson software AND Minnesota), I return zero results. However, each company in the Manta results list does list the state where the company is located.

In your search result list, you may see in parentheses after the company name (Branch) or (HQ), identifying the particular listing as being either a branch office or the company headquarters. To view information about the company, just click on the appropriate link.

10 Companies listed

Your Search Results on **"lawson software"**

Lawson Software Inc (Branch)
MN

Lawson Software Inc (Branch)
CO

Lawson Software Inc (HQ)
MN

Lawson Software Inc (Branch)

Home Find Companies: U.S. | Worldwide   Browse: Industries | Publishers

Manta > Find Companies > Saint Paul, MN > Technology & Communications > Computer Soft software > Lawson Software, Inc

Lawson Software, Inc

380 Saint Peter St Fl 1, Saint Paul, MN, United Sta

Phone: (651) 767-7000

Ticker Symbol: LWSN

URL: www.lawson.com

Trade Style Names: Lawson; Lawson Software

SIC: Prepackaged Software

Line of business: Prepackaged Software Services Custom Computer Programing

Lawson Software, Inc - Detailed Company Profile

Year Started: 1975

State of Incorporation: DE

URL: www.lawson.com

Location type: Headquarters

Stock Symbol: LWSN

Stock Exchange: NMS

Trade Style Names: Lawson; Lawson Software

NAICS: Software Publishers; Custom Computer Programming Services

Est. Annual Sales: $390,776,000

Est. Employees: 3,400

Est. Employees at Location: 900

Contact Name: Harry Debes

Contact Title: President And Chief Executive Officer

Click on a link for companies in that category.

After you click on the company name to view detailed company information, take note of the directory links on the top of the listing and additional categories on the details page right-hand side. Click on any of these links and you'll find a listing of companies that meet the category criteria. You can't download a list like you can in a typical D&B search, although you certainly can print the list, and it's a great way to get a snapshot of competitors and others operating in a particular industry.

Manufacturing Company Locator – ThomasNet

http://www.thomasnet.com

SAM TIP ▸
ThomasNet:

ThomasNet is the online version of the Thomas Registry key manufacturing directory.

1. Go to **www.thomasnet.com**

2. Use the top navigation tabs to choose your search type: products, companies, brands, or industry.

3. Enter your search term(s).

4. Click on the categories that appear right for additional information.

Who makes "stuff" in the United States and Canada? Who are the key suppliers to an industry? This is obviously great information if you are an entrepreneur and want to know who can manufacture your product. It's equally appealing if you're a company that sells to other companies and you'd like to easily and quickly pull up a list of organizations operating in a particular industry.

ThomasNet is the online version of the popular Thomas Register. The Register is a physical book considered the premier directory of North American manufacturers.

The ThomasNet search feature allows you to search by company name, product type, brand name, or industry. You can also use the ThomasNet directory to locate lists of companies that have been neatly organized into categories and subcategories. Click on a category in the Browse Categories section to access the directory.

When conducting a Brand Name, Product/Service, or industrial Web search, you'll notice various related categories that appear on the results page. Click on any of these links for additional information, companies, and products related to that particular category.

When conducting a Company Name search, once you've pulled up a list, you can modify your results by geography by choosing a state, or even enter a mileage range to a particular zip code and further restrict your results.

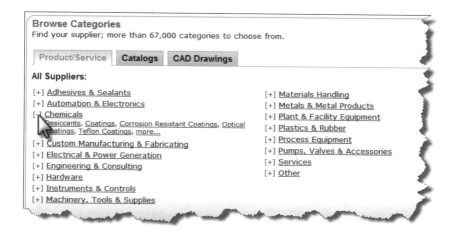

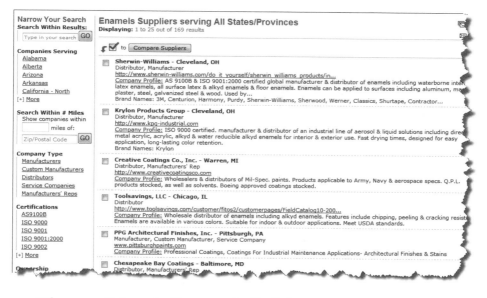

When you click on the Company Profile link associated with each company, you'll get a company detail listing featuring a brief company description and a link to the company Web site. In addition, you'll find estimated revenue figures and employee size, the key activities that a company is involved in and, with some listings, you'll find products that the company manufactures or sells.

Larger Company Information – Hoovers

http://www.hoovers.com

If you're looking for information on publicly held and larger private companies, one of the best resources around is Hoovers. A Dun & Bradsteet company, Hoovers leverages the D&B database to compile detailed company data including financial information, executive contacts, and more.

Although the site has links to search for companies by industry and geography, I would recommend just entering the company name directly into the search form. As there is no Advanced Search, you'll want to make sure to use Boolean and put quotation marks around multi-word company names.

If you search for information on a smaller company, you'll most likely find that Hoovers does have information, but you'll have to purchase a report to see the information. You'll know because when you click on a company name after a search, you'll either go directly to company information or you'll open up a browser window that asks you to subscribe.

For publicly held companies, the information is quite robust including detailed financial data and charts from the Edgar database. For larger companies, you'll find company overviews, competitor lists, executive compensation information, and even recent job postings.

For smaller companies, you'll find similar data as to what you would find in Manta (which also uses D&B data to power its database) including revenue and employment figures. Occasionally you'll also find a "Competitive Landscape" profile, that when clicked, provides some useful information.

Imagine meeting with a prospect and being able to site industry forecasts when you ask questions related to future company direction, competitive differentiation, etc.

SAM TIP
Hoovers:

Hoovers offers very good information on publicly-held and larger private companies.

1. Go to **www.hoovers.com**

2. Enter a company name in the main search form; use quotation marks around multi-word names.

3. After results appear, if Hoovers offers free information, you'll see it when you click on the company name; if not, you'll be asked to subscribe to see the data.

4. Click the various resource and tool links to see what free information Hoovers provides.

5. See if the company detail page offers a Competition field, with the option to click on a Competitive Landscape link; click on it to see a nice industry overview, forecast, and recent developments.

Competition

Competitive Landscape for Public Relations

Demand is driven primarily by the health of the US economy and corporate profits. The profitability of individual companies depends on the value of the creative services delivered and efficient use...

▶▶ **Read more about Weber Shandwick Worldwide's competition** across multiple industries

Competition

Now Viewing Weber Shandwick Worldwide's competition in: **Public Relations (primary)**

Compare Weber Shandwick Worldwide to its competition in: Select Industry... ▼ Update View

Competitive Landscape

Demand is driven primarily by the health of the US economy and **corporate profits.** The profitability of individual companies depends on the value of the **creative services** delivered and **efficient use of personnel.** Large companies have advantages in having multiple subsidiaries that offer different marketing services to large customers and some economies of scale in marketing. Small companies can compete successfully by specializing in a particular industry or geographic market. The PR industry is **labor-intensive:** average annual revenue per employee is less than $150,000.

▦ **Full Industry Overview For Public Relations**

Public Relations Industry Forecast

from Hoover's/D&B subsidiary First Research

The output of US advertising and related services, including public relations, is forecast to grow at an annual compounded rate of 2 percent between 2008 and 2013. Data Sourced: December 2008

Advertising and Related Services Growth Slowly Strengthens

First Research forecasts are based on INFORUM forecasts that are licensed from the Interindustry Economic Research Fund, Inc. (IERF) in College Park, MD. INFORUM's "interindustry-macro" approach to modeling the economy captures the links between industries and the aggregate economy.

First Research Industry Growth Rating

The First Research Industry Growth Rating reflects the expected industry growth

Recent Developments

Podcasts May Become Mainstream PR Platform - The US podcast audience is expected to nearly double from 2008 to 2013, which may increase PR agencies' use of podcasts to reach target markets. Over the next five years, the podcast audience is predicted to grow from 9 percent of US Internet users to 17 percent, according to market research firm eMarketer. By 2013, more than 37 million people will download at least one podcast per month.

Recession Causes Drop In Direct Mailing Campaigns - US PR firms' marketing strategies in 2009 may involve less direct mailing as firms try to cut costs. Spending on direct mailing campaigns fell 3 percent in 2008, the biggest drop in more than 60 years. Direct mail spending may continue to fall, possibly by as much as 9 percent in 2009, according to research firm Winterberry Group. Cheaper marketing strategies include targeted mailings, instead of mass mailings, and digital media.

Industry Divided on 2009 Forecast - Surveyed PR firms are split on revenue predictions for 2009: about one third predict growth, one third predict decline, and another third predict revenues to be flat. Firms predicting growth in 2009 expect corporations will need PR firms for crisis management, for social media, and for help maintaining visibility during the economic downturn, according to a survey by the Council of Public Relations Firms.

Visit Guidestar for detailed
information on non-profit
organizations.

1. Go to **www.guidestar.com**.

2. Enter an organization's
   name and a city or state
   into the main search form.

3. Click on a result, and then
   on the organization's overview page, click on a tab for
   additional details.

4. You will need to register to
   access detailed information;
   some data is only available
   to premium members.

5. Form 990 data is a non-
   profit's tax filing and
   contains detailed information on revenue, expenses,
   compensation, investment
   performance, and more.

Non-Profit Financials – Guidestar

http://www.guidestar.org

There are well more than one million non-profit organizations in the United States, many with multi-million dollar
budgets. So there's a good chance that no matter what you
sell, a non-profit organization might need your product or
service.

Because of their special tax status and because many
non-profits are funded via public trust, financial information
available regarding non-profits is almost on par to what's
available on public companies. Everything from annual revenue sources and expenses to executive compensation can
be found by using Guidestar, the pre-eminent source of non-
profit financial data.

To use, go to www.guidestar.org and conduct a search using the search box on the site's home page; enter in an organization's name and a city or state. If you don't find the result
you want, try entering the name in differently, for example,
St. Jude's Hospital might be Saint Jude's Hospital.

If you want to search by geographic location, click the
Advanced Search link next to the main search button. Once
in Advanced Search, just choose a state and Guidestar will list
all of the non-profit organizations within that state. On the
results page, you can further refine your search by city.

For information about a non-profit, just click the result
link and you'll see an overview page that lists the organization's contact information and other key facts. Click on the

Contact Information:		At a Glance:	
Greater Twin Cities United Way		Category:	P Human Services / P99 Human
		Learn More >	Services - Multipurpose and
Also Known As:			Other N.E.C.
Former Name(s):			
Physical Address:	404 S Eighth St	Areas Served:	
		Year Founded:	2001
	Minneapolis, MN 55404 1804		
Web Address:	www.unitedwaytwincities.org		
Blog Address:			
Contact E-mail:	▓▓▓▓@unitedwaytwincities.org		

General Info	Financials	Forms 990 & Docs	Programs & Help	People	News

various tabs for detailed information. For example, the People tab lists information on the executive director and key staff and board members. Form 990 allows you to download an organization's tax returns, featuring revenue and expense information. NOTE: you will need to register to see detailed information, and some of the data is only available to paying Premium members.

Use this information carefully when making a warm call on a non-profit; you obviously don't want to "blurt out" how much money the executive director made last year. Yet armed with this data, you can ask great questions, craft highly relevant proposals, and make superb impressions with your organizational knowledge.

Pending Patents – Patent Application Database

http://patft.uspto.gov
(Note: no www in URL – choose Patent Applications Quick Search)

Imagine a sales call where you walk in talking about how your company can help distribute a product your prospect hasn't even introduced yet? How quickly could you turn a cold sales call into a warm one if you were able to show your prospect detailed drawings of the new technology *their* competitor will be introducing in the next year?

You can find every patent issued and almost all patent applications through the U.S. Patent Office online database. You can search by company name, individual's name, or even industry if you'd like to get a list of new technologies for a particular industry.

To search for pending patents, go to the Web site and enter the information you desire. Note that if you're searching for a person's or company's name, you'll want to put it in quotation marks.

Use the site's automatic Boolean terms to enter more than one word or name. Enter the most important term, typically the company name, product name, or industry in the Term 1 field. In the Term 2 field, enter any additional information (e.g., if you entered the company name in the Term 1 field, you might want to enter the product type in the Term 2 field).

After hitting the Search button, you'll see a list of patent applications relevant to your query. To read the full patent application, just click on any of the listed links.

When reviewing a patent application, note that the company you're researching may in fact just be mentioned in someone else's patent application. You can tell who the patent application is for by reviewing the owner information upon clicking your selected link.

Let's look for pending patents for Lawson Software.

Once you click on a patent to read it, take note of a tab on the upper part of the page called "Images." When you click on this tab, you'll receive an image of the full patent application including any charts, graphs, tables, or CAD drawings. It's truly an image of the full patent application as submitted to the patent office.

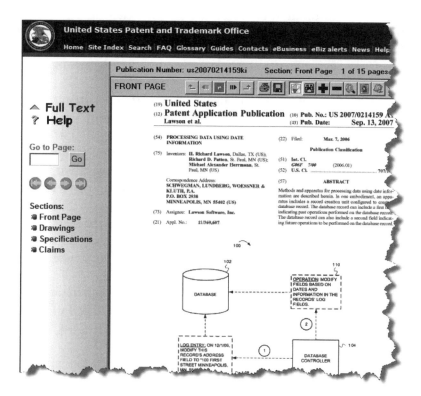

PATENT SEARCH NOTE: To see the full patent image, you'll need special TIFF reading software which you can download for free. For a list of places to download patent viewing software, visit: **http://www.uspto.gov/web/menu/plugins/tiff.htm**

Patents – Google Patent Search

http://www.google.com/patents

Google has an excellent patent search engine and it uses the standard Google interface you're used to. It's simple to use and it's much easier to get drawings and abstracts versus the U.S. Patent Web site.

Go to **www.google.com/patents** and enter the name of the company you're interested in on the search form. Remember that if it's a multiple-word company name you should use Boolean quotations (e.g., "widget corporation").

On the results page, click on any patent link for additional information. Once on the Google patent page, you can easily click and download additional information about your chosen patent including the patent Abstract, Drawing, Description, and/or Claims.

To easily search for information within a particular patent, just scroll down on the Google patent results page and look for a search form titled "Search Within This Patent." Type in any word or phrase within this search form and Google will search for results only within your selected patent.

For additional search options, click the Advanced Patent Search link on the Google Patent home page (the link is right next to the Search button). The Advanced Patent Search feature gives you additional search options, including the ability to search for patents by date. This can be helpful if you want to see what new patents a company has issued.

Here's an example of a Google Patent Search on my former employer, Digital River. I clicked the Drawing link:

SAM TIP 🖈
Google Patents:

Google Patents is a quick and easy way to locate and view existing patents and search for information within a patent.

1. Go to **www.google.com/patents**

2. Enter the name of the company you're researching in the search box. If it's a multiple-word company (e.g., "widget corporation") make sure to use quotation marks.

3. On the results page, click on any patent that appears.

4. Click Abstract, Drawing, Description, and/or Claims for additional information about the patent.

5. Read the patent online, or download a PDF file.

6. Scroll down the page and use the search form that allows you to search within a patent.

7. Use the Advanced Patent Search feature (next to the Search button) and limit your patent search by multiple criteria, including dates.

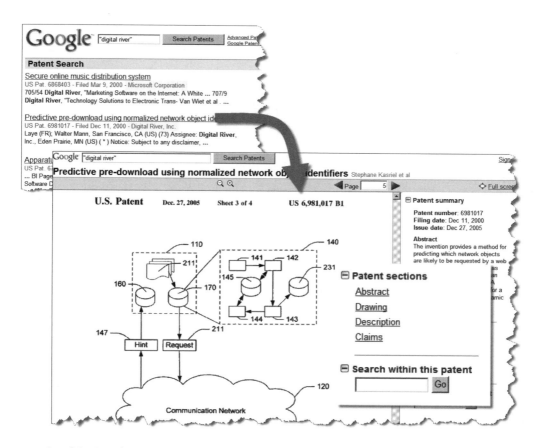

On this Google Patents results page, there are a number of patents listed, the first one from Microsoft and the second from Digital River. This means that the first one, the Microsoft patent, references a product or patent of Digital River.

Related Firms – TouchGraph Graphical Company Relationships

http://www.TouchGraph.com/TGGoogleBrowser.html
(Note: web address is case sensitive)

We discussed earlier in the *Yahoo Tip Company "Friend Search"* section how you can use the "link:" query to find what Web sites are linking to each other with the assumption that if

TouchGraph gives you
a graphical representa-
tion of Web site relationships. Knowing these
relationships can provide
a snapshot of a company's
friends, vendors, customers,
partners, and even competitors.

1. Go the Web address under
   the header (or **www.touch-
   graph.com**, and choose
   the "TouchGraph Google"
   button on the right).

2. Enter the Web site address
   you're interested in and
   click the "Graph It" button.

3. Sites that appear either
   directly or indirectly link to,
   or have related content to,
   your chosen site.

4. Click on any of the images
   to move the graph around
   and see linking relationships.

5. Click any of the listed sites
   on the left side to see additional information about
   the site, including a Web
   address.

someone is linking to a company, they are probably a friend, supplier, or customer of that company (or a disgruntled customer or employee).

TouchGraph is a tool that graphically shows you who's linked to a company's Web site, and also who's linking to the company that links to the company's Web site, and so on. You can get a snapshot of a company's "friends" with this valuable online program.

Note: Web site links are important because if you want your Web site to appear high in natural search engine results, one of the key criteria search engines use is how many sites link to your site. If your site does not rank high and if your site does not have many direct linking relationships in TouchGraph, have your marketing team initiate a linking campaign and get your company's "friends" to link to your company's site.)

To use TouchGraph, just go to the TouchGraph site and enter the name of the Web address you'd like to learn about. You must have Java enabled on your computer (most computers do; if you don't, you can download it at www.java.com).

After a few seconds, an animated chart appears showing site relationships. You can click on any of the images that feature a Web page. With your mouse, you can move the chart around to see different relationships. You can even click on any of the Web site names to get information about that site and click again to visit it.

On the left-hand side you'll see a list of all sites that link to or relate to your chosen site. You can click on any of these links for information about the site, including the Web address so you can visit the site in a new browser window.

Following is a TouchGraph chart of Weber Shandwick, the PR agency where I used to work. The chart shows who is linking to Weber's site, who links to the sites that link to Weber's site, sites that are related to Weber's site and who is linking to them, and so on.

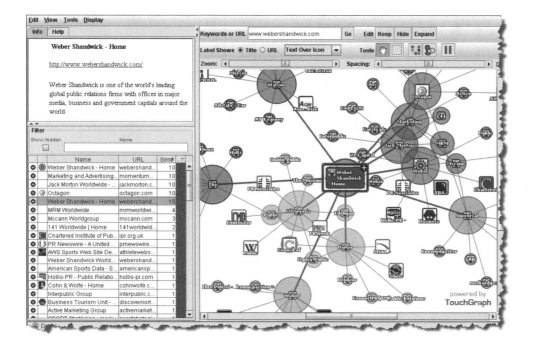

Local Business News – *Business Journal*

http://www.bizjournals.com/search

Most salespeople don't have the luxury of only calling on larger publicly traded companies where company news is easily found online or via major news outlets. In fact, most salespeople spend their time calling on privately held companies that exist in relative obscurity.

"There's nothing out there on private companies" is then the excuse I often hear when talking to a salesperson about practicing the "Fourth R." However, as you know from previous sections, there is a lot of information available on private companies, as long as you know where and how to search.

A great place to look for news on private companies is the *Business Journal* news archives. *Business Journals* are located in more than forty markets throughout the United States. Typically, local *Business Journals* cover mid- and small-sized companies in much greater depth than local dailies. Oftentimes

SAM TIP ↖

Biz Journals:

Business Journals are located in more than 40 markets across the U.S. and include articles on local companies, many of them private.

1. Access article archives at **www.bizjournals.com/ search**

2. Enter the company or executive name in the form.

3. Make sure to use quotation marks with multiple words (e.g., "widget corporation").

4. To sort your results, choose the "Sort by Most Recent First" or the "Most Relevant First" link directly above the search result listings.

5. Choose the "Articles," "Companies," or "Others" tab to locate additional information.

6. **NOTE:** The Companies tab shows information the *Business Journal* has gleaned via its articles and it may include company details, financials, key executives, and more.

an article in a *Business Journal* that profiles a local company will provide accurate revenue and employee figures, recent deals, and in-depth information on key executives.

Think of how much more effective your sales letter and sales call will be if you're able to reference a quote you read in the *Business Journal* from the CEO of the company you're calling on. Think about the great conversation starter you could have by referencing an article where your client is featured.

To access *Business Journal* archives, go to **www.bizjournals. com/search** and type in your keywords (use Boolean for a better search and be sure to use quotation marks around companies with multiple names such as "widget corporation").

On the results page, you can sort by relevance or date by choosing the "Sort by Most Recent First" or the "Most Relevant First" link, located directly above the results. Here are article results on my former employer, Digital River, sorted by date:

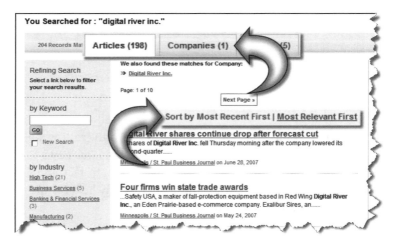

Another great feature of the BizJournals search is they compile information about companies featured in articles and make the information easily accessible by clicking the Companies Tab. Data gathered can include company overviews, financials, key executives, and more. If there is more than one company with the same name, you can click the company you want and news written about that specific company will appear.

If you want to refine your company searches even further, use the various search options on the left side of the results page. You can limit or expand your searches by industry, geography, and more.

Local Company News – Newslink.org

http://www.newslink.org/statnews.html

Almost 80 percent of all companies in the United States have fewer than twenty employees. Many of these companies are located in the suburbs or rural areas.

Therefore, it's only logical that as a salesperson, you'll sometimes call on a relatively small company located in a relatively smaller town. Where can you find information on small firms? How can you practice the Platinum Rule and the "Fourth R" if no news articles show up in Google, the major daily newspapers or even in the *Business Journal*?

Local newspapers provide a wealth of detailed information on local companies and people. Newslink is a gateway to local media with searchable archives.

1. Go to **www.newslink.org**

2. Find the U.S. Newspaper header, and click the "By State" link.

3. Click on one of the publication links.

4. Once on the newspaper's site, find a Search Form or an archive link; it's usually on the top or left-side navigation.

5. You may need to click the Advanced Search link to get older articles.

6. Enter the company name and see what appears.

The good news is local newspapers are filled with articles profiling businesses and business leaders. Whether it's an article on your target company that discusses a recent merger, or an article about your target executive and their coaching success for the local youth soccer team, you can find great material to help ensure your sales call is relevant so you can build rapport.

What kind of impression would you make if your opening comment to your prospect is this: "I was reading the local newspaper Web site before coming in and, hey ... congratulations on your seventh grader winning the area soccer tournament. That must have been a lot of fun to coach."

To find local articles of this type, you can use Newslink newspapers by state search (**www.newslink.org/statnews.html**), a gateway to almost every newspaper in North America featuring a searchable article archive. Then you can use each newspaper's own search engine to see if there has ever been an article printed about your target company or business executive.

To search for a newspaper article, choose the state, choose the publication you're interested in, and click on the link to go to its Web site. Once at the site, find that publication's search feature, which will usually be a search box on the upper navigation or an archive link on the left-side navigation. Conduct a search on your company and see what appears.

Below is a list of publications in Minnesota that Newslink.org found:

Minnesota newspapers

Major metro:
- **Minneapolis-St. Paul:**Pioneer Press
- **Minneapolis-St. Paul:**Star Tribune

Daily:
- **Albert Lea:**Tribune
- **Austin:**Herald
- **Brainerd:**Dispatch
- **Crookston:**Times
- **Duluth:**News-Tribune and Duluth City Guide
- **Fairmont:**Sentinel
- **Faribault:**News
- **Fergus Falls:**Journal
- **Hibbing:**Tribune
- **Mankato:**Free Press
- **Marshall:**Independent
- **Moorhead:**Forum
- **New Ulm:**Journal
- **Owatonna:**People's Press
- **Red Wing:**Republican Eagle
- **Rochester:**Post-Bulletin

Let's pretend I'm calling on a bank in Crookston (it's a small town). You think the local branch has ever been profiled in *USA Today* or even the *StarTribune* (Minneapolis-St. Paul)? Probably not. However, do you think they made the *Crookston Times* when they sponsored a local event, when they hired a new VP, when they opened a new location? You bet.

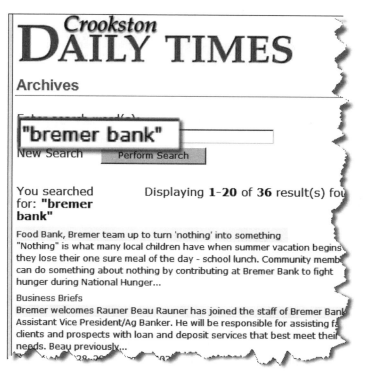

Company Job Openings – Indeed

http://www.indeed.com

An excellent way to find out what's going on inside a company—and possibly where a company is headed in terms of new products or market—is to look at its job postings.

For example, if a company is advertising for an engineer who speaks Chinese, that's a pretty good bet they're entering the China market. If they're looking for a sales representative

indeed ™
one search. all jobs.

what	where
"general mills" AND marketing	
job title, keywords or company name	city, state, or zip

"general mills" AND marketing jobs

▶ ✉ Save this search as an email job alert

Financial Services Admin Asst
General Mills - Minneapolis, MN
areas of **marketing** and referrals for Financial Services. Coordinate seminars, including
marketing of the... as assigned by **General Mills** Federal Credit Union...
From General Mills - 9 days ago - save job - more actions

iMarketing Manager
General Mills - Minneapolis, MN
is a highly motivated **marketing** professional with a B... **marketing** or communications and a
strong interest in Advertising, **Marketing**, Interactive **Marketing** or...
From General Mills - 10 days ago - save job - more actions

Sr. Consumer Insights Associate
General Mills - Minneapolis, MN
name of the **General Mills marketing** research function... exciting career opportunity at...

or marketing person with specific industry experience, you can probably guess that the company is going to start selling its products and services to that market.

One of the most comprehensive online information sources for job postings is Indeed (**www.indeed.com**) because it's actually a meta-search engine of job posting sites. Thanks to Indeed, you don't have to search job postings from multiple sites; Indeed does all of the work for you.

To search for company listings using Indeed, just type the name of the company. You can also include a state, city, or zip code.

If you receive several search results, and you will for larger companies, you may want to conduct a second search and this time either use Indeed's Advanced Search program (the link is located right next to the Search button), or use Boolean logic and craft a more complex search query. For example, if you only want to know what types of expertise a company is looking for from its marketing people, you would enter the name of the company (use quotes for multiple word companies) AND marketing.

Here's an example of this search for General Mills:

A very helpful tool Indeed offers is the ability to register for e-mail alerts. Following a search, just click on the "e-mail job alert" link, enter your e-mail address, and any time Indeed finds a new job posting, you'll receive it via e-mail.

If you're a salesperson, set up an Indeed e-mail alert on your most important prospects. Based on the type of individual the company is looking for, you can tailor your sales calls and presentations to where you believe the company is going in the future.

If you're an account manager, set up an Indeed e-mail alert on your client's competitors. Send your client a note when their competitor is looking to hire someone with specific talents and experience. Or, if you want to provide incredible value to your existing client, set up an Indeed e-mail alert on your client and when they're looking to hire someone, make a referral from your network. Your client will remember you, and if your reference is hired, they'll be grateful for many years to come.

Museum of the Internet – The Way Back Machine

http://www.archive.org

Web sites change. One of the beauties of the Web is that you can update your Web site on a daily basis for virtually no cost. Unfortunately, this constant changing of information can make finding information difficult if you're a salesperson or account manager and you're looking for data that was online a few months back.

Companies change too. Companies are acquired. Web sites that were once filled with information might no longer even exist. Have you ever called on a division of a company that was its own firm prior to being acquired? Wouldn't it be

SAM TIP
Internet Museum:

View historical Web sites, or sites that no longer exist (e.g., the company was acquired) through the "Way Back Machine."

1. Go to **www.archive.org**

2. Enter a Web address.

3. On the results listing, click on a link to see what the site looked like on the corresponding date.

123

nice to see what the company was, what the products were, and how it operated prior to the acquisition?

You can go back in time and find old Web site versions with the "Way Back Machine" (**www.archive.org**).

Think of the Way Back Machine as a virtual museum of the Internet. Find previous versions of product catalogs and manuals. Look at the issues companies were dealing with years ago. Find Web sites of companies that no longer exist or that have been acquired.

Using the Way Back Machine is very easy. Just enter the Web address you're interested in, hit the "Take Me Back" button, and see what appears.

You'll get a listing of past Web sites that the Way Back Machine has archived. Click on a link and see what the Web site used to look like. Often the complete Web site has been archived, meaning that the links still work and the graphics still appear.

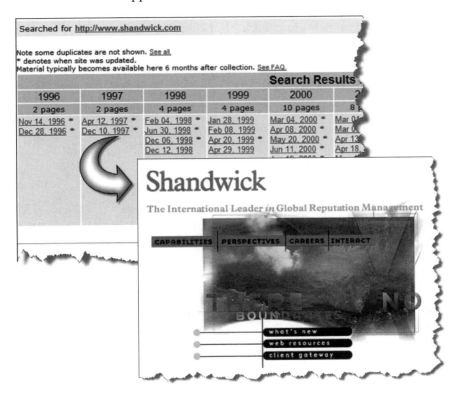

Here's a perfect example of using the Way Back Machine. Let's say that I needed to find information about the public relations agency I used to work for, but the Web site is nowhere to be found because the company was acquired. I can type in the old Web address into the Way Back Machine, and get a listing of dates when the Web site was updated. By clicking on a date prior to the acquisition, I access a fully working site complete with information on executives, clients, and more.

The Real Live Web: Blogs (online diaries) – Google Blog Search

http://blogsearch.google.com
(Note: no www in URL)

Blogs are real-time online Web logs, or "diaries," on just about any topic imaginable. Anyone can create a Blog, it's easy, and it's free. There's no editor; people can write what they like (and they do). In addition, Blogs often have a community section where visitors can contribute to the discussion via chat rooms and postings. Blogs also are a great source of information when researching companies.

Blogs have a major impact on companies. Don't think so? Go to a Blog search engine like **Blogsearch.google.com**, type in "Microsoft" and see what appears.

In the tens-of-millions of Blog posts featuring Microsoft, you'll find Blogs from employees giving you the inside scoop of what's going on at Microsoft's Redmond headquarters. You'll find Blogs about how to better use Microsoft's products. You'll find Blogs complaining about Microsoft. And you'll find Blogs where people reminisce about their Microsoft products.

When I counsel companies that sell a consumer product, I always recommend that they have a person frequently search Blogs to find out whether anyone has posted negative comments about the company's products. If you can learn about a problem early on that a Blogger is complaining about,

Blogs, or Web logs, are online "diaries" created and updated by individuals who are passionate about a particular topic.

You can use a Blog Search engine to locate information about a company.

1. Go to **www.google.com**

2. Click the More tab on the upper navigation, and choose Blog Search (or, you can access directly by going to **http://blogsearch. google.com**).

3. Enter a company or person's name in the main search engine and see what information exists.

4. Use Google's Advanced Blog Search link (next to the Search button) for better searching.

5. Use the Google Alerts button (envelope icon on the left side of the results page) to set up an alert whereby you'll receive an e-mail anytime your search terms show up in a new Blog posting.

you have the chance to rectify it. Respond poorly or do nothing and the negative comments will spread through the Web like wildfire.

(A note to those who have been paying attention: you may be asking yourself, "If I can find it via Google, why is this Invisible Web?" The reason is that although you can find Blog postings using a traditional Google search, because many of these Blogs are obscure, they may be far down the list of a standard Google search. By using the Google Blog Search feature, you're specifically limiting your searches to information contained in Blogs; you're filtering out all non-Blog content).

As a salesperson, how can you make the best use of Blogs? Use them to find "inside" information! Maybe a company employee has a Blog and you can learn what's really going on inside a firm. You might learn about a new product the company is going to introduce because a Blogger visited a booth at a trade show. You might find a former employee's Blog where he or she shares what they learned, who they reported to, and what they did at the company.

As an account manager, how can you take advantage of Blogs to provide exceptional value to your clients? Maybe the company's customers are praising or vilifying the company's products. Find out first, let your client know, and help them plan how they might thank the positive opinion, or appropriately react to the criticism.

A number of Blog search engines will help you search for content within Blogs, and I find the Google Blog search to be one of the best. The number of current Blogs on the Web is

approaching 100 million and Google claims to index a large majority of them.

Once at the Google Blog search, you can use the search engine just like you would Google. Make sure to use Boolean Logic searches discussed earlier for better results. I also recommend clicking on the Advanced Search link (directly next to the main search button) to help narrow down your search by keyword, phrase, posting date, and more.

Type in the name of a company, or even a person, that you're interested in learning about and there's a chance you might get lucky and find something valuable. If you get too many results, re-enter your search but this time add information related to what you desire (e.g., sales or a company's divisional name).

On the search results page, you'll see options on the left side that allow you to sort by the date of the Blog posting. You can also save yourself a lot of time by subscribing to a Blog alert (the envelope icon on the left side). Enter the name of the company you're interested in, and any new Blog content Google Blog Search finds will be sent to you via e-mail.

Twitter is a tool that allows people to instantly communicate. You can often find information about what's going on at a company by searching for "Tweets."

1. Go to:
   http://search.twitter.com or use the the search on **www.twitter.com**

2. Enter the name of a company; for multi-word names, put within quotation marks.

3. If it's a larger company, you'll most likely receive many irrelevant results. Use the Boolean minus sign tip to remove words and the corresponding results (e.g., "-stock" will remove results with the word stock in it).

4. For more refined searching, use Advanced Search; the link is located next to the main search button.

5. If you think someone is on Twitter and you'd like to find the person's account, enter in his or her name without spaces (e.g., samrichter).

6. To see what others are saying about another account, in the search form, enter the @ symbol followed by a name (e.g., @samrichter).

7. **Follow me on Twitter.** I promise to only share interesting information. Find me at **http://twitter.com/samrichter**

Instant Updates – TwitterSearch

http://search.twitter.com (or use the search on www.twitter.com) (Note: no www in URL)

What's the rage about Twitter? Everyone from celebrities to politicians to CEOs to junior high-school kids now have Twitter accounts. In 140 characters or less (the amount of space you have when you send a "Tweet"), here's a definition: ***Twitter is an instant messaging tool that allows you to send very brief updates to people who have chosen to "follow" your "Tweets"*** (that was 132 characters with spaces).

Is Twitter a fad, or is it here to stay, forever changing the way people communicate and think about personal privacy? I don't know. What I do know is that it can be a valuable "Fourth R" Sales Intelligence tool.

When I first joined Twitter, I thought I would get inundated with updates about what people are buying at the grocery store, whose children were ill, etc. However, it's been quite different. I have chosen to follow people from whom each day I receive a plethora of valuable information, a lot of which I use as I craft proposals and counsel my clients on how to build successful businesses.

There's a tremendous cultural shift going on right now. When I grew up, there were certain things you kept private. What's happening today at an incredible pace is a major change from privacy to "if it's not posted online, it never happened." Especially with those younger than 25, if it's not communicated on a blog, in a MySpace account, or instantly via Twitter, then from a peer's perspective, it never occurred.

This shift toward instant communication provides a wealth of useful information for those looking to learn more about the inside workings of a company. Through Twitter, I've "met" a lot of people with unique insight, linking to interesting Web sites, and sharing information that I would never have known. Because you can send a "Tweet" from your cell phone, I've received instant updates from people listening to an expert's keynote address at an industry conference, from staff people "reporting" on a management team meeting, even from board members discussing private issues at a board meeting!

From a "Fourth R" perspective, the good news is all "Tweets" are searchable. Not just the ones to which you subscribe, but literally, you can search ALL "Tweets" from the hundreds of millions of messages sent every day.

Go to **http://search.twitter.com** and enter the name of a company in the search form, using quotation marks around multi-word names. If you want to do some real power searching, use the Twitter Advanced Search. You'll find the link next to the main search form.

If you're searching for information on a larger company, you'll probably receive many irrelevant results. For example, in searching for information on Best Buy, you'll find results related to music, computers, etc. Just use the Boolean minus sign to remove words and the corresponding results (e.g., "'best buy' –music" will show all Best Buy results, but will remove the ones with the word music in them).

So what can you find? I was giving a demo of Twitter and used the Best Buy example above. After a few uses of the minus sign, I started to find some very interesting results. One was a "Tweet" about store layoffs. "So what" you say?

I didn't realize it at the time, but I had found an employee giving *"inside information"* about what was happening at Best Buy, a day before it was announced to the public!

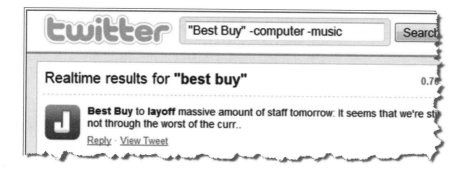

Company Meta-Search – Samepoint

http://www.samepoint.com

Samepoint advertises itself as a "social media search engine;" however, I find it to be so much more. When you enter in a company name at **www.samepoint.com**, you receive results placed into various categories pulled from many different sources, which in a sense, makes Samepoint a very powerful company meta-search engine. For example, Samepoint can pull blogs, instant Twitter messages, Web site results, the latest news, documents downloads, even personal profiles like LinkedIn all in one search (more on LinkedIn in the "Invisible Web - People" chapter). I've been really amazed with the information that Samepoint can quickly find.

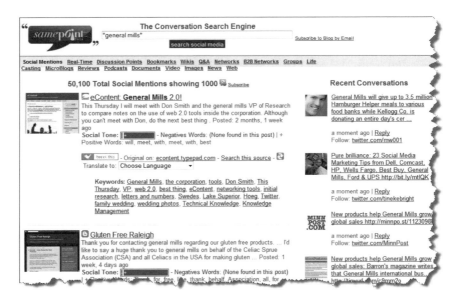

For example, entering a large company name into Samepoint delivers thousands of relevant results. In fact, it can get a bit overwhelming. For example, a search on "General Mills" delivers more than 50,000 Social Mentions. Under the Micro-Blogs category, we find almost 1,000 people discussing General Mills. In the B2B Networks category there are almost

6,000 employee LinkedIn postings. And in the News category, there are more than 100 current news articles.

The beauty of Samepoint is it also works when searching for information on smaller companies. Instead of having to use multiple search engines and techniques where, quite often, you won't get any results, in Samepoint you can save a tremendous amount of time because results are consolidated in one engine.

For example, I serve on the board of directors of ARANet, a small yet growing company, which also has a division called Adfusion. I searched Samepoint to see what it could find on either name. What I received in seconds (including a Twitter response I made to someone's post an hour before I grabbed the screen shot) would have taken me probably 15 minutes or more to find using multiple search engines.

Imagine if I were a salesperson having my first meeting with the ARANet team. I would be armed with information on what bloggers think of the company's unique online marketing tools. I would see a study that showed effectiveness of the company's product. I would even be armed with executive names by looking at employee's LinkedIn profile abstracts.

For company Sales Intelligence—literally you could do your search just minutes before a meeting—Samepoint is an excellent and fast "Fourth R" tool for your arsenal.

SAM TIP
Samepoint:

A meta-search tool, Samepoint finds everything from blog postings to the latest news to employee networks and more, all in one search.

1. Go to:
   www.samepoint.com

2. Enter the name of a company; for multi-word names, put within quotation marks.

3. On the results page, click on the various category links so you can see all that Samepoint found.

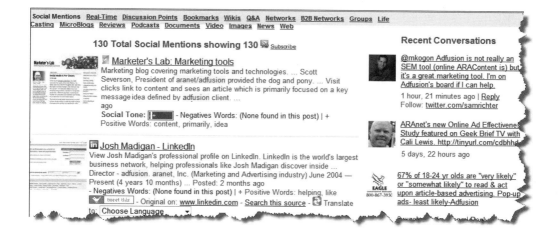

CHAPTER FOURTEEN

The "Invisible Web" – Industry Information

> "You can put yourself at a distinct competitive advantage in comparison with many salespeople by becoming familiar with these [trade] publications. Use them to keep abreast of industry trends. You should understand and be able to adapt to the business environment faced by your customers."
> – Stephan Schiffman, *The 25 Sales Habits of Highly Successful Salespeople*, Holbrook, MA: Bob Adams, 1994.

When making a cold call or when you're meeting with an existing account, it's imperative that you have an understanding of your client's industry and the issues he or she is facing.

Is your client's industry growing? Is it consolidating? Is outsourcing an issue your client has to contend with?

It also may be important to understand the industries where your client does business, and the companies within those industries. If you can help your client resolve issues and be more successful with his or her customers, you'll ultimately be more successful and provide more value to your client.

Is the industry your client sells into seeing massive growth? Alternatively, is the industry your client sells into dying and do the companies in that industry need to create new products or identify new markets to survive?

By keenly understanding the external opportunities and threats affecting client and company, you are able to construct a pitch and a proposal that is relevant to your client's needs. In addition, by understanding your client's industry, you can provide ongoing value, strengthen your relationships, and offer solutions to problems. In-depth understanding of your client's industry is what can help transform your business relationships from client/vendor to client/valued business partner.

The good news is that the Web is filled with industry information. You can get a wealth of data using search engines like Google and Yahoo by entering search queries that include the name of the industry you're interested in followed by words like "trends" or phrases like "current issues." Unfortunately, because there is so much industry information available via popular search engines, it can often take a lot of time to sift through the search results.

An easy and fast way to get industry information is to find industry Web sites that have a high likelihood of housing Invisible Web pages. Such sites can often be found via popular search engines, but the underlying information is invisible because it's behind a password-protected area or is generated dynamically.

The following sites feature in-depth, credible, and objective information related to industries. Most of the sites use online search tools to help you identify information sources for your chosen industry. Some will point you to industry research reports. And some feature more general information related to specific industries.

Association Search – Association of Associations

http://www.asaecenter.org/Directories/AssociationSearch.cfm

There is a tremendous amount of industry information available via popular search engines. If you enjoy surfing through thousands of search results, that might be the way to go. I, however, prefer someone else to do the hard research work for me. A timesaving method of gathering industry information is through industry associations.

Why do associations exist? One of the big reasons is to provide information to members. If I'm interested in infor-

SAM TIP
Associations:

Why do associations exist? To give information to members.

If you're interested in an industry, locate the industry association and see what's available on their Web site, and what they might send you.

1. Go to the Web address underneath the header (or go to www.asaecenter.org, click "People and Groups" then choose "Directories," and then click the "Gateway to Associations" link).

2. Enter an industry name (e.g., plastics) in "Association Name Contains" search box.

3. Click on a result listing.

4. Visit the selected association's Web site.

5. Contact the association to see what kind of information they will send you.

mation on an industry, instead of spending hours online, I find an association and visit its Web site, a place usually filled with industry information including current issues, additional resources, back issues of newsletters, and more.

When I'm finished searching, I might also then pick up the most powerful research tool ever invented, the telephone, call the association and ask for additional information.

Ask for membership information and a sampling of what members might receive. Often you'll receive a copy of the most recent trade journal, some survey information, and events calendars.

If the person who answers the association telephone is reluctant to send you information, mention that you are interested in attending or exhibiting at the upcoming trade show or advertising in the association trade magazine (which you should probably do).

Many times an association will not share information with just anyone. However, a person or organization looking to spend money with the association is treated differently. Sometimes you can even receive member directories and copies of members-only reports. Thus a tip is to mention to the person at the association that you might be interested in advertising in their industry journal, or exhibiting at the trade show.

Finding an Association is relatively easy. Just go to the American Society of Association Executives Web site association search page at **www.asaecenter.org/Directories/AssociationSearch.cfm.**

Once at the search page, enter the name of the association you're interested in; make sure to use the search form box that says "**Association Name Contains.**" Click the "Search" button and a list of industry associations that meet your criteria will appear. Click on any link and you'll have the full contact information for that association.

As an example, let's say I want to sell into the printing industry. I'll enter "Printing" in the "Name Contains" field, find a key association, and visit the site online (look at the information I receive, HINT: "Member List" equals "sales leads"):

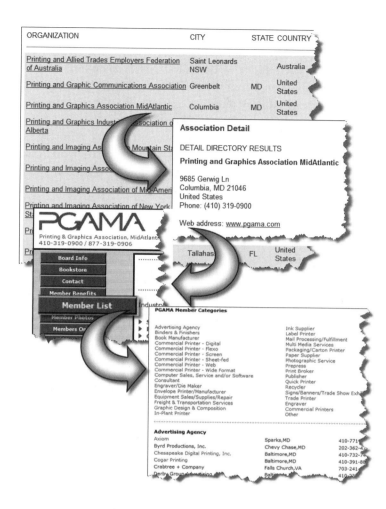

INDUSTRY ASSOCIATION HINT: Do you belong to your industry association? Most likely yes. Do you belong to your client's industry association? Most likely no.

I spent a number of years in advertising and even owned my own advertising agency. I belonged to the Advertising Federation and the Public Relations Society of America and other industry groups and, looking back, I received very little value out of my memberships in my industry associations, except for the free beer at the annual golf outing.

What I should have done is belong to my clients' industry associations. I had clients in the medical device industry, the entertainment industry, the real estate industry, and more. Why didn't I belong to those associations?

How much client value would I have been able to provide if I had been attending their trade shows, if I had been reading their industry publications and e-mail newsletters, if I had been learning about their key issues?

Want another benefit of joining your clients' industry association? When you join an industry association, you often get a little book. It's called a Member's Directory. **I call it Sales Leads with full contact information.**

Industry Data Gateway – Valuation/Industry Resources

http://www.valuationresources.com/IndustryReport.htm

The "Invisible Web" is filled with vortals or vertical portals. A "vortal" is a *portal*, a one-stop source of information, about a particular *vertical*, a subject or topic.

When doing industry research online, a helpful site to find is a *vortal of vortals*, or a one-stop source of information on finding industry one-stop sources of information. Industry Information Resources is one such vortal of vortals as it features direct links to industry resources divided by industry code.

(NOTE: The government classifies industries using a code Standard Industrial Classification (SIC) code. SIC codes have been around for a long time and many sites use them, but there are not enough of them so the government created North American Industry Classification System (NAICS) codes. See the "Sam Tip" for how to locate codes).

Industry Information Resources provides links to resources from more than 250 industries. Click on an industry to locate resources that address a variety of industry topics, including industry overviews, issues, trends, outlooks, and even financial benchmarking and valuation data.

To access the service, go to www.valuationresources.com/ IndustryReport.htm. Although the home page looks a bit over-

SAM TIP
Industry Resource:

Industry Data Gateway features links to information on more than 250 industries including trend reports, valuations, and more.

1. Go to the Web address under the header (or to **www.valuationresources.com** and click on the "Industry Research" tab).

2. Use your browser's Find function (simultaneously press the Ctrl and F keys).

3. Enter the name of the industry in the search box and click the Next button. Continue to click Next until the industry that you want appears.

4. Click the link to the Vortal page about that industry.

5. Choose any of the links on the page for information about the industry.

whelming, it's actually easy to quickly find the industry you want.

Simultaneously press the Control Key (Ctrl) and F to open up your browser's Find function. Enter the name of the industry on the search form and click the Next button.

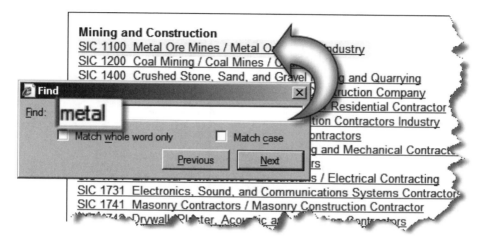

Your browser should automatically take you to an industry and its corresponding code on the page. If it is the industry you want, click the link. If not, click the Next button on your browser's Find function and go to the next industry containing your term.

Some of the sites that Industry Information Resources link to charge for information; however, a majority of the resources provide valuable free information.

For example, if I'm making a sales call on a firm in the bakery industry, spending one minute on Industry Information Resources can provide me links to a wealth of data I can use to learn about an industry and make a great first impression during my cold call:

SAM TIP
SIC and NAICS:

To find an SIC code, visit **www.osha.gov/pls/imis/sicsearch.html**

To find a NAICS code, visit **www.census.gov/epcd/www/naics.html**

The NAICS site also features an SIC-to-NAICS code converter.

Wholesale and Commercial Bakeries
SIC 2050 / NAICS 311800

Industry Overview, Issues, Trends, and Outlook

Baking Business
Industry Statistics
http://www.bakingbusiness.com/industrystats.asp
Industry statistics and information. Available free online.

International Dairy-Deli-Bakery Association
"How to Open and Manage a Profitable Bakery" Resource List
http://www.iddba.org/ Select "Industry Resources"
Lists books, periodicals, videos and association contacts. Available free on

Compensation and Salary Surveys

American Bakers Association
Salary & Benefits Survey
http://www.americanbakers.org/committee/SalaryBenefits.htm
Provides regional breakdowns of key industry and distribution positions in the
wholesale baking industry; includes division & corporate positions and plant

Industry Data – Encyclopedia of American Industries

http://www.referenceforbusiness.com/industries

Imagine your next client meeting where you're sharing industry statistics and knowledge that your client might not even have. Do you think your credibility will reach a new high?

Understanding the history, issues, and future of your client's industry is the quickest way to ensure you're looked at as a business partner versus a vendor. You can quickly get an overview of just about every industry by using the online Encyclopedia of American Industries database.

The Encyclopedia is a comprehensive guide to industries in every realm of American business. The database, created by the Thomson Corporation, covers more than 450 manufacturing industries, and features more than 500 essays about non-manufacturing and service industries.

Go to **www.referenceforbusiness.com** and click on the Encyclopedia of American Industries link. Take note of the other information resources available on the page as they may be beneficial to your organization.

Once on the Encyclopedia page, click on a category and then scroll down to find the appropriate sub-category or SIC code. You can also use the search engine at the top of each page to locate entries that include your search terms. Make sure to use quotes around industry phrases so you don't return hundreds of non-relevant results (e.g.,"medical devices").

SIC 2321
MEN'S AND BOYS' SHIRTS

INDUSTRY SNAPSHOT

Sales of men's and boys' shirt reached $6.5 billion in 2001. Although knit shirt continued their dominance of the sector, woven dress shirts made slow increases. Men's knit shirts sold 686 million units, and men's woven sport shirts accounted for 253 million units. Although casual dress was still prevalent in corporate America, economic uncertainty and widespread layoffs were key in bringing back a more polished look to U.S. offices and service industries. Management no longer had to entice workers with casual dress policies and workers felt projecting a more professional image would be a wise decision in the increasingly competitive market for jobs in the early 2000s.

One important issue affecting the industry was cost. Shirt manufacturers in the early 2000s had greater competition for consumers dollars because of less disposable income. Manufacturing costs, however, continued to rise with shirt makers forced to find ways to save in other areas to keep costs low. Continuing an important trend of the 1990s, shirt manufacturers moved production to more affordable factories overseas. The closing of Hathaway's, the last major U.S. shirt manufacturing plant in 2002, marked the end of U.S. domestic shirt production.

Click on a result and get an overview of the industry. Note that some of the data are based on older reports, so use the information cautiously. A nice feature is on the bottom of each industry report where you'll find a list of other relevant industry readings.

SAM TIP ↖
Industry Articles:

FindArticles lets you search
for articles from industry
publications, magazines,
and newswires. You can
locate great industry trend
information, plus information about companies and
people.

1. Go to **www.findarticles.
com**

2. Enter your search terms into
the main search box.

3. Choose "Free Articles Only"
to restrict your search to
the free content.

Industry Articles (Company Ones, Too) – FindArticles

http://www.findarticles.com

There's nothing more impressive during a sales call than to reference your client's industry and mention a trend, statistic, or issue that your client may be facing (and that you know how to solve). Even better is when the information you reference comes from a reputable source, a publication your client most likely reads.

Imagine calling on a prospect whose company produces plastic parts for automobiles. How impressive is it when you site recent trends and new products mentioned in the latest issue of *Automotive Design and Production*? How much more credible are you when you can discuss how your firm has done projects similar to the ones mentioned in *Product News Network*?

ALL BNET | ARTICLES | LIBRARY | STOCKS | DICTIONARY

"plastics industry" A IN   free and premium articles ▼   🔍

free and premium articles
free articles only
premium articles only

Arts
Autos
Business
Health
Home & Garden
News
Reference
Sports
Technology

The good news is there are ways to access these types of articles in an easy-to-use search engine. FindArticles.com (**www.findarticles.com**) offers the Web's largest collection of articles from credible industry and general sources. The site claims to have indexed more than ten million articles.

Some of the articles are available to FindArticles' premium subscribers only. However, they have literally millions of credible industry articles searchable and available for free.

Go to the **findarticles.com** home page and in the search engine, type in the name of the industry you're interested in; for example, "plastics industry." You can conduct a Boolean search to narrow your search even further (e.g., "plastics industry" AND automotive AND trends).

To limit your search to the freely available articles, just choose "Free Articles Only" from the pull-down menu next to the search form. You can also limit your search to specific categories.

FindArticles is also a good search engine to use when you're looking for articles on companies or people. Just use the Boolean techniques discussed earlier, such as putting the name of a company or a person within quotes.

Industry Articles II (Company Ones, Too) – Access My Library

http://www.accessmylibrary.com

We'll discuss in Chapter XVI that some of the best information is locked up in expensive databases typically only available to large organizations with substantial resources. Then in Chapter XVII, we'll discuss what types of premium information sources are available at public libraries. There is one site, however, that lets you tap into premium information sources without being a big company employee or without having to visit a public library.

Gale, one of the best business information companies around, makes available a portion of its premium information database for free at AccessMyLibrary.com. This article database features similar content sold to big companies and public library systems.

Just like with FindArticles, imagine the great first impression you make with a new client when you quote a statistic from an industry journal. Think about the value you can provide by sending your client a recent product news release from your client's competitors.

To use the database, go to **www.accessmylibrary.com** and enter an industry term in the search form. You can also search for companies or people; however, except for press releases, I've noticed that the results aren't as current as industry searches.

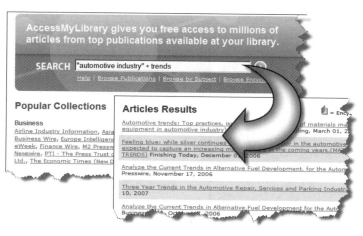

Alternatively, click on any of the publications listed in the "Popular Collections" area, which is broken out by category. You can also locate and search individual publications by using the alphabetical publication listing located beneath the "Browse All Collections" section.

Your search results will include articles from industry trade journals, newspapers, general publications, and newswires. I've found that in general, some of the information available for free is older than what you would find if you were paying for database access. However, the broader the search (e.g., a general industry search), the more relevant and up-to-date results you'll receive, although a broad search does return many press release results.

When you click on an article, you'll be asked to register with AccessMyArticles. During the registration process, you're asked to select your local library. Here's where the site gets a bit cumbersome to use.

For the first thirty-days, you'll be able to use AccessMyArticles with no restrictions. You can click on any search result and instantly view the full article online.

Following the thirty-day period, you'll be asked to either purchase the article, or enter the library card identification number from the library you chose during the registration process. Unfortunately, I don't typically have my library card with me when I'm using the site and quite a few libraries don't participate in this system.

My work-around is if I use the site and I'm past my thirty days, I just register again under a different e-mail address. Then my thirty-days start over again and I can use the site like

I would any search engine. (You may have to clear your Web browser's cookies to eliminate remnants of past registrations prior to re-registering).

Industry Blogs – Google Blog Search Revisited

http://blogsearch.google.com
(Note: no www in URL)

When you're practicing the "Fourth R," any industry news can be good news because news you have related to industry trends and issues can be used in the sales process to build rapport and ensure your sales pitch is relevant to your prospects and clients.

Industry Blogs are one of the most up-to-date sources of industry news. Blogs, or Weblogs, are online "diaries" of information created by people who are passionate about a specific topic. Not surprisingly, there are many people passionate about specific industries.

You can use the Google Blog Search to locate Blogs where individuals spend a great deal of their own personal time gathering and disseminating information about a specific industry or industry topic. Certainly when reviewing an industry Blog, you should be skeptical and review entries closely to see whether there is a bias (such as when the Blog is created by one of the leading companies within an industry simply to promote its products). More often than not however, an industry Blog truly is a collection of valuable articles, news feeds, and commentary about a particular industry.

To find an industry Blog, go to **http://blogsearch.google.com** and choose the Advanced Search link located directly next to the main search button. Look for the "In Blogs" section, and then enter in an industry name in the "with these words in the Blog title" field. If you wish, enter in additional keyword(s) or phrase(s) in the appropriate fields. In this example, we're looking for the phrase "medical device" but we're only going to search Blogs that are specific to diabetes.

SAM TIP
Industry Blog:

A Blog Search engine is a great way to find industry information, written by people who are passionate about their subjects.

1. Go to **www.google.com**

2. Click the More tab on the upper navigation, and choose Blog Search (or, you can access directly by going to **http://blogsearch. google.com**).

3. Click Google's Advanced Blog Search link (next to the Search button).

4. Look for the "In Blogs" section, and then enter in an industry name in the "with these words in the Blog title" field.

5. If you wish, enter in additional keyword(s) or phrase(s) in the appropriate fields.

6. Instead of searching for information from millions of Blogs, you limit your search to only Blogs specifically about your chosen industry.

By limiting your search to Blogs where the industry name is in the Blog title, you are limiting your search to Blogs where the majority of the information is specific to that title or industry. So instead of searching tens of millions of Blogs, we're restricting our search to only Blogs that focus on our area of interest. In the example below, you can see that each Blog relates to "diabetes" and we only searched those specific Blogs for the phrase "medical device."

Industry Blogs are constantly updated with current industry news, company press releases, and company news. You can also choose to have Blogs monitored by using the Blogs Alerts feature on the left side of the results page. Enter your search query, and Google will e-mail you the next time it finds the keywords featured in a Blog.

Market Research Reports – MarketResearch.com & Google

http://www.marketresearch.com

Big companies contract for and spend hundreds of millions of dollars each year on research reports that help predict trends, outline major issues, and provide information for solid business and strategic planning. The same companies that create these market research reports also produce similar reports that they sell online.

MarketResearch.com is your "online shopping mall" for market research reports covering just about any industry. You can search by category or keyword for a report, and when you conduct a search, you'll receive an abstract of what's in the report and a link for additional information.

For example, let's suppose that I work for a company that sells wireless networks and I've been tasked with identifying new markets for our services. I have a hunch that the health care market, and in particular, hospitals, might benefit from our products.

I visit MarketResearch.com and enter wireless AND hospital in the keyword search form and a number of great results appear:

(**NOTE:** MarketResearch.com has a very good Advanced Search plus the ability to refine a search, so if you don't find what you're looking for right away, use those features).

More than 140 reports turned up in my search, and the first few look very promising. Unfortunately, the one I want costs $3,950. Now it's possible that I might just pay for the report, as I'm sure it has some great information. However,

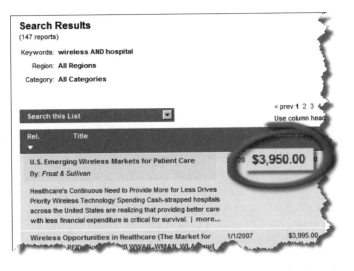

what if I'm not sure? That's a lot of money to spend when I'm not even sure this is the right market for us. Instead of getting frustrated, I try a little trick.

I use my mouse and highlight the report name and then I right mouse-click and choose Copy.

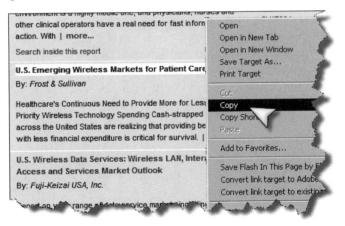

Then I visit Google, put my cursor in the search form, right-mouse click and Paste the exact name of the report into Google. So we treat the entire report name as a single phrase, I put quotation marks before and after the report name. Then I hit "Google Search."

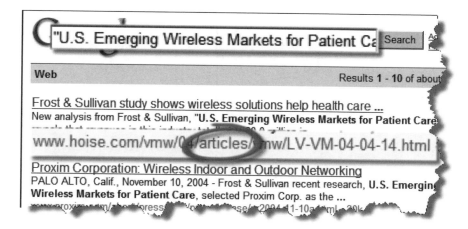

I returned hundreds of results, many being other Web sites selling the same report for close to $4,000.

However, what **I'm looking for are industry Web sites or trade associations that may have purchased the report and referenced it** in a story they wrote about wireless networking and how it's impacting the hospital industry. Basically, I'm looking to see if I can find the bulk of the information featured in the report for free.

A trick when doing this is to search for the mention of the report in some of the later Google listings. Therefore, you might want to go through a few pages of Google results before you take a chance at clicking on a link. Another trick if you return a number of results is to add the phrase "press release" or the word "article" to your search, as this will limit the search results to an article or press release about the report.

In particular, the type of link I'm looking for is one where the abstract doesn't mention a product for sale, or in the Web address associated with the link I don't see words like "product catalog" or "for sale." Rather, the types of results I'm looking for will contain the word *article, graph, chart,* or something to that effect in either the result abstract or result Web address.

One of the sites that appeared in my search result was www.hoise.com. The result's Web address actually has the word "article" in it, which probably means that the Web page is an article that features the market research report that I want.

Frost & Sullivan study shows wireless solutions help health care professionals meet need of the hour

Palo Alto 03 March 2004 *Cash-strapped hospitals in the United States are finding it increasingly difficult to provide patients with anything more than the standard levels of medical care. Rising patient volumes, acute staff shortages, and a rapidly aging population are not only c_____ ing ___tient quality ___ care, but als____ s_____*

By spending a few minutes carefully reading the Google results abstracts, by studying the Web addresses, and by clicking on a few links, I am usually able to find a free article or a press release that references the report I'm interested in. Typically, I don't find the entire report, although I have successfully done that. However, more than half of the time I am able to find an article that references enough of the report to help me in my sales strategy, sales planning, and enough, frankly, to determine whether I actually might want to buy the full report from MarketResearch.com in the future.

IMPORTANT NOTE: The MarketResearch.com/Google trick highlighted above only works some of the time. And even when it does, it is very unlikely that you will get the bulk of the data from a research report in something you find for free on the Web. **Therefore, if you have a sales call with an important prospect, or if you are doing business planning or strategic planning and the type of information contained in the report is critical to your success, then bite the bullet and buy the report; I guarantee you'll be happy you did.**

Hidden Research Reports – Google Filetype: Search

http://www.google.com

Although technically not the Invisible Web because you're using Google, a great way to find industry research reports is to use the Google filetype: search, as described in Chapter IX.

Oftentimes professional research reports get posted online for people to download because they are too large to e-mail. Sometimes industry groups or even companies post reports online for members or employees to download.

Posters of these reports often think that if they only give the download link to specific people, the report is secure. However, if you remember what happens with the Google "vacuum cleaner," if something gets posted online and it isn't behind a properly secured username and password, Google may eventually find it.

It's easy to find these reports using the Google filetype: search (filetype colon). Just type an industry name followed by the word *industry*, into Google, using quotation marks (e.g., "paper industry"). Add words like *trends, issues, revenue, technologies*, etc. that you think might appear in a research report.

Next, type in filetype:pdf, which will limit your search results to just PDF files, which is a fairly typical format for a research report. You can also try filetype:ppt for PowerPoint slides, or filetype:doc for Word documents.

SAM TIP ➤
Search for Research Reports

There are millions of research reports online, many of them meant for a "private" audience. You can sometimes locate these reports by using a Google filetype: (colon) search.

1. Go to **www.google.com**

2. Enter an industry name followed by the word industry, into Google, using quotation marks (e.g., "paper industry").

3. Add additional words that might appear in a report, such as issues, trends, etc.

4. Add filetype: and then pdf (e.g., "paper industry" + trends filetype:pdf).

5. Try other filetypes including doc (Word document) and ppt (PowerPoint file).

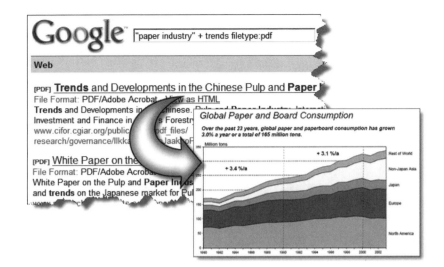

Review the search results to see if the abstract looks like a report. If it is, click on the link and download the file. You'll be amazed at the types of professional research reports you can find online using the filetype: method.

Market Research Tools – Third Wave Research

http://www.thirdwaveresearch.com/mrttwr

Occasionally you'll stumble upon an invisible Web site featuring free resources and tools and you'll wonder if it is too good to be true. Third Wave Research is a for-profit research firm that sells in-depth reports on products, industries, and markets. They have a number of free resources, however, that can be very beneficial to business development professionals.

When you visit the site, you'll see an impressive area of research options. To access the detailed data, you do have to pay.

However, Third Wave does provide free top-level data with some of its tools that can help you in creating customized sales proposals. In particular, the Household Spending, Product Line Planner, and Business Profiler tools offer some great data.

SAM TIP ▶
Research Tools:

Third Wave Research offers free research tools that provide some great information for sales calls and proposals, particularly if your clients sell directly to consumers.

1. Go to **www.thirdwaver-esearch.com/mrttwr**

2. Choose one of the report options.

3. In each report, follow the prompts and use the pull-down menus and geographic selection to create your report.

4. You will be asked for a username and password.

5. You can choose to register, or just click the "To Continue ..." link to immediately access your report.

NOTE: When you are ready to access your chosen report, you will see a login screen. You can register for free; however, a link on this page also allows you to go directly to your report without registration.

Using the Household Spending Tool

These reports provide a household spending overview for particular products. This kind of data can be very helpful when making a sales call to a company that sells into a specific market. Obviously, it is also very helpful when preparing a sales proposal and you need to show you have a solid understanding of a prospect's (or existing client's) market and customer spending habits.

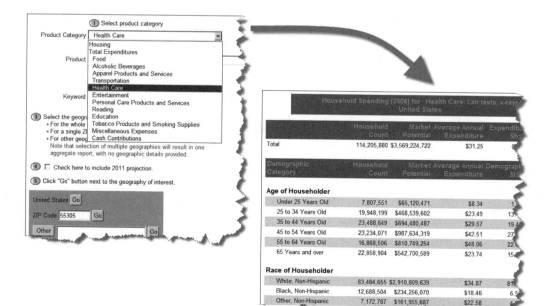

1. On the main page, click on the Household Spending link.

2. Choose a product category and then a product from the pull-down menus, or just enter a keyword.

3. Click on the "Click Here to Include 2011 Projections" box if you want to identify spending trends for the particular product.

4. **NOTE 1:** You can only click on the United States "GO" button if you want a free report. By entering a zip code, you will be asked to purchase the report.

5. **NOTE 2:** On the screen following clicking on the "GO" button, click on the "To Continue without Logging In" link to access your report without registering.

Using the Product Line Planner Tool

These reports are helpful if you need a solid understanding of sales by product type. Imagine being armed with this data during a prospect call to a client who sells your referenced product, or sells to companies that sell your referenced product. How credible would you seem armed with this data? Alternatively, how impressive would it be to reference these charts in a proposal or plan to an existing account? (Just right-mouse click on a table, copy, and then paste a table directly into your proposal.)

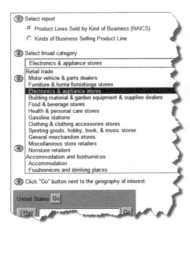

1. On the main page, click on the Product Line Planner link.

2. Choose either the "Product Lines Sold by Kind of Business" or the "Kinds of Business Selling Product Line" radio button.

3. Choose a Broad Category and then a Specific Category using the pull-down menus, or enter a keyword.

4. Click the United States "GO" button for national data, or click the "Other" tab and select a geographic region.

5. **NOTE:** All Product Line Planner reports are free. However, the data are from 1997 so use the Product Line Planner for base planning purposes only.

6. **NOTE 2:** On the screen following clicking on the "GO" button, click on the "To Continue without Logging In" link to access your report without registering.

Using the Business Profiler Tool

These reports are very helpful if you're a salesperson entering a new territory and you want to know what types of businesses are located within a specific geographic region. In addition, you can reference these reports during a cold call if you're meeting with a prospect who you know is looking to enter a new market. Imagine the value you could provide a prospect, or existing account, if you print out the report and present it.

Business Profile (1999/2000) for ZIP Code = 55401
Total Businesses = 1,011

Category	Count	Percent
Number of Employees		
1-4 Employees	524	51.8%
5-9 Employees	205	20.3%
10-19 Employees	128	12.7%
20-49 Employees	95	9.4%
50-99 Employees	35	3.5%
100-249 Employees	18	1.8%
250-499 Employees	3	0.3%
1,000 or More Employees	3	0.3%

Category	Count	Percent
NAICS Industry Sector		
Utilities	3	0.3%
Construction	16	1.6%
Manufacturing	69	6.8%
Wholesale Trade	72	7.1%
Retail Trade	49	4.8%
Transportation & Warehousing	6	0.6%
Information	66	6.5%
Finance & Insurance	67	6.6%
Real Estate & Rental & Leasing	37	3.7%
Professional, Scientific & Technical Services	372	36.8%
Management of Companies & Enterprises	12	1.2%
Admin, Support, Waste Management, Remediation Services	53	5.2%
Educational Services	14	1.4%
Health Care and Social Assistance	20	2.0%
Arts, Entertainment & Recreation	37	3.7%
Accommodation & Food Services	62	6.2%

1. On the main page, click on the Business Profiler link.

2. Click the United States "GO" button to receive business profiles for the entire nation.

3. Or enter a zip code and click the "GO" button to restrict your search to a specific area.

4. Or click the "Other" button and select multiple zip codes, metropolitan areas, counties, cities, etc. Following your selection, click the "GO" button.

5. **NOTE:** All Business Profiler reports are free. However, the data are from 1999 and 2000, so use the reports for base planning purposes only.

6. **NOTE 2:** On the screen following clicking on the "GO" button, click on the "To Continue without Logging In" link to access your report without registering.

7. **NOTE 3:** Once in the report, click on the small graph icon to pull up a chart of the specified data.

Industry Media Lists – Publist

http://www.publist.com

A superb way of learning about an industry is through industry trade journals and magazines. Public relations firms often charge lots of money to create a list of industry publications for clients. Although not as thorough as a public relations firm, you can get a good grasp of the publications serving a particular industry via Publist.

Publist features a database of more than 150,000 magazines, journals, newsletters, and other periodicals. You can easily search for publications from around the world specializing in particular industries or topics. Publist is free to use; however, registration is required.

Let's say that I have been assigned a new client in the plastics industry. I'd like to get up to speed on the industry prior to my initial sales/account call. Or let's pretend that my

SAM TIP ◥
Associations:
_____

Knowing which industry journals and magazines focus on your industry, your client's industry, and your client's customer's industry is imperative if you want to provide value to prospects on existing relationships.

You also need to know this information to help with your advertising and public relations strategies.

1. Go to **www.publist.com**; you will need to register for free

2. Type in a broad search term related to the industry you want (e.g., plastics).

3. Free registration is required to access the list.

4. Use the Advanced Search feature if you want to get more specific and narrow your search. It is located under the search form on the main page.

company has come out with a new IT solutions product that serves the plastics industry and I want to generate publicity prior to making cold calls.

Either way, I need to know which trade publications are read by those in the industry. This will tell me which publications I need to become familiar with, and help me determine where I ought to be sending my press releases.

By entering "plastics" in the search form on Publist.com's home page, I instantly learn about more than 120 national and international publications serving the plastics industry.

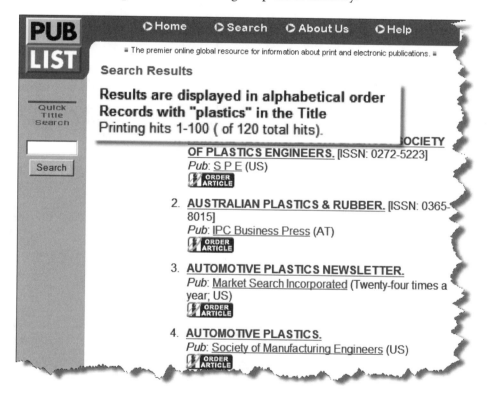

For more detailed searching, use Publist's Advanced Search feature, found directly under the search form on the main page. The Advanced Search feature allows you to limit your search by publication titles, subject, country, and more.

SAM TIP
Free Journals:

Subscribing to and reading a trade journal is the best way to immerse yourself in an industry. You can get free publications covering dozens of industries.

- Go to **http://smallbiz-trends.tradepub.com**

- On the left-side navigation, search by industry or click the "Publications by Name" link to search by title.

- Click any publication.

- Click the "Subscribe Free" or the "Request Now" button, and fill out the form to receive your free journal.

Free Trade Journals – TradePubs

http://smallbiztrends.tradepub.com
(Note: no www in URL)

If you really want to immerse yourself in your client's industry, you should subscribe to and read your client's industry trade journals. If your client ever visits your office, it's impressive if they see a number of industry journals on your desk. Alternatively, on a client visit, throw an issue in your briefcase and make sure your client sees it as you take your notes out.

The true benefit comes when you actually read the physical publication. You'll be able to reference material you've read during your client conversations, and you'll really make an impression. In addition, there's great value in the pictures, charts, and graphs found in a physical publication.

You can get FREE subscriptions to industry trade journals at **http:// smallbiztrends.tradepub.com**. To find a journal, use the category selection on the left-side navigation. You can also search by title by clicking on the "Publications by Name" link, again on the left-side navigation.

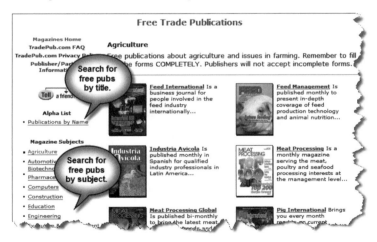

When you find a trade journal you want, just click the journal title/picture where you'll access more detailed information about the publication. If you determine you want it, click the "Subscribe Free" or the "Request Now" button, fill out the form, and within a few weeks you'll start receiving your free subscription. NOTE: Make sure you give yourself some time as it can take up to ten weeks for you to receive your first issue.

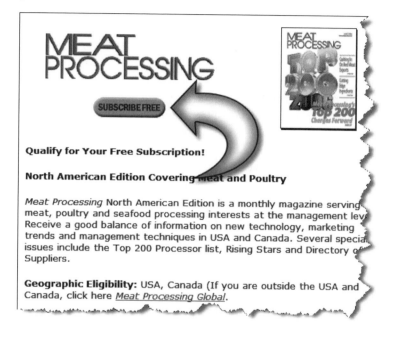

Foreign Market Research Reports – Export.gov

http://www.buyusainfo.net/adsearch.cfm?search_type=int&loadnav=no

As Thomas Friedman so eloquently describes in his book *The World is Flat*, we live in a global inter-dependant economy. To thrive, even small businesses must consider exporting, importing, and/or partnering with overseas firms as viable growth options. However, it can often be difficult to find information on foreign markets when it comes time to construct a business plan and sales strategy.

The good news is that there are literally hundreds of thousands of research reports on doing business with foreign countries covering virtually every industry. The U.S. government, the largest producer of research in the world, provides a free online library of these reports through the Market Research Library at Export.gov.

Registration is required to access the database, but searching and downloading are free. You can search for reports by using the industry pull-down menu. You can search by region of the world, country, date range, and type of report.

You can also search by keyword. Just type in a keyword to search report titles, or click the "Search the Document Body" check box to receive the maximum number of reports related to an industry. You can even sign up for automatic alerts to be notified whenever a report that covers the industry you're interested in is added to the library.

Here's a look at some foreign market research reports related to the cell phone industry.

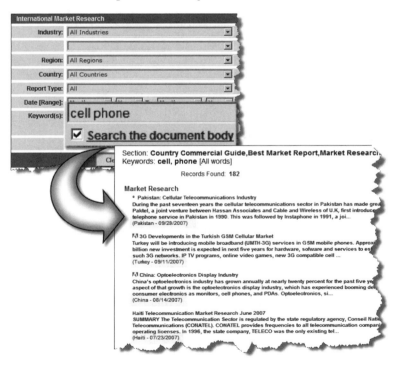

Business Meta-Search Engine – Biznar

http://www.biznar.com

Biznar allows you to search multiple site simultaneously like a standard meta-search engine, however, Biznar limits its sources to business Web sites, blogs, wikis, and the Invisible Web. Each search is done in real-time as if you were entering the search term on each individual Web site yourself.

For best results, use the Advanced Search feature and start your search with a broad industry term, for example, "medical device industry." For more recent articles, choose a date range.

After clicking the "Go" button to conduct your search, it may seem like the search engine stalls. This is normal so be patient while Biznar searches its sources. You can track your

search status by watching the "sources complete" meter.

On the results list, you can see the source on the right side. Under many of the results is a star rating, showing how relevant the result is. To open a result, just click on it.

SAM TIP
Business Meta-Search

Simultaneously search business Web sites, business sites on the Invisible Web, government sites, business blogs and more.

1. Go to **www.biznar.com**

2. Use Advanced Search. Enter the name of an industry; keep your search fairly broad (e.g. enter a term like "plastics industry") as you can always enter more terms later.

3. Choose a date range to limit your results to a specific time period.

4. Wait a few seconds while Biznar searches its various sources.

5. Notice the star ratings underneath the results, telling you how relevant the result is to your search query.

6. Review the categories on the left side and sort results by topic, sources, author, date, and more.

7. Click the box in front of any result and save it for later access, which you can do by clicking on the "My Selections" link.

On the left side of Biznar's results page, you'll notice a number of different categories and subcategories. These allow you to sort results by topic, source, publication, author, and date. To sort results, just click on any of the categories/sub-categories.

Another neat feature is the ability to click on the box in front of each result. When you do this, the result is saved. You can conduct future searches and access any of the saved ones at anytime during your session, by clicking the "My Selections" link.

SAM TIP
Salaries:

Knowing someone's approximate salary is helpful if you're selling to them, or need to figure out a company's cost structure.

1. Go to the Web address under the header. You will need Java installed on your computer. You can download it at www.java.com.

2. **Step 1:** Select geography.

3. **Step 2:** Select an occupation. If it's not listed, find one that is "close enough."

4. **Step 3:** Select a work level, or approximate experience level, using the pull-down menu. Choose multiple levels by selecting a level, clicking on the **"Add to Selection"** button, and then going back and choosing another level.

5. **Step 4:** When you've loaded your levels, click the **"Get Data"** button and view your results.

6. Increase by 2 to 3 percent per year from the listed year and multiply the hourly rate by 2,080 to get an annual figure.

Salary Figures – BLS Compensation Survey

http://data.bls.gov/PDQ/outside.jsp?survey=nc
(Note: no www in URL – web address is case sensitive)

Knowing the average salary for an employee can be helpful in a sales call or client plan. Certainly, it's beneficial if you sell insurance, financial services, or home mortgages. But even for the salesperson who sells widgets, or for the account manager who serves the Widget account, knowing general salary statistics prior to a sales call or proposal can be important when trying to figure out what your pricing ought to be.

In the service industry specifically, "human capital" or employee expenses are typically an organization's largest cost. Knowing your prospects' costs can be beneficial when tailoring your sales message.

Several Web sites offer salary figures (a Google search on "salaries" returns millions of results). However, when reviewing some of these sites, it's difficult to know from where they compiled the data, and how relevant and accurate the information actually *is*.

Many salary-related Web sites, in fact, base their data on surveys. I don't know about you, but I have fun when I receive a survey asking how much I make (I answer in the millions). I hope that a good survey company removes my answers; however, my point is that survey data *are* based on self-reporting and the data can be skewed.

The U.S. government's Bureau of Labor Statistics produces a very slick and easy-to-use tool for salary information. The database allows you to choose a geographic area, a job title, and even experience level to learn what people are earning.

To use, go to the BLS salary calculator tool, visit the Web site at **http://data.bls.gov/PDQ/outside.jsp?survey=nc** (web address is case sensitive). Choose a geographic area, and then in the right window, choose an occupation by using the pull-down menu and/or by entering a keyword into the field.

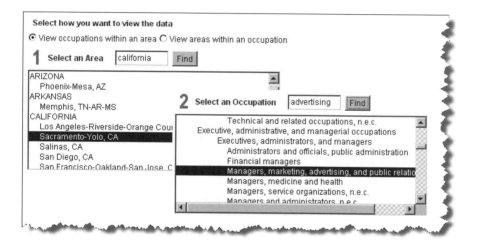

Next, use the Work Level pull-down menu to select experience levels. Select a level, then click the "Add To Your Selection" button. You can select as many experience levels as you'd like.

When you're finished adding experience levels, click the "Get Data" button and retrieve your results.

The data are complied using government statistics, tax figures, and surveys. When I present around the country, I often conduct a search using someone in the audience and typically, the results I get back from the BLS database are a solid match.

You must have Java enabled on your computer to use the BLS database. The only drawback I find is that the job titles aren't broad enough, so too often I'm using a title that's only close to what I really want.

In addition, the data are sometimes a year or two old so you'll need to add 2 to 3 percent per year to get a more up-to-date figure. Finally, the database lists the salaries as an hourly wage so you'll need to multiply by 2,080 (workable hours per year assuming a forty-hour work week) to get a good understanding for the annual salary.

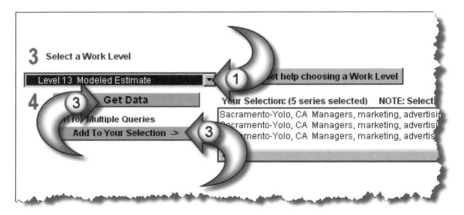

Area	Occupation	Level	DataSource	Year	Period	Hourly Rate	
Sacramento-Yolo, CA	Managers, marketing, advertising, and public relations	Level 05	**Modeled**	2004	Jul	$23.97	**Typic** F1=5; F4=2; F7=1;
Sacramento-Yolo, CA	Managers, marketing, advertising, and public relations	Level 09	**Modeled**	2004	Jul	$34.33	**Typic** F1=6; F4=3; F7=2;
Sacramento-Yolo, CA	Managers, marketing, advertising, and public relations	Level 07	**Modeled**	2004	Jul	$29.49	**Typic** F1=6; F4=3; F7=1;
Sacramento-Yolo, CA	Managers, marketing, advertising, and public relations	Level 11	**Modeled**	2004	Jul	$42.68	**Typic** F1=7; F4=4; F7=3;
Sacramento-Yolo, CA	Managers, marketing, advertising, and public relations	Level 13	**Modeled**	2004	Jul	$65.21	**Typic** F1=8; F4=5; F7=3

CHAPTER FIFTEEN

The "Invisible Web" – Personal information

"Be totally knowledgeable about the prospect. Your knowledge of the prospect and his or her business is critical to completing the sale."
> – Jeffrey H. Gitomer, *The Sales Bible*, New York: William Morrow and Company, 1994.

Creating a personal connection during a sales call is one of the keys to success. Knowing the likes and dislikes of your existing clients is critical as you provide personalized service and value.

There are hundreds of books that teach salespeople and account managers how to connect with prospects and existing clients. A theme in almost every one is "ask questions." However, asking good questions is an art form. The top five percent of salespeople and account managers brighten up a room and can make any prospect feel "at home." Unfortunately, the other 95 percent of us feel, and often look, uncomfortable trying to come up with something—some question—to break the ice.

In Minnesota, the standard "cold enough for you?" is good for just about any situation. However, for the 95 percent of non-superstars, coming up with the next question can be awkward. Worse is when you launch into a series of what can be perceived as "canned questions." You look phony and instead of listening to you, your prospect or client is thinking about the sales training seminar you must have recently attended.

An easy way of impressing your prospects and existing clients and increasing your comfort level is by asking questions in areas where you already know your client has an interest. People like to talk about themselves. So make it easy and ask questions relevant to your client's life or business.

How impressive will you be if your question relates to a charity your prospect donates to? You think you could create a connection with an existing client if you ask about a relevant after-work activity or hobby? Or play "six degrees of separation" and ask questions about a person both you and your prospect know.

The good news is there are numerous ways to find information on people using the Internet. Practicing the "Fourth R" in relation to people information can be fun and, once you do it a few times, easy as well.

The following pages highlight a number of Invisible Web sites that offer great information on people. Some of the sites help you find commonalities between groups of people, while others are geared to search for information on a specific person. I'll also review some of the sites discussed earlier and highlight how they can be used for locating information on individuals.

IMPORTANT NOTE: To ensure your prospects or existing clients don't think that you're a stalker, it's critical that you use information you find about them very carefully. For example, if you find information about the success of your prospect's children, you don't walk into a first-time sales call and start your greeting with, "Hey ... congratulations on your sixth-grade daughter winning the talent show." Besides freaking out your prospect, you could end up with a restraining order.

Rather, when you're going to mention information that you found on your prospect or existing client, use some tact. Don't just blurt out what you found. Instead, use the information that you gathered to ask better questions.

Using our example, you know that your prospect has a sixth-grade daughter, so when you walk into your prospect's office, look for a picture. Then, motioning to the photo, say, "Is that your daughter?" You already know the answer is going to be "yes" and then you can engage in a conversation you know your prospect cares about: his or her family.

Another way to use the information you found is to be honest about how you found it. People respect that you took the time to research prior to a sales or existing client call, so don't be afraid to mention it.

Using our example again, you could say: "Before I meet with any company or potential client, I like to do a little Internet research to see what I can find. Besides all of the great material I found on your company, I thought that recent article in the local newspaper about your daughter winning the talent show was great. You must be very proud." Then you can engage your prospect in a conversation you know he cares about: his daughter.

Search Engine People Search

Popular Search Engines

As discussed in Chapter V, popular search engines like Google, Yahoo, MSN, and Ask offer powerful search capabilities and can provide relevant and focused results *if* you know how to search. Following are some reminder tips about effectively using search engines when searching for people information.

Quotes: When searching for the name of a person, remember to put the person's name in quotation marks. Enter William Scott Johnson in a search engine and you'll return every result with the word William, the word Scott, and the word Johnson somewhere on the page. Enter "William Scott Johnson" and those three words must be next to each other, in that exact order.

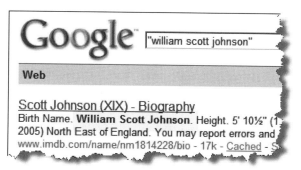

Combo Search: Narrow your search by entering your prospect's name and associated relevant terms. Entering "Jim Smith" in Google returns 1.1 million results. Add Minnesota to the search (e.g., "Jim Smith" AND Minnesota) and it's down to 52,000. Add banking to the search (e.g., Jim Smith AND Minnesota AND banking) and you're down to 766 results. Add "vice president" (e.g., "Jim Smith" AND Minnesota AND banking AND "vice president") and you're down to a few hundred relevant results.

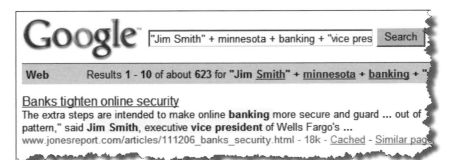

SAM TIP
ZabaSearch:

Locate contact information, including birthdates and even unlisted phone numbers!

1. Go to **www.zabasearch.com**

2. Enter a person's name; do not use quotation marks.

3. Choose a state.

4. If you receive too many results, use Advanced Search.

5. Click the Map It tab for a Google Map of the person's address.

6. Click the ZabaSearch/ Google link to see Google results for the person.

7. Use ZabaAlerts to receive an e-mail anytime the site finds new or updated information.

Remember, you may need to use the + sign instead of AND, or, for most popular search engines, you can skip the AND altogether as long as you're using quotes correctly.

Contact Information – ZabaSearch

http://www.zabasearch.com

A number of Web sites can help you find a person's phone number and address. Some good ones include 411.com (**www.411.com**) and the Online White Pages (**www.whitepages. com**). My personal favorite, however, is ZabaSearch (**www. zabasearch.com**).

Why? Although ZabaSearch is unfortunately filled with links to sites where you have to pay for information, it does offer some nice features not found through other sites, including date-of-birth information, direct links to Google search results, and even unlisted phone numbers.

Using ZabaSearch is easy. Just enter the name of the person you're interested in finding, choose a state, and click the search button.

NOTE: Do not use quotation marks around the name. Just enter the person's first and last name.

If you receive too many results, click on the Advanced Search link to the right of the search tab. On the Advanced Search, you can choose a city and/or a birth date, which will help limit your search results.

Once on the search results page, you'll see numerous links next to each name. The two that I find helpful are also free: 1) The Map It link which will open up a Google Map of the person's listed address, and 2) The ZabaSearch/Google link under the results listing, which will open up a new window featuring the sites that Google has indexed related to people with that name.

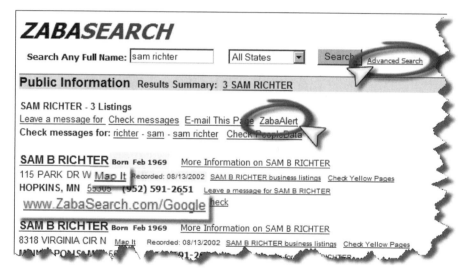

On the result listing page, you'll find an address and a telephone number, which is usually the person's home information. On many of the results, you'll see when the data was last updated, which is obviously crucial if you want to see the latest information. Many of the results also include the person's birth date.

Finally, make sure to check out the ZabaAlert feature. You'll find it near the top of the search result page. With ZabaAlert, you can enter your e-mail address and ZabaSearch will send you an e-mail each time it finds or updates information about your chosen person.

People in the News – Newslink.org Revisited

http://www.newslink.org/statnews.html

Unless you're calling on an executive at a large organization or publicly traded company, it's unlikely that a major newspaper has written a story about your prospect. You might get lucky doing a "news search" using one of the major search engines, but more than likely, your search will turn up empty; or if your prospect has a common name like "Nancy Smith," you might end up with hundreds of thousands of results. This is especially true if your prospect is an executive in a small to mid-size private firm.

There are news sources that might have information about your prospect, especially if your prospect is an executive at a firm or involved in the community. If you remember from the company search section, Newslink.org (http://www.newslink.org/statnews.html) is a directory of searchable newspapers and news sources from around the country.

Where a large metropolitan newspaper wouldn't cover a story about an executive being promoted or their kid's soccer team winning the regional championship, a local newspaper is often the place you can find relevant information about a prospect that you can use in your sales call. Remember that people buy from people. How better to show your prospect that you care about them than by referencing something that is very important to your prospect—news about themselves.

Let's take a friend of mine, Louise Anderson, CEO of Anderson Performance Systems. Louise's company is in Hastings, Minnesota, a smaller town just outside the Twin Cities metropolitan area.

SAM TIP
Local People News:

It's unlikely that your prospect has been written about by a major news organization. It's likely, however, that your prospect has appeared in their local newspaper (e.g., wedding announcement, charitable donation, etc.).

1. Go to **www.newslink.org**

2. Find the U.S. Newspaper header, and click the "By State" link.

3. Click on one of the publication links.

4. Once on the newspaper's site, find a Search Form or an archive link; it's usually on the top or left-side navigation.

5. You may need to click the Advanced Search link to get older articles.

6. Enter the person's name and see what appears.

Using Google in a general search, I found 64,200 results on "Louise Anderson." When doing a Google News Search, I found four results, none of them related to a Louise Anderson in Minnesota. So I tried Newslink.org.

On the Newslink.org home page, I clicked on the "By state" link underneath the U.S. Newspapers header. I clicked the Minnesota link, and a list of Minnesota newspapers appeared. Knowing that Louise's company is in Hastings, I scrolled down and in the Non-Daily area clicked on the "Hastings Star Gazette" link.

Once on the newspaper's site, what I looked for is a Search Box, where I then typed in "Louise Anderson;" note the Boolean quote marks so I treat the words as a single phrase.

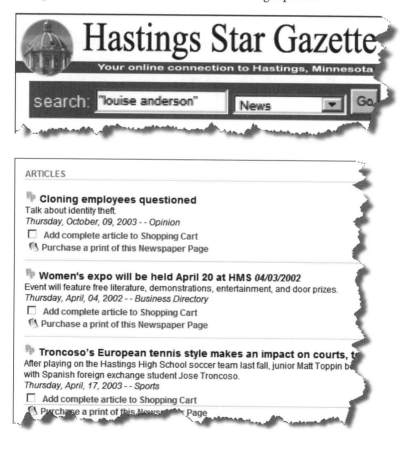

As you can see, a number of search results appear, all about the Louise Anderson that I care about, all of which I can read and then reference during my sales call. (Note that I do have to pay $1.95 per article as unfortunately, many smaller publications now charge to access archived articles.)

For example, the first article about "cloning people" is a letter to the editor about a book that Louise wrote. Don't you think it would be a good idea for me to buy that book and read it (or at least scan it) so I can reference it during my call? The second article references an exchange student who is a tennis star at the local high school who happens to be staying at Louise's house. Could I reference that?

Taking a few minutes of time to reference a prospect prior to a sales call can pay incredible dividends during the call. By referencing stories about Louise and her company, how important do you think I make her feel during my meeting? Assuming my product or service is something that Louise needs, what's the chance she'll read my material or call me back for a second meeting?

Colorful Demographics – CensusScope

http://www.censusscope.org

If you have a client or prospect that sells directly to consumers, a great way to customize a sales presentation is to show that you understand their customers. The good news is demographic data is relatively easy to find online.

Demographic data typically includes information related to population, education, income, race, and other factors. The Federal Government, the largest producer of demographic information in the world, makes its data available for free via numerous Web sites. In fact, typing "U.S. Census" in a popular search engine returns tens of millions of results (have fun).

The most popular site for U.S. demographic information is the U.S. Census Web site at **www.census.gov**. Unfortunately, there is so much information at census.gov that it can be overwhelming, and the data is not always well organized.

SAM TIP ➤
Demographic Data:

U.S. Census data provides an accurate snapshot of people in a geographic region. CensusScope is an easy way to find census data, and you can instantly produce graphs that can be copy/pasted into documents.

1. Go to **www.censusscope. org**

2. Choose one of the four report tabs on the top navigation.

3. Choose a report from the left-side navigation.

4. Using the pull-down menus on the lower left-side navigation, limit your report to a specific geographic area.

5. Right mouse click, Copy, and Paste graphs into your document.

6. Scroll down and locate the data. Left mouse click and highlight the data. Right mouse click and Copy.

7. Open an Excel spreadsheet and select one region. Right mouse click and choose Paste to input the data into your spreadsheet.

However, there are a number of Web sites that take U.S. Census demographic information and repackage it, making it easy to find and use. My personal favorite census site is CensusScope, **www.censusscope.org.**

At CensusScope, you'll find charts, trends, maps, rankings, and more for every U.S. geographic region. I like clicking on the "Map" tab, choosing a state, and then selecting a report. I can then further define the geographic area using the options on the left side navigation.

With CensusScope, you not only get the data in a table form but you also receive a color chart breaking out the information in an easy-to-understand visual format. You can then right mouse click on the chart and copy and paste it directly into your proposal or PowerPoint presentation.

For example, let's say I'm preparing a proposal for a company with customers in Colorado. In particular, my client is interested in attracting a younger audience. How impressive is it if my presentation contains a color chart showing the age breakout of people living in Colorado?

The chart below would have probably taken me a half hour to create in Excel. It took me less than ten seconds to locate, copy, and then paste using CensusScope.org.

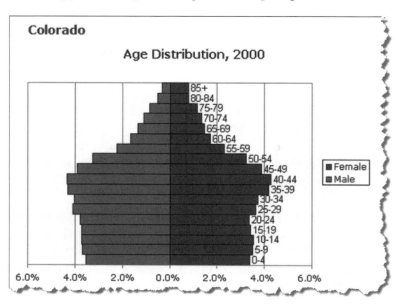

Psychographics – You Are Where You Live

http://www.claritas.com/MyBestSegments/Default.jsp
(Note: web address is case sensitive)

When customizing a proposal to show that you understand your client's audience, a great complement to demographic data is psychographic data. Demographic information is quantifiable population data. Psychographic information, on the other hand, measures attitudes, lifestyles, and behaviors.

Typically, companies pay tens of thousands of dollars for access to psychographic information. However, you can access basic psychographic data for free via Claritas' "You Are Where You Live" tool.

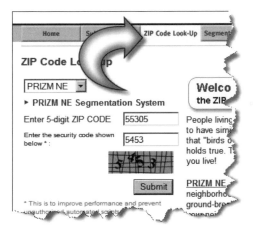

To get a free report, just go to www.claritas.com/MyBest-Segments/Default.jsp (web address is case sensitive) and click the **"ZIP Code Look-Up"** tab on the upper navigation bar.

Enter the zip code you're interested in, type in the security code that appears in the grayed out area, click the Submit button, and receive psychographic information about the people who live in your selected area.

Claritas breaks each zip code into five distinct segments. When you click on a segment, you get general information about the people from that segment in that zip code. For example, using my home zip code of 55305, I learn that the five types of people who live in my area are ...

Hopkins, MN 55305's most common PRIZM NE Segments are:	
Number	**Name**
02	Blue Blood Estates
21	Gray Power
03	Movers & Shakers
01	Upper Crust
22	Young Influentials

Click on the segment name for more detail.
Please Note: Segments are listed in alphabetical order by

SAM TIP
Psychographic Data:

Psychographic data are attitude, lifestyle, and behavior information about people in a particular area.

1. Go to the Web address under the header.

2. Click the **"ZIP Code Look-Up"** tab on the main navigation bars.

3. Enter a zip code.

4. Enter the provided security code. Click Submit.

5. Click any of the links to learn about the people who live in your selected zip code.

Since I'm no longer young and as my kids tell me, I have very little influence, I can't be a "Young Influentials." I'm certainly not an "Upper Crust," "Gray Power," or "Blue Blood Estates." So by default I must be a "Movers and Shakers"—which makes me feel pretty good.

Snapshot	Neighborhood Demos	Household Demos	Lifestyles	Media	Markets	Premium

03 Movers & Shakers   **BACK**

Movers & Shakers is home to America's up-and-coming business class: a wealthy suburban world of dual-income couples who are highly educated, typically between the ages of 35 and 54 and often with children. Given its high percentage of executives and white-collar professionals, there's a decided business bent to this segment: Movers & Shakers rank number-one for owning a small business and having a home office.

Social Group: Elite Suburbs
Lifestage Group: Midlife Success

2005 Statistics:
US Households: 1,806,132 (1.63%)
Median HH Income: $98,031

Lifestyle Traits
- Go scuba diving/snorkeling
- Eat at Bertucci's
- Inc. magazine
- Home study course by internet
- Porsche 911

Demographics Traits:

Ethnic Diversity:	White, High Asian
Presence of Kids:	No kids
Age Ranges:	35-54
Education Levels:	College Graduate
Employment Levels:	Management
Homeownership:	Mostly own
Urbanicity:	Suburban
Income:	Wealthy
Income Producing Assets:	High

By clicking on any one of the profiles, I can learn about the people in that segment. It's important to remember that the data are an average; it does not perfectly represent the people in a particular classification. Movers and Shakers does offer a decent snapshot of me and my family (except I don't drive a Porsche; does a Camry come close?).

Find A Tweeter – Tweepz

http://www.tweepz.com

As discussed in the Company Invisible Web section, Twitter is one of the fastest growing social networking sites. Millions are now "Tweeting" everyday—every hour for that matter—on topics ranging from what is going on in their personal lives (does anyone really care?) to important business information that can be invaluable when practicing Sales Intelligence.

The trick then is finding people who are "Tweeting" about their companies and/or industries and following them. The good news is there are a number of services that help you find "Tweeters" using a variety of search criteria.

My favorite search engine to locate "Tweeters" is Tweepz (**www.tweepz.com**). Tweepz works by searching the account information people set up when they open their Twitter accounts. Not all people include their place of work in their Twitter account information/biographies, but many do.

For example, if I was looking for people at Best Buy who are on Twitter, I would enter "bio:(Best Buy)". Entering "bio:" (bio colon) tells Tweepz that I want to search Twitter biographies and by putting Best Buy within parentheses, I tell Tweepz to treat those two words as a single phrase. Note that

there is no space after the colon. I can get more specific by entering job titles or even functions, e.g., "bio:marketing". If I wanted to find Best Buy employees in Minneapolis, I would use "bio:(best buy) loc:minneapolis" (for more search tips, click Tweepz's Advanced Search link).

Each result includes information from the found person's Twitter biography, a link to their Web site, and Twitter statistics including when the person's last "Tweet" was. Tweepz also provides a number of options for refining your results.

To learn more about a specific person, just click on the person's Twitter account name to see what kind of information he or she includes in "Tweets" (e.g., personal information, business information, or both). For ongoing Sales Intelligence, just "Follow" the person and you'll receive updates every time he or she "Tweets."

To follow someone, you need your own Twitter account, which is free and easy to set up. Once you have an account, just go to the Twitter page of the person you're interested in and click the "Follow" button. You'll receive updates on your Twitter page, via a Twitter desktop application (my favorite is Tweetdeck at **www.tweetdeck.com**), or via an RSS feed that you can easily set up by clicking the RSS button in Tweepz.

TIP: If you already have a Twitter account and don't want to clutter up your other updates, just set up a second account to use for Sales Intelligence and then follow prospects, clients, and your competition through the new account.

Employee Directories – Spoke

http://www.spoke.com

Imagine if you could use the Web to locate a company's employee directory? Unless the company made a big mistake and posted it online, you probably can't. Spoke.com, however, might be the next best thing.

According to Spoke, it has the nation's largest online database of business-to-business contacts, featuring more than 55 million people and more than one million companies.

SAM TIP ➤
Find a Tweeter:

Find people who use Twitter to share what's going on inside their companies.

1. Go to **www.tweepz.com**

2. Enter "bio:" (bio colon) and the company name. There is no space after the colon. If it's a multi-word company, put between parentheses e.g., "bio:(Best Buy)".

3. To find other terms within a person's Twitter biography, enter "bio:" and then the term e.g., "bio:marketing".

4. To search a specific geographic area, enter "loc:" and then the area e.g., "loc:minneapolis".

5. Click Tweepz's Advanced Search link for additional search tips.

6. On the results page, if you find someone of interest, click the person's Twitter name to learn more.

7. Sign up for a Twitter account if you don't have one, and then follow the person. You will receive instant updates on your Twitter account every time the person posts a new "Tweet."

8. Use a service like Tweetdeck (**www.tweetdeck.com**) to organize Tweets you receive.

9. Consider setting up a Twitter account just for Sales Intelligence and use it to follow prospects, clients, and your competition.

Spoke requires registration, which is free. Following registration, you can use Spoke's search engine to locate information on people, and more impressively, to locate a list of up to five company executives and five employees.

There are two drop down options on the main search form: Find People and Find Companies. To find people at a company, choose Find Companies and enter an organization's name. For common company names, you will see a result list where you will need to choose a firm by location.

On the company information page, you'll find a brief overview including estimated revenue and number of employees. You'll also receive a list of up to five company executives, and up to five employees. If you click on any of the names, you'll receive contact information for the selected individual.

To locate people and their job titles within a company, industry, and/or geographic area, use the Advanced Search feature—it's a small link next to the main search form. Enter any combination of a name, job, recency, job title, company,

Advanced Person Search

Find People | Companies

Name	
Title	Target Titles: -- Choose a Functional Area -- ▾ - Choose a Level - ▾

-- Choose a Functional Area --
Senior Exec
Engineering
Finance
Human Resources
Information Technology
Legal
Marketing
Operations
Procurement
Sales
Service & Support

Company	Done
Reachable only	Restrict resu...
Job Recency	Last 3 years
Industry	
Industry Keyword	
Revenue	
Number of Employees	
State	
Metro Area	

[Search] [Clear]

industry, industry keyword, revenue figure, employee figure, and geographic area.

When using the title search, you're presented with pull-down menu options, which make selecting the proper job function easy. For the industry search, Spoke provides prompts and keyword searches to help you identify the proper industry code. Other fields are also "guided menus" when clicked, giving you options versus free-form typing.

Note that you are required to use either a person's name, company name, or job title in your search, so you can't tell Spoke to find every company in a particular city. However, what you can do, for example, is tell Spoke to find job titles within every company of a certain size or industry in a specific city.

After you've entered your criteria, click "search" and Spoke will find results that meet your criteria. On the results page, you'll receive up to five employees who fit your search criteria. Note that because you only receive five results, you

Showing 1-25 of 25   Upgrade to se

Refine your results

[Save to List ▾]   [✉ E-mail Selected]   [More actions ▾]

[Update Search]

select   all, none   Validated

☐ **Patti Hart** ✉   6/2008
   Ceo at Lin Tv Corp

Name
[   ]

☐ **Bart Catalane** ✉   6/2008
   Chief Financial Officer at Lin Tv Corp

Title
[   ]

☐ **Scott Blumenthal** ✉   6/2008
   Executive Vice President Television at Lin Tv Corp

☐ Contact info

☐ **Vincent Sadusky** ✉   6/2008
   President at Lin Tv Corp

Recency
[Last 3 years   ▾]

☐ **Robb Richter** ✉   3/2008
   Vice President at Lin Tv Corp

Company Name
[Lin Tv Corp   ]

probably want to stick to searches that include a company name.

Click on the person's name and you'll get some information about the company, and possibly additional information about the person including a brief biography, job history, etc. Note that some people have quite a bit of information in their profiles while others have nothing. Again, contact information for the individual is provided. For some individuals, you will be provided with the company's general phone number. For others, you actually receive the person's direct dial. Spoke also offers a feature where you can click an e-mail icon and Spoke will facilitate an e-mail communication. However, you're only offered three connections via Spoke's free version, and you have to upgrade to a paid membership if you'd like to send e-mails to more than just the three contacts.

On any Find People or Find Companies result page, you have the option of refining your search by using the criteria listed in the Refine Search area. You have the ability to add and/or delete information from your original search, using the same options as featured in Advanced Search.

One point of annoyance is that Spoke only allows you to conduct a certain number of searches per day with its free service. The way around this is to register for multiple accounts using different e-mail addresses.

One note of caution: Even though Spoke says it has updated data on tens of millions of business people, you still must view the data with a critical eye. Because the information in Spoke is compiled using an automated "Web spider" versus a human-built database, it can be inaccurate, outdated, and sometimes humorous, especially when it comes to information on private companies and the people who work at privately held firms.

For example, as librarian Patricia Hoskins pointed out to me, if you type the name of a video company into the Spoke

SAM TIP
Search with Caution:

Anytime you're searching for information on private companies, ACT WITH CAUTION: the data might be outdated or just plain wrong.

It's imperative when you're searching for company/people information that you use multiple sources. Verify your data by searching newspaper or trade journal articles. Pick up the phone and call the company to verify accuracy. **The bottom line: search skeptically.**

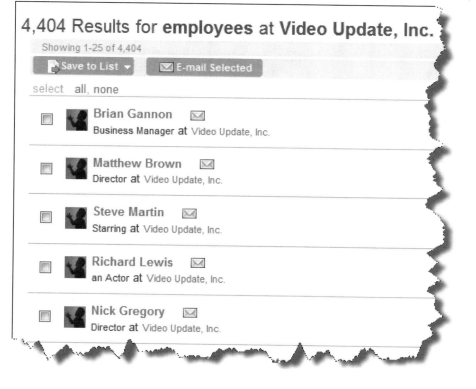

search engine, it reports thousands of employees. However, what Spoke reports as employees are actually actors who appear in the movies you can rent at its stores.

The Spoke "Web Spider" found a person's name (actor) associated with a company (video rental store) and the database system automatically assumed the person was an employee.

Where Are They Now – ZoomInfo

http://www.zoominfo.com

A number of "people search" Web sites have entered the market in recent years. In my opinion, ZoomInfo is the best free site available for locating information on business people, especially executives.

ZoomInfo is really a big Index Engine—a giant online vacuum cleaner—that searches the Internet for names of people. The search experts at ZoomInfo have used different algorithms to create profiles of individuals, their job histories, and where they are today.

Although ZoomInfo allows "People" and "Company" searches via its home page, the company search only provides you access to company and related Web sites, not the contacts at that company (ZoomInfo's Premium service offers that function, which we cover in later chapters).

The "People" search is quite good. To access it, make sure you choose the "People Search" tab off of the home page. Enter the first and last name of the person you're interested in. Note that ZoomInfo will automatically search for spelling variations of the first name (e.g., John, Jonathan, Jon).

Click Search and find the result. Click on the name of the result to learn more about that person.

If the name is a common name use ZoomInfo's Advanced Search. Click the Advanced Search link (directly to the right of the Search button), and enter the company name, or a portion of the company name, where the person works. The last field on the Advanced People search form is the name field;

SAM TIP
People Zoom:

Imagine a search engine that scours the Web but only looks for pages that contain information about people.

1. Go to **www.zoominfo.com**

2. Click the People tab.

3. Enter the first and last name of the person you're interested in finding.

4. Click Search and find the result. Click on the name of the result to learn more about that person.

5. If the name is a common name (e.g., Pat Smith), use Advanced Search.

6. Enter the company name, or a portion of the company name, where the person works.

7. The last field on the Advanced People Search form is the name field; enter the person's name.

enter the person's name. Then click the Search button to find results.

If you don't know the full company name, a quick way to get it is to use ZoomInfo's company search. Just click the "Company Search" tab off the home page. Type in a partial name of the company, conduct your search, and see how ZoomInfo has indexed the name. Use that exact name in the Company search field in the Advanced People Search.

Note that the Advanced Search offers a number of search options that look very intriguing; for example, the ability to search for job titles within a certain geography. However, to use these features, you need to be a ZoomInfo Premium member.

When you conduct a search using my name, a number of results appear. If you happen to know I'm the "Sam Richter" you're interested in because you know where I work, clicking on my name provides some solid results.

On the biography page, the menu areas will show the information that ZoomInfo has compiled including employment history, education, etc. Unfortunately, for many people, the majority of menu areas are blank. If you don't find great information in the menu area, click the "View Sources" link and you'll see portions of Web sites that ZoomInfo has gathered featuring information about your person.

Results 1-17 of 17 people		Sort By: Relevance (Default)
Name	**Title**	**Company**
Richter, Sam	Chief Executive Officer	SBR Worldwide
Richter, Sam	Senior Pitcher	Knights
Richter, Sam	Position In Sales	Ryan Chevrolet
Richter, Sam	Trainer	
Richter, Sam	Designated Hitter	
Richter, Sam	Catcher	

Mr. Sam Richter Edit

Chief Executive Officer

SBR Worldwide, LLC
Minnetonka, MN
✉ Contact this person

Employment History

▽ **Chief Executive Officer[3]**
SBR Worldwide, LLC
Minnetonka, MN
USA

▷ **President[3]**
James J. Hill Group / James J. Hill Reference Library

▷ **Senior Director of E-Business Marketing[2]**
Digital River , Inc. (NASDAQ: DRIV)

▷ **Group Director**
Weber Shandwick Company

▷ **Vice President, Creative Director**
J. Patrick Moore and Partners/Gerber Richter

▷ **Vice President and Senior Copywriter**
Cevette and Company Advertising

Board Membership and Affiliations

▷ **Board of Advisors**
Vortal Optics

▷ **Board Member**
ARANet

▷ **Speaker**
Vistage International Inc

Certifications

▷ **Board of Directors, Public and Private Company**
Saint Mary's University

▷ **Executive Leadership**
University of St. Thomas

Education

BA, School of Journalism and Mass Communication
University of Minnesota

Biography

Sam Richter, Chief Executive of SBR Worldwide (http://www.sbrworld...
SVP/Chief Marketing Officer at ActiFi (http://www.actifi.com) is an inte...
recognized expert on sales, marketing, and leadership. His award-wi...
i...

Web References

1. MCN : Tech Conference Breakouts
www.mncn.org/event_technology_ - [Cached]
Published on: 3/13/2008 Last Visited: 3/13/2008

Sam Richter, CEO of SBR Worldwide, is a nationally sought-after spe...
ranging from online searching to effective selling to value-based lea...
published author and has been featured in hundreds of publications, ...
programs, and radio shows. Sam has more than 20 years experience...
managing award-winning programs for some of the world's most fam...
six years, he was president of the James J. Hill Reference Library and...
the nonprofit local library into a national business resource, helping...
entrepreneurs access the information to live their dreams.

2. About Us - JJ Hill Library
www.jjhill.org/About_us/press_ - [Cached]
Published on: 8/14/2007 Last Visited: 12/11/2007

Sam Richter, president of the James J. Hill Reference Library, is resp...
the private, non-profit business research organization. Sam has more...
experience creating and managing award-winning programs for some...
most famous brands. He is a published author and has been featur...
publications, television programs, and radio shows. (click for more) ...

3. MCN : Tech Conference Breakouts
www.mncn.org/event_technology_ - [Cached]
Published on: 5/8/2006 Last Visited: 3/13/2008

Sam Richter, CEO, SBR Worldwide, LLC

4. cincinnati.bizjournals.com
cincinnati.bizjournals.com/twi - [Cached]
Published on: 12/31/2007 Last Visited: 1/1/2008

After six years as president of the James J. Hill Reference Library, Sa...
announced today will be his last day at the St. Paul organization.

Richter plans to devote time to his soon-to-be released book, Take th...
Calling.

He will remain CEO of SBR Worldwide, a consultancy for entrepreneu...
businesses.

"We've worked exceptionally hard over the past six years to transform...
a national resource, providing important and meaningful value to A...
entrepreneurs and small business communities." Richter said...

The Power of Networks – LinkedIn

http://www.linkedin.com

According to Wikipedia, "six degrees of separation refers to the idea that, if a person is one 'step' away from each person he or she knows and two 'steps' away from each person who is known by one of the people he or she knows, then everyone is no more than six 'steps' away from each person on Earth."

My personal goal is to get the Earth down to three degrees of separation, in which I get to anybody in the world within three phone calls or e-mails. I'll consider myself "uber connected" when I am one-degree away from the President of the United States, the Queen of England, and the Pope. With the Web, my goal is realistic.

For example, I am actually directly virtually connected to Barak Obama (I'm also directly linked to John McCain so my bases were covered during the last election), I'm three degrees from the Queen of England, and two from the Pope.

(The reality is I doubt President Obama would personally respond to an online request from me, and I don't know anyone well enough who will make an introduction to any of these people for me—at least I don't think so—but I am linked to people who know the Pope, and I am linked to people who are linked to people who know the Queen.)

In sales, your personal one, two, three, or six degrees of separation are your future earning power. Your network of contacts and your ability to nurture and build that network directly relates to your long-term success and career growth.

Why is having a powerful network so important for someone in sales and business development? If you don't know the answer, I suggest you get to a book store immediately and buy a book on networking. The reason networking is so important for anyone in sales is that a personal referral to a decision maker dramatically increases the chances that you'll get a meeting. Because the meeting request was suggested by a mutual contact, it dramatically increases the chances that your meeting will be a "warm" one.

Harvey Mackay is the guru of building and nurturing personal networks. In his numerous sold-out lectures and best-selling books, including the networking "bible" *Dig Your Well Before You're Thirsty*, Mackay talks about building a network of trusted individuals and then helping those individuals network with each other. Mackay has a number of great resources on his Web site (**www.harveymackay.com**) including his Memory Cards, which will help inspire you to build your professional network.

SAM TIP
Networking:

LinkedIn can help you build a virtual network of contacts, build your credibility, and help facilitate introductions. It's also a great site to find detailed information about prospects.

1. Go to **www.linkedin.com**

2. Register to become a member and complete your profile.

3. Start inviting people to join your network.

4. Enter a company name in the search box to see if someone in your network knows a person at the company.

5. If there is a LinkedIn relationship, request an introduction.

6. Complete the introduction forms and your request will be sent to your contact who can then forward and make the introduction.

7. Don't forget to make recommendations; people usually reciprocate and thus you can use LinkedIn to build your credibility.

The Web makes practicing "six degrees," Mackay's Memory Cards, and building your network easy. One of the best sites around for building your professional network, and it is also an exceptional "people research" site, is LinkedIn (**www.linkedin.com**).

LinkedIn is free to all registered users. You set up your own profile, your résumé, and then you can invite people into your virtual network. LinkedIn makes inviting people easy by allowing you to upload your contacts from programs like Outlook.

As you start building your network, you'll make connections with not only people you've invited and who have

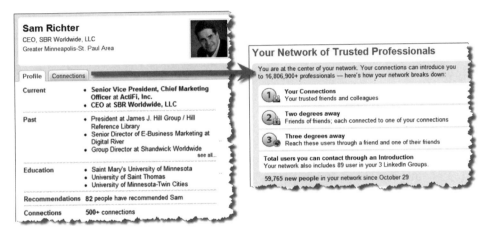

invited you (your first level contacts), but you'll also build connections with your contact's contacts (your second level), and your contact's contact's contacts (your third level). For example, as of the date I sent this book to the publisher, I have almost 2,500 people in my first level contacts. Those contacts have "introduced me" or linked me to nearly 850,000 people. My second level contacts have then linked me with nearly 17 million people. And my network grows by tens of thousands of people every month!

Another great feature of LinkedIn is people in your network can write a recommendation on your behalf that anyone who is a member can see. This ultimate third-party objective endorsement builds your credibility, enhances your reputation, and causes others to want to become part of your network. It's also great fun recommending others—saying nice things about clients, co-workers, colleagues, and friends—and then seeing what those people say about you when they reciprocate. (On a side note, once you build up a list of recommendations, if you're ever having a bad day, reading nice things that others say about you is the perfect pick-me-up.)

I build my LinkedIn network in three ways:

1. I invite people I know who are in my Outlook contact list to join my network.

2. When someone joins my network, I look to see who is in their network. If I recognize a name, I click on their name to open up their profile page. Then I click the "Add [Name] To Your Network" link. I use the form to write a personalized note, and ask the person if they would be willing to join my network.

3. I search for companies where I want to have a relationship to see if they have any employees who are LinkedIn members. LinkedIn alerts me if someone in my network has a relationship with a person at my desired company and I can then ask the person I know to make an introduction.

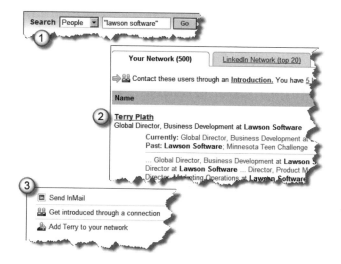

Making an introduction is, in my opinion, one of the most powerful tools available on LinkedIn. For those in sales and business development, or for anyone looking for a job or a contact, you can use the search engine to search for people who work at a company. Use the main search form and enter a company name. Alternatively, click on Advanced Search to open up LinkedIn's advanced search feature, which also lets you search by name, company, title, industry, location, etc.

Advanced Search

People Search   Reference Search

Keywords: marketing, business development	First Name:
Location: Anywhere	Last Name:

Title: vice president	Industry: ☐ Accounting
Current only	☐ Airlines/Aviation
	☐ Alternative Dispute Resolution
Company: lawson software	☐ Alternative Medicine
Current only	☐ Animation
School:	Groups: ☐ DFW Entrepreneur Network
	☐ James J. Hill Reference Library members
	☐ Market Research
	☐ TopLinked.com (Open Networkers)
	☐ Minnesota Networking Group

The search results will show names of LinkedIn members who meet your search criteria. For example, if you entered a company name, LinkedIn will list members who currently work for, or used to work for, the company. LinkedIn will let you know if the person is already in your network at the first, second, or third level. If you find a person you're interested in meeting, click on their name to open up their LinkedIn profile.

If the person is in your first level, you can contact him or her directly by clicking the "Send A Message" link, and LinkedIn will facilitate a connection.

If the person is in your second or third level, click the "Get introduced through a connection" link, and LinkedIn will show you a list of the people in your network who have a connection to the person you want to meet. Choose a person in your network, and via the LinkedIn request form, you can ask your contact to make an introduction for you.

It's important to note that with the LinkedIn free service, you can only request up to five introductions at a time. Before you can ask for additional introduction, you have to wait until your contact acts upon your request to clear a space in your queue. Therefore, you must use your introduction requests carefully and make sure to ask for introductions only from people you know and trust.

I have successfully used the "request an introduction" fea-

Compose your message to Terry (recipient):

Category: Business deal

Subject: I have a new venture opportunity for you

Message: [tips]

Terry,

At Lawson, I know you're constantly looking for new ways to provide value to your existing software clients. As information is key to your client's success, I thought you might want to know about a program we have at the Hill Library (your next door neighbor) that can provide your clients customized information services, and provide Lawson a new revenue stream.

I saw recently where you were quoted in the

Terry Plath
153

Headline: Global Director, Business Development at Lawson Software

Currently: Global Director, Business Development at Lawson Software

Previously: Market Development Director at Lawson Software; Development Director at Minnesota Teen Challenge; Director, Vertical Market Development-Professional Services at Lawson Software; Director, Product Marketing at Lawson Software; Director, Marketing Operations at Lawson Software; Manager, Strategic Planning at Lawson Software

Compose your note to Brett Norgaard (forwarder):

Remember, your note to Brett will be seen by everyone in the Introduction chain.

Note: [tips]

Brett,

I hope all is well. I was wondering if I could ask you for a favor. I see that you know Terry Plath at Lawson Software. I've got a business opportunity for Terry and I'm hoping you can

Brett Norgaard
42

Headline: CEO, Wire The Market, Inc.

ture a number of times. I have made numerous introductions to people in my network on behalf of others. When I need a contact at a company, my LinkedIn network has referred me to people I want to meet, and the entire process takes me literally a couple of minutes and a few mouse clicks. Because a number of people have recommended me and those recommendations are posted on my profile, when a new contact reads my profile, I have already established my credibility and built a positive reputation.

Now think about what I just said for a moment ...

In the days before LinkedIn, I had to personally know that a friend of mine knew someone at a company, and then I had to place a phone call and ask for the favor of an introduction. Or if I was lucky, I could get a phone number and call the person directly, mentioning that our shared friend encouraged me to call. This process took time, and I was limited in my network to only referrals from friends who I knew had relationships with a person or a company that I wanted to meet.

LinkedIn also lets you request connections directly without a referral, but you need to be very careful.

If you want to make a connection with a LinkedIn member and you do not want to ask someone in your network to make an introduction on your behalf, on the person's profile page you can click the "Add [Name] to your Network" link. The LinkedIn system will ask you how you know the person. You then choose the appropriate button, complete any requested information (for example, if you choose "friend," you're asked to enter their e-mail address for verification) and then send the LinkedIn invitation.

DO THIS VERY CAREFULLY. I do not recommend sending invitations unless you have some sort of relationship, for example, the person you want to meet used to work at the same company you did but you just did not know them, or you share a mutual friend who is not a LinkedIn member. If the person you contact thinks that you're "Spamming," they can report you to LinkedIn and for all future invitations, you will be required to enter in the person's e-mail address for verification, or worse, you can lose your account.

To help avoid the perception of Spam, take advantage of the text field to write a personalized note to the person you'd like to meet. Instead of using the pre-formatted introduction text that LinkedIn provides, write a brief message explaining why you want to meet and how linking will benefit the other person. By adding a personalized note, I've had great success linking with people I did not previously know, but because of

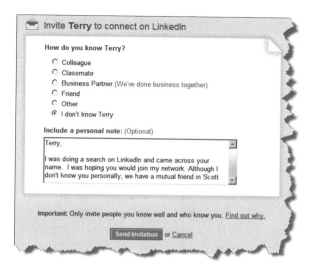

where they worked, their experience, etc., I wanted to add to my network.

When you search a company name via the main search form (choose Search Companies) or via Advanced Search, LinkedIn will also let you know if there are members who work at a company that are not in your network. If you are not connected at any level, LinkedIn will only give you a job title. You have to be a premium paying member to get their name and request a contact via LinkedIn's InMail system.

However, a trick to finding names is to highlight the job title and company, right mouse click and choose "copy." Then go to Google.com, insert your cursor in the search field, and right mouse click and choose "paste." Make sure the entire title and company are within quotation marks (e.g. "vice president of operations at Medtronic"). Click the "search" button and most of the time, Google will deliver the person's name.

With LinkedIn, my networking is now limited to only the size of my third level contacts and the overall size of the LinkedIn network. So now that I am on my way to multi-millions of third level contacts in my network and because LinkedIn now has more than 35 million members, my networking is now limited to well … pretty much any company in the world where there is an employee who is a LinkedIn member. Or saying it another way, as LinkedIn continues to

SAM TIP ➤
Join My Network:

Because you're taking the time to read my book, I already consider you a business partner.

So let me know how I can help you! If you would like to tap into my network …

1. Register to become a free LinkedIn member at **www.LinkedIn.com**

2. Search for "Sam Richter at SBR" by doing a People search.

3. Click "Add Sam To Your Network" and choose our relationship (e.g. Business Partner). If you are asked to enter an e-mail address, use sam@sbrworldwide.com.

4. In your note to me, mention that you're reading my book and what you think.

5. Once I've accepted and you and I are connected, return to my profile page (see #2).

6. Click "Connections."

7. If you see anyone I know that you'd like to meet, please request an introduction as I'd be happy to help you network.

grow, I will eventually have no limits on my potential network. In addition, via LinkedIn, my reputation and credibility grow automatically the larger my personal network gets and the more people who recommend me!

The final great LinkedIn benefit for those who practice the Sales Intelligence is that reading the profile of the person you want to meet gives you an incredible amount of information about that person. A member's profile typically includes work history, links to business and personal Web sites, hobbies, and non-profit organizations where the person volunteers. If someone is in your first level network you can also see their contacts, so you can reference a mutual relationship.

Many people include their educational background and even personal information like family members, hobbies, where they donate, and more in their profile. If you're fortunate enough to be meeting with a prospect who has a detailed LinkedIn profile, you probably have all the information you need to make your first meeting an exceptionally warm one.

There are many Web 2.0 applications available that make interacting with people easy, and fun. Facebook, Twitter, and others have made it exceptionally simple to build a network of online friends and colleagues. For the business person and especially the person involved in sales and business development, LinkedIn is the modern-day version of a physical Rolodex, only this Rolodex has no limitations on the number of cards it can contain. LinkedIn is also adding new features on a regular basis, from online applications like Twitter and blog linking to powerful advanced search functionality, meaning that it will continue to grow and become an even more powerful tool as you continue to build your online network.

Harvey Mackay stated it best when he described the power of networking:

"If I had to name the single characteristic shared by all the truly successful people I've met over a lifetime, I'd say it is the ability to create and nurture a network of contacts. Networking is an art form and can be learned by anyone."

I'd like to be a truly successful person, as I'm sure you would too. How about if we join each other's LinkedIn network? Find me at **www.linkedin.com/in/samrichter**.

Political Contributions – OpenSecrets

http://www.opensecrets.org/indivs

Although knowing a prospect's political persuasion isn't typically relevant for a sales call, it can be helpful on occasion. For example, if there is a politically charged current news event, it might be helpful to know if the prospect you're calling on is a Democrat or Republican so you can avoid saying anything that might be offensive (frankly, it's probably best to avoid any conversation related to religion or politics with your clients, but sometimes it cannot be avoided).

Another time when knowing the political persuasion of a prospect or client can be beneficial is if your company, or your client, does business with the government. Wouldn't it be nice to know who supports a particular candidate or a political action committee?

If you're a non-profit organization soliciting a business or individual for a donation, knowing a person's political persuasion can also be beneficial.

Most people would probably be surprised to know that corporate and individual political contributions are on the public record. However, because the data are stored in a database format, accessing the information is not easy via popular search engines.

One of the top search sites for political contributions is OpenSecrets, which has a powerful and easy-to-use search engine at **www.opensecrets.org/indivs**. You can search for current and past contributions, and you can search by company name for corporate contributions or by individual names.

The site also lets you search for contributors by candidate and it lets you identify lobbying groups. This can be very beneficial depending on your prospect's or client's line of business. For example, if your prospect or client is in the construction industry, it might be nice to know if they or any competitor supports a politician who is influential in awarding government projects.

To use the site for a general search, enter the name of a person or company, and then choose a location. Then select

SAM TIP ▶
Political Donations:

Knowing the political persuasion of your prospect can be beneficial. It could be critical if you or your client is doing business with the government, or if you're a non-profit organization soliciting a donation.

OpenSecrets is your gateway to U.S. political contributions.

1. Go to **www.opensecrets. org/indivs**

2. Enter the name of the company or an individual then choose a location.

3. Choose the years you'd like to search by clicking on the corresponding check boxes, or choose Search All Cycles.

4. Enter the given security key.

5. If you receive no results, try changing your year selection(s).

a year or years by clicking on the corresponding check boxes, or choose Select All Cycles. Finally enter in the given security code, click Submit, and conduct your search.

anderson	**LAST NAME** of donor (or last name, first name) *Use company name for soft money donations*
Minnesota ▾	**STATE** of donor
55305	**ZIP CODE** of donor
	OCCUPATION / EMPLOYER of donor
	RECIPIENT (Name of federal candidate, PAC, or party committee)

Note: *CRP does not provide street address or phone information for contributors.*

Election cycle(s) to search:

Select one or more of the following options:
- ☑ 2008
- ☐ 2006
- ☐ 2004
- ☐ 1990-2002 (include soft money)

OR
- ☑ Search all cycles

Order the results by:
- ◉ Name of donor
- ○ Amount donated
- ○ Date of donation

Golf Scores – USGA Golf Handicap and Information Network®

http://www.ghin.com

If you're searching for information on a business executive, there's a decent chance that he/she plays golf. If you know anything about golfers, you know that they are passionate about their game.

Imagine the great "small talk" conversation you can have with an executive at an initial business meeting if you know that the person is passionate about golf. Yes, you could easily just ask your prospect if they play golf, but by being unprepared, you risk that the answer will be "no." However, what if you already know the answer is "yes" and you are prepared with information?

One way to find out whether prospects enjoy golf is to see whether they're registered with the United States Golf Association Golf Handicap and Information Network. To find out, just visit **www.ghin.com**.

Once at the site, click the "Handicap Lookup" tab on the site's top navigation. Then choose the "Lookup by Name and State" section.

Choose a state, type in the person's name using the fields, and then click the Submit button. Here's a look at my good friend Murray Death's golf handicap.

SAM TIP ➤
Golf Handicap:

Golfers are passionate about their game. If your prospects play golf, you can find their handicaps at the USGA's Handicap Network.

1. Go to **www.ghin.com**

2. Click the "Handicap Lookup" tab on the upper navigation.

3. Enter the person's name and state to look for handicap index information.

4, Click the name for their score history, where they play, etc.

If the person has a registered golf handicap, you'll see their index along with the course where their score was last registered. Click on the person's name and you'll see a history of golf scores and course locations. The latter information can be especially valuable if you happen to know other people who play at the same course (remember a personal referral and recommendation is exceptionally valuable in the sales process).

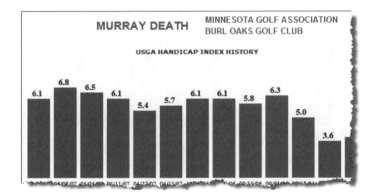

Click on the "View Index History" tab and get a graph of the player's handicap history (as you can see, Murray has been playing a lot of good golf lately).

A final benefit of knowing someone's golf handicap comes during the contract stage. For example, if by using the GHIN site you know that a person who claims to be a scratch golfer actually has an 18 handicap, you had better be wary during negotiations!

People Meta-Search – Pipl

http://www.pipl.com

Let me state up front—Pipl is downright scary in terms of what it can find. If you've gotten to this point in the book and you still think you might have a modicum of privacy left, Pipl will destroy that wishful thinking.

Pipl is a meta-search engine that simultaneously searches multiple search engines and information sources. Pipl's claim to fame is that it searches the "Deep Web" (another name for the Invisible Web) meaning that it's going to find results that popular search engines like Google and Yahoo won't find (or if they do, the results are not typically featured on the first few pages).

With Pipl, you can search for people by name, email address, username (e.g., you know the name the person uses in his or her blog even if it is not the person's real name), and phone number. For most searches, you'll want to use the name search option.

Enter in the first and last name of the person you want to search for, his or her city and/or state, and country (yes...Pipl will search internationally). Wait a few moments as the site searches its myriad of sources.

The result list will deliver content from multiple sites, including address records, court records, personal profiles, networking sites, public records, blogs, general Web sites, photo databases, archived records, email addresses, and more. Pipl will even retrieve documents such as PDF files where the name of the person for whom you searched appears.

The one big drawback I've found with Pipl is that there is no Advanced Search, and no ability to search within a search.

For example, my name isn't that popular and there is a lot of information about me online compared to the world's other Sam Richters. Yet if you don't know me or what I do for a living, you might get confused looking at Pipl search results for my name. You'd probably figure out quickly that the "Sam Richter" female softball player is not me. But you might be confused about the "Sam Richter" baseball player (not me; I can't hit a fastball), or the "Sam Richter" head of the Connecticut Communist Party (definitely not me).

Therefore, if I'm meeting with someone I don't know, before I do a Pipl search on the person, I'll use some of the other

SAM TIP
Pipl:

Pipl is a meta-search engine for people information, and it's very comprehensive.

1. Go to **www.pipl.com**

2. Search by name, email address, username, or phone number.

3. Enter the person's name and state; click "search."

4. If the person you're interested in has a common name, make sure to view other people-search sources first so you have a good understanding of the person, (e.g., what he or she does for a living).

pipl

Name Email Username Phone

sam	richter		MN	US	Search	Clear
First Name	Last Name	City	State	Country		

Sam Richter, Minnesota, United States

Contact Details

Sam Richter. 3030 Harbor Ln N #216, Minneapolis, MN.
⚲ Search Person ⌂ Map Address
whitepages.addresses.com

Sam Richter, ▓▓▓▓▓▓▓▓▓▓▓▓▓▓▓, Minneapolis, MN. (612) ▓▓▓ ...
⚲ Search Person ℄ Search Phone ⌂ Map Address
www.whitepages.com

Personal Profiles

Sam Richter, Ceo, Hopkins, MN, US...
Personal Profile - Konnects
www.konnects.com - Deep Web

Professional & Business

Sam Richter. SVP/Chief Marketing Officer, ActiFi. **Minnesota**... 🔒
People - Plaxo
www.plaxo.com - Deep Web

Sam Richter, MN, US, ... 🔒
Professional Profile & Networking - LinkedIn
www.linkedin.com

Web Pages

Nationally renowned keynote speaker, seminar presenter, and author on leadership , sales improvement, and using the Web to find.
Sam Richter — SBR Worldwide
www.speakermatch.com

News Articles

In the top of the seventh inning, with runners on second and third, Allegany-Limestone intentionally walked **Sam Richter**. The umpires told Richter to go to ...
Dunkirk falls in a game under protest
Fri, 24 Apr 2009 - Evening Observer

Blog Posts

Sam Richter, President/CEO, SBR Worldwide, LLC.
02 Turning Cold Calls Warm: The Key to Building Strong Business ...
www.wsradio.com

Documents

Sam Richter. CEO. SBR Worldwide. 612.655.3397 sam@sbrworldwide.com .... **Sam Richter** is an internationally sought-after speaker on a variety of business ...
Put the Develop Back Into Development
www.mncn.org

people-search techniques discussed in this book. I want to get a good picture of who the person is, where he or she works, a bit about the person's history, etc., before I dive into Pipl. For one, I don't want to waste my time in Pipl trying to guess who my prospect is. More importantly, I don't want to find a piece of information that I assume is correct, and during an important sales meeting when I bring it up, I learn that it's wrong and actually is associated with a different person with the same name.

So, if the person you're researching is "Joe Smith," good luck; research the person using other means first so you understand what to look for once you're in Pipl. If the person you want is "Joe Buphutnick," then it's probably safe starting with a Pipl search.

House Values – Zillow

http://www.zillow.com/

If you're selling financial service products, insurance, or if you're a non-profit organization that relies on individual donations for your revenue, it can be very beneficial to know the value of a person's home. Imagine how relevant you can make your sales presentation or donor solicitation if you know a bit about your prospect's net worth, assuming that the value of a person's home provides a "guesstimate" of their net worth and possibly even their lifestyle.

To find the value of virtually any home in the United States, just visit Zillow at **www.zillow.com**. You can search for home values by entering an address, or even just a city if you don't know an address but you want to see the value of homes in a particular area.

NOTE: If you don't know a person's home address, there are many Web sites where you can search for addresses by entering a person's name. My favorite is **www.411.com** or **www. zabasearch.com**.

SAM TIP ↖
Home Values:

You can often tell a person's net worth by the value of his or her home.

1. Go to **www.zillow.com**

2. Enter an address plus a city, state, or zip. If you need to locate an address, try **www.411.com** or **www. zabasearch.com**

3. On the address result page, click the address link to find price information and, in some markets, a "bird's-eye" view of the home and area.

4. Scroll down to locate detailed information about the home, including sales data.

5. Enter the security ID code and get property tax information.

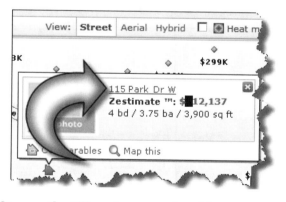

Once on the Zillow site, enter the address or even part of the address if you know it. The city, state, or zip code is required. A line drawing will appear showing various neighborhood home values, and if the address you entered is correct, a listing of the home you're interested in, its value, and details including the home's size. Here's the Zillow report for my home.

115 Park Dr W, Minnetonka, MN 55305

ZESTIMATE™: $█12,137

Photos | Bird's Eye View | Map View

See Bird's Eye & Map View

Click on the address of your selected home, and you'll find additional information including the change in value during the last thirty days. Click on the Bird's Eye View tab and in many cities, you'll see a high resolution home photograph

Public Facts	
Residence:	Single family
Bedrooms:	4
Bathrooms:	3.75
Sq ft:	3,900
Lot size:	28,045 sq ft / 0.64 acres
Year built:	1949
Year updated:	2000
# Stories:	1
Total rooms:	10
Basement:	Finished
Roof type:	Asphalt
Exterior material:	--
View:	Territorial
Parking type:	Garage - Attached
Covered parking spaces:	2
Heating source:	Gas
Heating system:	Forced air
Cooling system:	Central
Appliances:	Dishwasher, Dryer, Freezer, Garbage disposal, Microwave, Range / Oven, Refrigerator, Trash compactor, Washer
Floor covering:	Carpet, Hardwood, Slate
Rooms:	Breakfast nook, Dining room, Family room, Laundry room, Library, Master bath, Mud room, Office, Recreation room, Walk-in closet
Architecture:	Split-level
County	

(courtesy of Microsoft Live Search; the photos are taken from airplanes). You can even click on the directional links to see home photos from different angles. Some listings also feature Google Street Level View photos.

If you look at the photo of my home, you can see my car in the driveway. If you look very carefully, you can see that we left the dog in the backyard again.

Scroll down on the page, and you can see a list of home facts. The information comes from city records, so depending on the amount of information available at the city where they home is located, the data can be quite detailed.

Click on the Charts and Data link on Zillow's left side navigation, and you'll get a graph showing the home's value over time. There is also a listing of the percentage of homes in the area that have a higher or lower value.

If you enter the security id number directly under the market value chart, you'll even see recent sales data, and the taxable assessment of both the land and building. By the way, you'll see that my home's value has dipped a bit with the fall of the recent housing market, so if you're interested in buying my home, now is a great time. Just e-mail me with an offer.

I'll admit, having all of this information is a bit scary, and I'm pretty sure you don't want to use it in a sales call even if you're selling financial services, insurance, or soliciting a donation. Because if someone told me he had this information on me and my home, I'd throw him out of my office and report him to Homeland Security for fear that he was a spy!

However, in all seriousness, this can be valuable information if you are interested in a person's net worth, neighborhood, and lifestyle.

You obviously don't meet with a prospect and in the first few minutes of your conversation, mention that you think her house is overvalued. Yet having information on a person's home can give you an understanding for what her interests might be; for example, you see that she lives next to a lake so she may enjoy boating. It might also help guide your conversation; for example, if she tells you she has no budget, yet she lives in a $3 million home (which actually might explain why she has no budget).

More important, I thought I'd ruin the rest of your day because you're going to spend the next few hours on Zillow. com researching your own home, plus your neighbors', colleagues', friends', and relatives' homes.

> *"Give people a fish and you feed them for a day; teach them to use the Internet and they will not bother you for weeks!"*
> – Author Unknown

CHAPTER SIXTEEN

Premium Information Sources

"Deep customer knowledge and breakthrough insights about the client's underlying processes are the backbone of every customer-intimate organization today."
– Michael Treacy and Fred Wiersema, *The Discipline of Market Leaders*, Reading: Perseus Books, 1997.

I hope that by the time you're at this chapter, you have a new appreciation for the value of information, how to apply it in a sales call, and how to find relevant, credible, and objective business information using popular search engines and the Invisible Web.

Sorry to burst your bubble. Even though you're now an expert at using popular search engines and accessing Web sites most people don't even know exist, your new talent still only gets you a fraction of the business information that is available online. In fact, if you work for a small company, chances are your larger competitors already have access to this information, putting you at a distinct disadvantage.

Let's go back 1,000 years. Who had the power of information 1,000 years ago? It was the royalty and the clergy, and they held on to the information very tightly, not wanting to share it with the populace. A tiny minority had access to the best information and they used it to rule for centuries.

Then in 1436, Johannes Gutenberg invented a little machine called the printing press. (It probably really wasn't Gutenberg who invented the printing press. In fact, the Chinese had invented movable type approximately 400 years earlier. Nevertheless, Gutenberg is popularly credited with the invention.)

With the printing press came books. Those books had to be stored somewhere, so libraries were created. Public libraries, private libraries, school libraries; for hundreds of years, it didn't matter if you were a king, a president of a big company, or a person with a dream, if you wanted access to information, you went to the library.

Even when computers first became popular, it was still a fairly level information playing field. For example, in the 1970s, if you were an entrepreneur with a dream and you needed market research data for one of your inventions, you had to go to the public library. Similarly, if you were the CEO of a large company, and you needed market statistics for one of your new products, you sent someone to your local public or university library.

The level information-playing field started its dramatic change in the late 1980s.

With the World Wide Web becoming a popular sales and marketing tool, there was a mad rush to digitize information. There was this popular perception that the World Wide Web would make every word ever printed at any time free and easy to access for everyone and if you weren't getting your information online, you'd be left out.

Virtually every organization in the U.S. was trying to figure out how to digitize its content and get it online. Governments, academia, and private industry made a mad rush to build Web sites and get content online for all to view. Newspapers, magazines, trade journals, and other content-producing organizations started digitizing content and making it available for free to anyone who had access to a Web browser.

The CEOs of many of these content companies then started to look at their financial statements and saw red numbers—rather large numbers—associated with their online initiatives. They saw that the costs of digitizing and organizing content, Web site creation and hosting, not to mention legal and marketing costs, were getting out of hand. So they decided that their online content sites needed a revenue stream to support them.

For many, their first try at creating revenue for their free online content sites was to try the banner-advertising model. These content companies would place banner ads on Web sites with the hope that site visitors would see the ads, click on them, and thus generate money for the content company.

Unfortunately, many of these content-rich sites didn't have enough visitors to justify a banner-ad model. How many people are actually visiting *Meat and Processing Digest* online and of those, how many are clicking on banner ads that generate five cents per click for the publication?

So, many of these content Web sites starting requiring registration to access information, with the hope that they'd be able to sell the user database. The content companies hoped that the registered user list could be sold just like direct mail lists.

However, by requiring registration to access the content, these sites joined the ranks of the Invisible Web. Remember, Google can't register, so much of the content behind the registration page became invisible to Index search engines.

Thus, the sites did not attract as many visitors. In addition, with anti-spam laws, the selling of customer lists became a business many organizations didn't want to enter. Therefore, a new business model had to be found.

What the online content industry has seen over the past few years is a growing number of Web sites that used to offer free content now charging site visitors to access the online information. For example, take a guess at how many trade journals—a credible information source on trends and issues in an industry—offer information online at no charge. Eighty percent? Fifty percent? Well according to the American Library Association, how about 8 percent?

Why? Think about it for a moment. Trade journals make money via subscriptions. In general, not enough people visit a trade journal Web site to make banner advertising or registration an effective business model. Therefore, the trade journal sells access to information via the physical publication or via subscription databases.

Every day another site that once offered free information is now beginning to charge for it. Even some government offices now charge you to access information online; they've taken the "free" out of the Freedom of Information Act.

Following are some of the key subscription-based business information databases you and your business can purchase to ensure you're getting the most credible, relevant, and objective business information that you can use and apply in the sales process. The databases all feature sophisticated searching tools for locating information on companies, industries, and individuals.

Subscription prices for database access vary from company to company, with some offering time-based subscriptions (monthly, quarterly, or annually) and some offering per-use pricing models. Some subscriptions are for individuals only and some provide information for an entire department, sales team, or even company.

Dun & Bradstreet for Salespeople – Company Search and Lists

http://www.dnb.com/us/dbproducts/sales_marketing/

Dun & Bradstreet is a familiar name to most business owners because of its credit report database. D&B also has some very powerful tools for businesses, and in particular, salespeople. Specifically, D&B offers a number of company research and list building databases. You can access D&B's sales offerings via its home page at **www.dnb.com**, or directly at **www.dnb. com/us/dbproducts/sales_marketing**.

The D&B list building programs allow you to research companies and build sales lead lists using just about any variable you can think of. You can search by company name, executives, geography, industry, employee size, revenue, and more. You can also easily sort your lists, export them, and easily import the data.

D&B also offers a number of other tools designed to help salespeople and sales managers practice the "Fourth R" and help turn cold sales calls into warm sales calls.

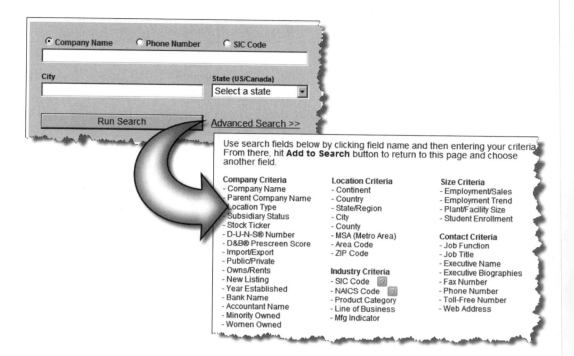

In particular, the following two products can be very beneficial to sales organizations in companies of all sizes:

- **MarketPlace Gold** – Provides fairly comprehensive information that helps you analyze markets and create targeted lists. MarketPlace Gold comes on a DVD so you can easily format and output the data with all members of your sales team.

- **Family Tree Finder** – Helps salespeople identify business relationships among current clients and prospects. One of the easiest ways to turn a cold sales call into a warm one is to make the sales call a personal referral. Family Tree Finder helps you identify relationships, and then you can ask your current clients if they would allow you to use them as a reference for prospect calls.

InfoUSA – Company Search and Lists II

http://www.infousa.com

InfoUSA is a similar product to Dun & Bradstreet, although InfoUSA markets itself primarily as a list-building resource. They do offer a number of pre-packaged company and consumer lists that you can purchase, and its database allows you to custom build your own sales lead lists.

Just like with any list building database, the accuracy of InfoUSA's data are only as good as the self-reported information that businesses give to InfoUSA and the date at which InfoUSA last updated the company information. Thus, it's important to use multiple sources of information, for example, newspaper or trade journal articles, to round out your knowledge about a particular company.

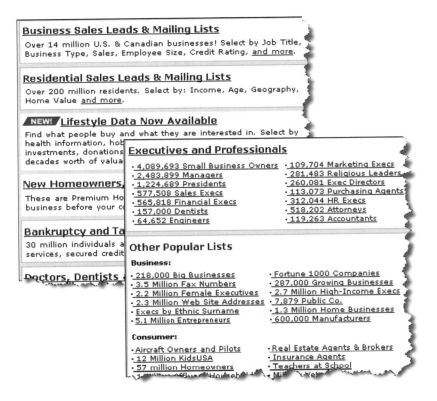

Business Sales Leads & Mailing Lists
Over 14 million U.S. & Canadian businesses! Select by Job Title, Business Type, Sales, Employee Size, Credit Rating, and more.

Residential Sales Leads & Mailing Lists
Over 200 million residents. Select by: Income, Age, Geography, Home Value and more.

NEW! Lifestyle Data Now Available
Find what people buy and what they are interested in. Select by health information, hob
investments, donations
decades worth of valua

New Homeowners,
These are Premium Ho
business before your c

Bankruptcy and Ta
30 million individuals a
services, secured credit

Doctors, Dentists

Executives and Professionals
- 4,089,693 Small Business Owners
- 2,483,899 Managers
- 1,224,689 Presidents
- 577,508 Sales Execs
- 565,818 Financial Execs
- 157,000 Dentists
- 64,652 Engineers
- 109,704 Marketing Execs
- 281,483 Religious Leaders
- 260,081 Exec Directors
- 113,073 Purchasing Agents
- 312,044 HR Execs
- 518,202 Attorneys
- 119,263 Accountants

Other Popular Lists

Business:
- 218,000 Big Businesses
- 3.5 Million Fax Numbers
- 2.2 Million Female Executives
- 2.3 Million Web Site Addresses
- Execs by Ethnic Surname
- 5.1 Million Entrepreneurs
- Fortune 1000 Companies
- 287,000 Growing Businesses
- 2.7 Million High-Income Execs
- 7,879 Public Co.
- 1.3 Million Home Businesses
- 600,000 Manufacturers

Consumer:
- Aircraft Owners and Pilots
- 12 Million KidsUSA
- 57 million Homeowners
- Real Estate Agents & Brokers
- Insurance Agents
- Teachers at School

Hoovers – Company Details

http://www.hoovers.com

Hoovers is well known by salespeople as a credible and affordable company information source. Many people don't know, however, that Hoovers is actually owned by D&B. In fact, it looks like a lot of what D&B offers is available via Hoovers and vice versa; the packaging is a bit different but they seem to be accessing the same data sources.

As described earlier, Hoovers does allow free company searches on its home page at **www.hoovers.com**. For larger companies, both public and private, Hoovers does return some de-

---

Lawson Software, Inc.

(NASDAQ: LWSN)

380 St. Peter St.
St. Paul, MN 55102-1302 (Map)

Phone: 651-767-7000
Fax: 651-767-7141
Toll Free: 800-477-1357

http://www.lawson.com

Hoover's coverage by Josh Lower

BUILD A REPORT

Overview

Lawson Software just wants to bring a little law and order to managing enterprises. The company makes enterprise resource planning software for the health care, professional services, retail, public sector, and telecommunications industries. Its applications handle such tasks as distribution, procurement, human resources, customer service, professional services automation, and accounting. The company also offers consulting, implementation, and maintenance services. Co-founders Richard Lawson and John Cerullo collectively own about a third of the company. Lawson agreed to acquire Intentia International in 2005.

Key Numbers

Company Type	Public (
Fiscal Year-End	May
2005 Sales (mil.)	$335.2
1-Year Sales Growth	(7.8%)
2005 Net Income (mil.)	$5.3
1-Year Net Income Growth	(33.7%)
2004 Employees	1,579
1-Year Employee Growth	(5.7%)

Key People

Chairman	H. Richard Lawson (Subscribers see complete biographies -- view sample)	Job Openings
President, CEO, and Director	Harry Debes	

---

cent information including company location, revenue, a company overview, and links to purchase additional data.

When researching smaller private companies, Hoovers will let you know whether they have information on the company and will provide a direct link to purchase the information.

Hoovers is a solid choice for salespeople, especially if what is needed is detailed information on a one-off basis. The database is easy to use, the information is quite comprehensive, and the price is affordable.

ZoomInfo PowerSell – People Search

http://www.zoominfo.com

In the Invisible Web section, we discussed the free version of ZoomInfo and its ability to locate millions of business people using a proprietary index search engine specific to locating individuals and their business relationships. The free version is nice, but it is limited to searching for a specific person, meaning that you have to know the name of the person at the company.

However, ZoomInfo's premium version, PowerSell, offers some powerful people-searching tools that allow you to search for individuals at a company without knowing the person's

name. You can build a list of company contacts using a wide variety of criteria, from job titles (including board members) to recent job changes to even keyword searches with terms like "vested stock options" (imagine if you were a financial advisor and you could search for only executives with a recent investment change). You can even search broader job title categories like "executives" or "mid-management," and ZoomInfo also highlights the last time the information was updated.

Unlike the free version of ZoomInfo, PowerSell allows you to save search results, and even download lists. You can even create and save your own virtual Prospect List for easy access at a later time, from any computer.

When you click on any of the names in the ZoomInfo results, you get a "biography" of the individual culled from Web sites that ZoomInfo has indexed and organized. Many times this biography includes information on the person's career activities and even outside activities, for example, non-profit board memberships. This type of information can be a wonderful icebreaker when you first meet with a prospect, quickly helping to warm up the cold call (e.g., "Are you still on the Board for the Children's Home Society? What a great organization. Do you know....").

You'll also note that the biographical information contains full contact information *including* e-mail address.

LexisNexis – Company and Industry Info

http://www.lexisnexis.com/busdev/

LexisNexis is one of the more famous names in company and industry information databases. They have a number of different products tailored to specific job titles and functions. You can see the full list at **www.lexisnexis.com**.

Lexis offers a number of products designed for business development professionals found at **www.lexisnexis.com/ busdev**. Three of LexisNexis' products are *particularly* beneficial for the sales professional wanting to research prospects prior to sales calls and/or account meetings.

LexisNexis *AlaCarte!*™

Improve your business one search at a time

Research | Business Intelligence | Search by Source(s)

Edit Search | New Search | Save Search

Search Results for: **"insurance industry" and trends**

News (494) | TV News Video (0)

⚘ **Add to Cart** 🛒   **Clear All**

Results Sorted by Relevance
◄ 1 - 10 of 494 ►

☐ **Keep on Working; Improved data management and automation of manual processes are key to helping workers' compensation carriers build share in an increasingly competitive market.**
INSURANCE & TECHNOLOGY - 9/1/2007 - LENGTH: 1453 words
A: Gary Baxter, MEMIC: Currently, the major challenge facing MEMIC and other workers' compensation carriers is how best to retain and acquire high-quality customers in a soft market. MEMIC's customers place a high value on our loss control and claims services so we're not that susceptible to undercutting...

View now for $3.00

☐ **GP indemnity fees set to rise by up to pounds 250**
... 9/7/20...

- **Company Dossier** – Provides basic and in-depth business information on more than 35 million global companies. Each report delivers a detailed company overview.

- **Industry Dossier** – Provides detailed industry information on more than 1,000 industries. These easy-to-read reports feature credible and objective business data combined with current market information.

- **LexisNexis AlaCarte!** – The free search engine allows you to search for company data, company information, industry news, and more. You only pay for the articles you need. LexisNexis AlaCarte! features access to more than 20,000 information sources not found on the free Web (sites not accessible to popular search engines). As the average cost to download a document is $3, this service is a good one for the salesperson who does not need a constant supply of information.

Dialog Select – Company and Industry Info II

http://www.dialog.com/products/openaccess

A powerful search tool is Dialog Select. Thomson owns Dialog, thus Dialog accesses many of the Thomson business resources for its content. The Dialog Open Access product allows you to search for free and then pay for specific articles via credit card.

To start your search, go to the Open Access main page at **www.dialog.com/products/openaccess**. Then choose a category from the various options.

Once inside a particular category, follow the instructions to select a database and conduct your search. Like LexisNexis, you can search and view result abstracts at no charge. If you want to download an article, just click on it and go through the payment process. Most articles cost between $1 and $5.

Dialog Open Access is a solid database featuring thousands of credible news and industry sources. It's a great place to locate specific articles on new products and detailed industry information. For an investment of a few dollars, you can really make an impression during your sales call by referencing an obscure trade journal or new product introduced by your prospect or a competitor.

SAM TIP
A Name Can Be Good:

Just having a credible name with some background information can be helpful when conducting a cold call, especially the initial sales call when you often get a "gatekeeper" (e.g., a receptionist or assistant).

If you do call a company and the gatekeeper says: "I'm sorry, he's no longer at the company," you can at least sound surprised and ask for the new person with that title.

The likelihood of success increases dramatically when you have a name versus the blind call and question of "Can I speak to the person in charge of ..."

DIALOGSELECT
OPEN ACCESS

NEW SEARCH   COST   LOGOFF   HELP   all categories ...

Search results: **657** titles in **Company News: Search by Company Name** (results greater than 500 are unsorted)

Estimated cost for selected titles: US $ 13.35   Actual cost will be as shown or lower.

select all none   Select titles on this page, then click [Purchase Selections] (You will still have a chance to cancel!)

☑ 1 **Digital River buys Netgiro.** - September 17, 2007 - Business & Industry® - *US$4.45*

☑ 2 **Capcom Entertainment Selects Digital River to Manage North American E-Commerce Operations.** - May 25, 2007 - Business & Industry® - *US$4.45*

☑ 3 **Credit Suisse Disruptive Technology Portfolio: Digital River's Ties To Microsoft And PC Industry Raise Concerns Among Investors; Stock price takes 9% plunge, biggest of all Disruptive Technology Portfolio companies.** - May 19, 2007 - Business & Industry® - *US$4.45*

☐ 4 **Digital River Inc forms e-commerce agreement with Skype.** - April 02, 2007 - Business &

Business & Company Resource Center – Company and Industry Info III

http://www.gale.com/BusinessRC

One of the more popular company and industry subscription databases is Thomson/Gale's Business and Company Resource Center. BCRC is used by professional researchers and librarians and can be found in corporate libraries throughout the globe. The databases leverage Thomson's incredible information repositories.

Using the Business and Company Resource Center is quite easy. You can search for company data, industry information, or articles simply by choosing one of the icons off the database's main page. The Advanced Search icon is very powerful, too.

If your company has a consistent need for high-end information, you may want to consider a corporate license. You can get a free trial by visiting the Web site at **www.gale.com/BusinessRC/request.htm.**

Factiva® SalesWorks™ – Company, People and Industry Search

http://www.factiva.com/segment/sales.asp

Factiva is a subscription database company that offers customized and complex information management systems to larger firms. A Dow Jones & Reuters Company, the Factiva business information collection features more than 10,000 authoritative sources including the exclusive combination of *The Wall Street Journal*, the *Financial Times™*, Dow Jones and Reuters newswires and the Associated Press, as well as Reuters Fundamentals and D&B company profiles.

For sales teams, Factiva offers a number of products, its flagship sales information product being the SalesWorks database. SalesWorks includes an impressive collection of company, industry, and executive news and information to help sales professionals find relevant information about prospects.

SalesWorks is sold on a corporate license basis, so it probably only makes sense if your company has multiple people involved in sales and business development.

Standard & Poor's NetAdvantage – Company, and Industry Data

http://www.netadvantage.standardandpoor.com

Standard & Poor's NetAdvantage is a comprehensive source of business information, independent research, and commentary on stocks, bonds, funds, and industries.

The database offers powerful searching and screening tools to facilitate competitive intelligence, planning, due diligence and M&A activities. It also offers concise industry overviews with forecasts and other helpful statistics. In addition, NetAdvantage provides company information on more than 85,000 privately help companies.

The service allows you to create lists and it's easy to download information that then can be uploaded into CRM systems, or other data management tools.

CHAPTER SEVENTEEN

Power Research for Individuals

As discussed in the previous chapter, more and more of the best information available online is moving towards a subscription model. It's necessary because the cost of producing, maintaining and distributing content online is becoming prohibitively expensive for the smaller information publishers. It's even getting difficult for the smaller publisher to break even financially with a subscription model that they themselves create and maintain.

Thus, the "charging for access to online information" model has spurred the growth of an entire industry—the content aggregator industry. What has happened is content aggregators have approached the information publishers and are paying them for the rights to digitize content and make it available via a subscription database, along with content from other publishers.

Many of the content providers are thrilled with this model as they now have eliminated an expense, digitizing and making available the content, and turned it into a revenue stream. Content providers are paid up front by the content aggregator or paid every time someone accesses content via the aggregator's subscription database.

Over time, many of these content aggregators have been bought by larger content aggregators, who have been bought by even larger content aggregators. So today, in the "Internet Age," the "Age of Information," in a sense we've gone back to the way we were 1,000 years ago. The very best business information is "locked up" in the hands of "kings" or a few very large content aggregator companies.

The Thomson Company is one of the largest content aggregators in the world. (In the previous chapter, did you notice how many times Thomson was referenced as the owner of one of the highlighted premium databases?) Dun & Bradstreet is another powerhouse in the world of business information. In a sense, they're the "clergy and royalty" of today's information world in that they own a good percentage of the really good subscription business information, and they make it available only to those with the means to pay.

Now I want to be clear; I'm not bashing the Thomson Company or Dun & Bradstreet in the least. To the contrary, because I chose to highlight a number of their products, I obviously think they're both wonderful companies that provide an exceptional service. If you're a business serious about information and competitive intelligence, you should be purchasing products from Thomson and D&B.

You've got to be a very large company like Thomson or Dun & Bradstreet to make available the digital information that they offer. The costs to digitize, aggregate, keep current and disseminate the amount of information in the Thomson and D&B libraries is incredible, with technology, legal, sales, marketing, and customer service expenses continually on the rise.

So if you're Thomson or D&B, where do you put your sales and marketing efforts? If I were a commissioned sales representative, I'd package my company's databases and sell them for tens of thousands of dollars, if not more, to large companies.

Not only would my commission check be greater, but my sales process would be easier too. These larger firms, typically companies with more than 100 employees, already understand the value of information and have the resources to pay for the best data sources.

Unfortunately, that leaves the individual entrepreneur and small business in a quandary. In addition, remember, more than 90 percent of firms in the U.S. have fewer than twenty employees.

In today's globally competitive marketplace, it's not uncommon for a twenty-person firm to compete against a

2,000-person firm for the same piece of business. Yet the business development and sales teams at larger firms have a competitive information advantage.

Yes, as a small company you can use some of the subscription databases highlighted earlier. You may choose to purchase information on an as-needed basis, or your company may even bite the bullet and subscribe to a premium database offering corporate-wide use.

However, because large companies subscribe to multiple premium databases including even more expensive ones than highlighted in the earlier chapter, they have access to better, more relevant, and more credible business intelligence and market information than smaller competitors. While the small firms are left surfing the free Web or occasionally purchasing an article or research report, the big firms have access to the latest company and market intelligence and oftentimes, they have in-house library and librarians/researchers. They have the "clergy and royalty" on their side.

If you're the next Bill Gates, Michael Dell, or Richard Branson with a dream, how can you possibly compete against wealthier competitors with greater resources? If you're a salesperson for a mid-size company selling a commodity-type product and your competitor is a Fortune 500 firm, can you possibly get the high-end premium business information you need to differentiate you (remember, people buy from people) and your firm?

The good news is that you can.

There is a place where "equal access to the best information" is the mantra. There is a place where you have access to the same or similar premium subscription databases as big companies pay big dollars to access, and you get them for free (because you've already paid for them). That place?

Your local public library.

Your Tax Dollar-Funded Sales Assistant – The Public Library

http://www.publiclibraries.com

When was the last time you visited your local public library? When you were in high school or college (it's okay, you don't have to be embarrassed)? Or are you like the many adults who truly enjoy visiting the public library, browsing material, and occasionally checking out a book to read over a lazy weekend?

When was the last time you visited your local public li-brary for business research? Whether you are an occasional or frequent visitor to your local public library, if you're like most people, you probably didn't realize that your local library is a hidden jewel of business resources.

For the salesperson in particular, your local public library might be the sales assistant you've been begging your boss to hire. Best of all, you've already paid for your new "sales assis-tant" via your tax dollars and it is ready to go to work for you, twenty-four hours a day, seven days a week, 365 days a year!

As you've learned by reading this book, while popular search engines and the Invisible Web can be used to find an incredible amount of valuable business data, the really good stuff is behind cyber lock and key in premium subscription databases. It's the sales professional who knows how to access all three—search engines, the Invisible Web, and premium databases—who is going to effectively practice the "Fourth R," provide value via the Platinum Rule, and quickly locate the information necessary to make all sales calls warm ones.

By practicing what you've learned in this book, you now know how to make the best use of search engines like Google and Yahoo, plus locate valuable data on sites that popular search engines can't access. The third leg of the stool, pre-mium subscription databases, is also right at your fingertips through your local public library.

Every public library in the country subscribes to pre-mium subscription databases. In fact, many of the databases highlighted in earlier chapters are available for free via your local public library. Your personal tax dollars and your company's tax dollars have already paid for these databases, so make sure you use them and get your money's worth.

It gets better. Some of the same or similar databases that Fortune 500 companies are paying millions of dollars to access **you can possibly get free of charge via your own home or office computer as long as you have a local library card!**

So how can you find out what premium business databases your local library offers? Just ask! To locate your local library, go to **www.publiclibraries.com**. Choose your area and then find out which public library serves your home, and if your office is in a different city which one serves your office.

PUBLICLIBRARIES.COM
Public Libraries, Building Blocks of Our Community!

Minnesota Public Libraries

This page contains a list of public libraries in Minnesota. If you do not see a link to your local branch library, please ch

City Name : A B C D E F G H I J K L M N O P Q R S T U V W X Y Z

City	Library Name	Library System	Address
Ada	Ada Public Library	Lake Agassiz Regional Library	107 4th A
Adrian	Adrian Branch Library	Plum Creek Library System	214 Maine
Aitkin	Aitkin Public Library	East Central Regional Library	110 1st A
Albany	Albany Branch Library	Great River Regional Library	400 Railro
Albert Lea	Albert Lea Public Library	Albert Lea Public Library	211 E Cla
Alexandria	Douglas County Library	Douglas County Library	720 Fillmo
Annandale	Annandale Branch Library	Great River Regional Library	30 Cedar S
Anoka	Rum River Library	Anoka County Public Library	4201 6th A
Apple Valley	Galaxie Library	Dakota County Library	14355 Ga
Appleton	Appleton Public Library	Pioneerland Library System	323 W S
Arden Hills	Arden Hills Library	Ramsey County Library	1941 W
Arlington	Arlington Public Library	Sibley County Library System	321 West
Atwater	Atwater Public Library	Pioneerland Library System	318 Atlan
Aurora	Aurora Public Library	Aurora Public Library	14 West
Austin	Austin Public Library	Austin Public Library	323 Fourth

If for some reason, you can't find your library via publiclibrary.com or you get a "page cannot be found error," use Google and Boolean logic to find your library.

In the Google search form, just type in the name of your city (make sure to use quotation marks if your city is more than one word), your state, and then "public library." If your city has a public library with a Web site, it should appear as one of the top five search results.

It's important to learn which library resources are available to you so you can take advantage of all of them. As long as you live or work in the geographic area served by a particular library, you can access that library's resources. In some areas, you can access the resources at every library regardless of where you work or live, as long as you have a library card from one of the libraries in the area.

The quickest way to find which premium business databases your library subscribes to is to visit your library's Web site. Again, use publiclibraries.com or the Google method described above.

Once you're at your library's Web site, you'll want to locate a link, tab, or button that says "databases." For some libraries, this link or tab might be called "electronic resources," "online reference," "research tools," or even "library holdings." If you can't find the link right away, most library Web sites have a search engine on the home page that allows you to search the Web site. Type "database" in the search engine and see what appears.

Now that you're in your public library's online databases, there are two key questions you need to answer: 1) what business databases does the library subscribe to, and 2) where can you access the database, at the library, via your own computer 24/7, or both?

Sometimes libraries make it easy to identify which databases include business information because the library creates a directory structure and houses its business databases in a category link typically labeled "business." Sometimes, however, when you click on a library's database offerings, you're presented with a huge list of databases, many of them with names that aren't familiar. So here's a quick trick to determine which databases offer business information.

When you're on the Web page featuring the long list of databases, go to your Web browser's menu and locate the "Find" option (in Internet Explorer, it's under the "Edit" menu). Select and open the "Find" tool and type the word "business" in the search form. Click the "Find Next" button (on some browsers it might be the "Find" or "Search" button) and you'll see all of the databases that feature business information.

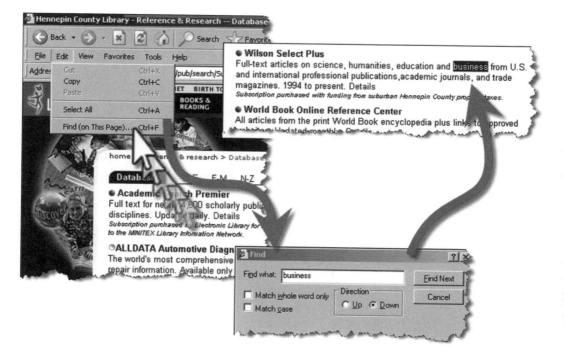

The next question you need to answer is whether the particular database you want is available remotely, meaning that you can access it via your home or office computer any time of day, or whether you need to visit the library in person to use the database. Some libraries put a label right next to the particular database that says "In Library" or "Remote Usage." For some libraries, you need to click on the database name to see if you are prompted for an identification code.

If the database you want does prompt you for an identification code, all you'll need is your library card, where you'll find your library ID or code number on the front or back of your card. Don't have a library card? As long as you have a driver's license or proof of address, you can visit your local library in person and get one free.

Consider your library card the "cubicle next to your office." Your library card is your sales assistant ready to help you with Sales Intelligence to turn every sales call into a warm one, where you have the information you need to differentiate yourself, your company, and help you close the deal.

The types of "sales assistants" or business databases are going to vary from library to library. Again, this is why it's important to find out whether you can get access at multiple libraries. Your library most likely subscribes to one or more of the following databases:

- **ABI Inform** featuring a wealth of business information from newspapers, research reports and industry trade journals.

- **Business and Company Resource Center**, which is the same database, described earlier, that many larger organizations subscribe to.

- **Business Source Premier** features access to trade publications, business magazines, country reports, industry surveys, and more.

- **Dun & Bradstreet Million Dollar Database** is a version of the D&B database profiled earlier. The D&B Million Dollar Database contains detailed public and private company information on firms with more than $1 million in sales or more than twenty employees. It typically provides full search functionality but limited downloads.

- **EBSCO Business Source Premier** features company and market reports and trade journal articles from more than 2,000 publications.

- **Gale's Ready Reference Shelf** is a directory of more than 300,000 organizations, publications, and databases.

- **Hoovers** is the same database described earlier, although some libraries only provide access to the free Hoovers version.

- **Kompass International Business Directories** is an international directory of companies.

- **Mergent Online** features detailed financial information on publicly held companies.

- **ProQuest** provides access to more than 8,000 magazines and newspapers from 1970 to present.

- **ReferenceUSA** is basically the same library version as the InfoUSA profiled earlier. ReferenceUSA via libraries typically allows full searching capabilities but limited company record downloads.

- **Regional Business News** features selected articles from business publications across the United States.

- **Wilson Select Plus** features articles on science, humanities, education, and business from U.S. and international magazines and trade journals.

Again, the databases above are the types of databases found at public libraries. Few libraries subscribe to all of these databases and certainly, libraries subscribe to databases not listed above.

Although your public library may soon become one of your relied-upon business success tools, your "sales assistant" isn't without its problems (just like those human sales assistants). Some of the issues you should be aware of when using local library business databases include:

- **Business database subscriptions are very expensive.** If you happen to live in a larger city or county that heavily supports libraries via local taxes, then you're probably in luck in that your library most likely features four to eight premium business databases. If, however, you live in a smaller community, you're probably limited to just a few databases. Also, know that libraries review subscriptions on an annual basis. Database costs are increasing at double-digit levels while simultaneously in many communities funding for libraries is flat or even declining. There is no guarantee that databases you have available and rely on today via your public library will be there tomorrow. On a side note, this is a key reason that in my opinion, businesses should support library funding.

- **Seats might be limited.** Many premium business databases are purchased on a per-seat license meaning the number of people who can use a database simultaneously is limited. So, for example, if you live in a community with one million residents and your library only subscribes to five seats of a particular database, there's a decent chance you will not be able to access a database at a particular time. This is especially true during business hours, thus you may need to limit your searching to after-hours. If you're a salesperson who can plan accordingly, that should work just fine. If you're a salesperson who waits until the last minute to conduct the "Fourth R" prior to a sales call, you might get burned.

- **You need time to conduct your research via libraries.** To practice the "Fourth R", you most likely have to search multiple databases to get what you need. You might use one database for company information and another for industry trends. Give yourself twenty to thirty minutes for each prospect search or longer if you have to wait for a particular database seat to free up.

- **Customer service can be limited.** Because the library is the one subscribing to the database, if you need help, you most likely will not be able to contact the database company directly. When you are stuck, make sure you call your local librarian, as they are trained information experts whose mission is to help you access information. However, know that librarians are busy and you may not be able to connect with a librarian familiar with business resources when you need him or her.

Even with the limitations highlighted above, your local public library is the great leveler of the information playing field. Through your public library, you can access the same types of premium business information sources that your larger competitors are accessing.

You also have access to expert researchers, librarians, who are more than happy to help you find the information you need. In addition, don't forget to check your local public library for training programs. Many libraries offer free classes on how to best use the library's business resources.

Search for Research – Your University Library

Besides public libraries, another place to access information typically not found on the "free Web" is your college or university library. For example, did you know that according to the American Library Association, more than 1.5 million academic titles have been published since 1970, yet less than

2,000 are available for free online? Many of these are available
through your local university library.

In addition, most universities spend substantial sums
on premium subscription databases. Most of these databases
are only available to current students and faculty. However,
many schools make portions of premium databases available
to the public or to alumni. Typically, all that is needed to access these databases through a home or office computer is an
alumni or alumni association ID.

To locate your college or university library, use Google
and in the search form enter the name of your university (remember to put the name between quotation marks) followed
by the word "library."

Clicking on the Web site link brings me to the university
library home page. On your school's home page, look for a
link titled "alumni" or another similar title and see if you,
assuming you're an alumnus, have access to any premium
databases.

Finally, don't forget to make note of the contact information at your local college or university library. If you're looking for an obscure piece of information, particularly if it's
related to an industry, you might do well to contact the university librarian to see if he or she can help you locate it. Remember that your university librarian has probably helped
many faculty members and students research business infor-

mation for school projects, research reports, or even university-funded business enterprises.

Low Cost Research – HillSearch

www.hillsearch.org

Since 1921, the non-profit, private, James J. Hill Reference Library in St. Paul, Minnesota, has been providing entrepreneurs, small business, mid-size companies, business students, and non-profits access to and assistance in finding the practical business information needed to succeed. The Hill Library has literally served millions over the past 86 years and hundreds of thousands of businesses can credit their success to information found at the Hill Library.

In 2003, the Hill Library launched a series of online programs designed to provide individual entrepreneurs and individuals at small businesses access to premium business information resources through their own computers. One of the programs, HillSearch (**www.hillsearch.org**), is a great, low-cost tool for the individual involved with business development, sales, and client management. You can get a HillSearch trial at **www.hillsearch.org/trial**.

HillSearch offers numerous premium business databases all in one easy-to-access interface. HillSearch offers two search methods, OneSearch, which looks and works much like a standard search engine, and CustomSearch, which helps guide your business research towards specific resources.

OneSearch is a power research tool that instantly searches millions of company articles, industry articles, and news stories. If you want to use individual databases and HillSearch resources, just click on the CustomSearch tab. You'll see the various premium resources that you can click on and immediately access. Alternatively, you can search for business information by topic.

When you access an individual database, you'll be using the same high-end research resources that your competitors at large organizations have access to.

SAM TIP
HillSearch:

The Hill Library's HillSearch membership program is a powerful, low-cost business research program available to individuals.

1. Go to **www.hillsearch.org**

2. Sign up for a free trial at **www.hillsearch.org/trial**

3. Become a member for a low annual fee with monthly payment options available.

4. Use the OneSearch tool to instantly search virtually every key newspaper, magazine, business wire, and trade journal.

5. Use CustomSearch to search individual databases and powerful data resources.

6. Use the Live Help feature anytime you're having difficulty using HillSearch or finding what you want online.

(Notice I didn't say "are using" because it's highly likely that your competitors don't understand the concepts of Sales Intelligence, the "Fourth R" and warm calling, so now that you understand it and have access to the tools to practice it, you have the competitive edge.)

Many of the HillSearch databases are found via your local public library at no charge. However, depending on your library system and what they subscribe to, your only access to a specific database might be through HillSearch. Plus with HillSearch, all of the databases are located in one resource, thus the price is probably worth if for the convenience.

HillSearch is only available to individuals and only those at small firms. HillSearch also includes tools for helping to prepare a business plan, marketing program, and strategic programs including financial calculators and benchmarking resources, thousands of sample downloadable business plans, and more.

One of my favorite HillSearch features is that if you ever get stuck and need assistance with your search, you're one click or phone call away from a Hill Library Business Information Specialist. If you can't find what you want, just click Online Chat in HillSearch and enter into an instant message chat session with a business information expert. With the Online Chat system, you can actually let a Hill Librarian "take hold of your browser" and guide your search. You can sit and watch as the Librarian visits Web sites, uses different advanced search techniques, and teaches you how to use a particular site or online database. When you're done, you receive an e-mail transcript with a list of visited sites.

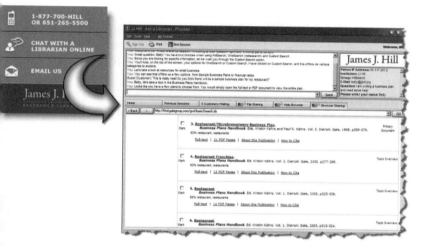

CHAPTER EIGHTEEN

Putting It Together: The Warm Call

> "Rainmakers never waste a sales call: They always have a precall plan. It is typical for a Rainmaker to spend three hours planning for a fifteen minute sales call."
> – Jeffrey A. Fox, *How to Become a Rainmaker*,
> New York: Hyperion, 2000

In his book, *Selling the Invisible*, Harry Beckwith discusses a number of sins poor salespeople commit. Many of these sins are a direct result of salespeople trying to conduct a cold call, versus a warm one. Some of the examples that Beckwith cites as the reasons customers can't differentiate one company, or one salesperson, from another include:

- **Poor voicemail messages.** If you haven't done your homework, there's a good chance you'll leave a rambling voicemail message completely irrelevant to your prospect's interests. With the "Fourth R," you can cite an industry issue, a recent company event, a quote from the CEO; something that will interest your prospect and encourage a return call.

- **Making a bad impression.** When you're unprepared, you're nervous and unsure of yourself. If you're like most people, these internal emotions express themselves with a weak handshake, avoidance in making eye contact, and a belief that you have to start talking to break the silence. Practice the "Fourth R" and you go into every meeting confident and secure in the knowledge that you're going to provide great value. This self-confidence shows in everything you do and say.

- **Being unprepared.** Beckwith says that decision-makers will give you fifteen minutes for you to make your case. Don't waste that time having your prospect explain to you their business strategy and competitive issues. Instead, impress your prospect with what you already know, and spend the first fifteen minutes proving your relevance and enhancing your credibility.

- **Talking about features instead of benefits.** If you're unprepared, chances are you immediately start talking about your product's features because you have the need to talk about something (e.g., look at the quality material in our product). If you've practiced the "Fourth R," however, you have an understanding of what your prospect cares about, and you customize your presentation to focus on the direct benefits your product or service will have on your prospect's business (e.g., this product will help you solve the issue that you're currently facing).

Beckwith is 100% correct when he states "customers aren't looking for reasons to do business with you, they're looking for reasons to get rid of you." When you're unprepared—when you go into a meeting cold—you're "winging it" and your only chance for success is to be a fast talker and thinker or to get very lucky. When you're unprepared, you're giving your prospect (and your existing clients) every reason to get rid of you.

When you're prepared, when you practice the "Fourth R," when you have a Platinum Rule mindset, you don't leave your meetings to chance. Instead, your sales calls and client presentations are highly relevant, what you're offering provides great value, and you're almost guaranteed of making a superb impression. The "Fourth R" will help you differentiate yourself and your company, you will be remembered, and you will make it difficult for your prospects and clients to get rid of you. How could anyone get rid of someone who provides so much value and so many relevant solutions?

By getting this far into the book, you now have a great appreciation for the value of Sales Intelligence, the "Fourth R" and information, how to find it, and how to use it to turn cold sales calls into successful warm calls. Finding the information becomes the easy part now that you know how to effectively use tools like Google, the Invisible Web, premium databases, and your local public library.

The challenge now becomes knowing how to organize and apply the information that you find. When practicing the "Fourth R," it is critical that you organize your research in a way that can be easily accessed and modified.

Many companies have spent thousands, if not hundreds of thousands of dollars, on sophisticated Customer Relationship Management systems (CRM). The theory for a CRM system is that it provides every person within an organization details about each customer interaction.

For example, a good CRM system will let you know what products a customer has purchased from your company, how many times they've called customer service and what the outcomes were, the prospects of the customer purchasing additional products, and when the customer was last called by a salesperson. Most companies with CRM systems also input information regarding potential prospects, to help sales management track opportunities and the likelihood of closing future business.

One of the problems with how most companies use CRM systems, however, is they include only "internal" customer data. So for example, when a customer calls an account representative, the CRM system will quickly tell the representative what the customer has purchased, but it tells the representative nothing related to what the customer cares about.

Using the CRM system alone, the representative knows virtually nothing about the customer's business issues, competition, market environment, for example. As you now know, this "external" information is critical to providing relevant value to clients and building deeper relationships.

The basic use of a CRM system allows the account representative to sell a new version of a product. But maybe what the customer really needs is a completely different solution based on their business issues. Because the company's CRM system doesn't include external notes fields that are intuitive, or if they do exist people aren't trained how to use them effectively (they aren't trained in the "Fourth R" or even how to ask basic questions related to external factors), the account representative misses an outstanding opportunity to provide value to the customer and increase profits for his or her company.

The good news is that you can easily create a different kind of CRM tool using something as easy as a simple spreadsheet, or something more sophisticated that is integrated with a traditional CRM system. Instead of a Customer Relationship Management system, however, this version of CRM is really a Client Research Management tool.

The Other CRM – Client Research Management Tool

As we've discussed throughout this book, imagine how impressive it would be if, when speaking with a prospect or client, you're able to reference a recent article about them, a journal article related to one of their key business issues, or a newspaper article about a competitor.

If you create a Client Research Management Tool and update it on a regular basis, knowing what's important to your clients and prospects and how you provide relevant and valuable solutions to their business issues is always a quick read or click away.

Creating a CRMT is simple (CRMT – we'll add the "T" on the abbreviation so as not to confuse it with the other CRM). You can use a spreadsheet format, or, if you collect a lot of data and like to print articles rather than abstracts, create a searchable document. At a minimum, enter "Fourth R" data as notes in your contact management software.

For example, if you use Microsoft Outlook, you can enter data into the Notes field and it becomes instantly searchable. If your company already has a CRM system, you should be able to create your own custom fields where you can enter your research directly into the software, making it easily searchable and usable by all within your firm.

Your CRMT can be simple, incorporating basic information that you should be able to find using the techniques described in this book. Alternatively, it can be more complex, incorporating not only information that you can find, but also information that you'll gather over time by networking, by asking great questions, and by listening carefully.

A superb example of a CRMT is the "Mackay 66" from top-selling business author and probably one of the world's top network experts, Harvey Mackay. You can download the "Mackay 66" for free plus some other helpful free tools at **www.harveymackay.com**.

Following is an example of a completed CRMT in spreadsheet format showing the key fields for the information that you will want to collect and update. You probably will want to customize and create your own version of a CRMT that incorporates fields that are particular to your company and/or industry, but in general, your CRMT should probably have data fields that include:

- Company Name

- Customer Name (the contacts you have, and make sure to identify decision-makers, influencers)

- Address, phone, e-mail, and Web site information

- Core products/services offered by the company

- Annual company revenue and employees

- Additional company information; e.g., company history, corporate donations, company mission

- Top competitors

- Key industry and market data and projections

- Company executive biographies

- Client personal information; e.g., hobbies, political and religious affiliations, birthdays, anniversaries, donations, favorite sports teams

- Key business issues; e.g., what's going on with the company, its customers, and its industry that is getting in the way of them achieving their objectives

- Benefits and/or value that you can provide; e.g., how can your company's products/services help the client resolve their key business issues, and what experience you have to prove it

It's important to note that your CRMT will grow over time. Obviously once someone becomes a client, you add information to the CRMT that you've gathered through questions and personal interaction. But as you look at the following chart, you'll note that a great deal of the data can be found using the techniques and resources highlighted in this book and at the Warm Call Center (**www.warmcallcenter.com**).

CRMT and Warm Call Selling Scripts

You've got the information, it is well organized, so now what? The only reason to do all of this work is if you're going to apply the "Fourth R" in a meaningful way that helps you deliver bottom-line results.

At the end of the day, your success still comes down to your ability as an individual salesperson, business development officer, and/or account manager. The "Fourth R" is a major part of the puzzle, but it's still your talent that is going to close the deal. No matter how much great information you have on your clients and their issues, you're still the one who has to determine when to use the information to prove your relevance, increase your credibility, and provide client value. That takes tact, and it takes time to master.

The "Fourth R" is not some sort of magic bullet that immediately starts generating money for you. You're not going to start automatically closing deals on the first sales call or prospect meeting. The "Fourth R" is not even necessarily going to shorten the sales process.

What I do know from experience, however, is that if you practice what you've learned in this book, you're much more

SAMPLE CLIENT RESEARCH MANAGEMENT TOOL (CRMT)

Company Name:	Widget Corporation
Customer Name:	Joe Smith
Address:	1234 Widget Lane Minneapolis, MN 55305
Phone:	612-345-6789
E-mail Address:	jsmith@widgetcorp.com
Company Web Site:	www.widgetcorp.com
Core Products/Services:	Widgets are sold to the automotive industry. Widgets are used in the manufacture of a car's air conditioning system.
Annual Company Revenue:	$22 million
Number of Employees:	56
Additional Company Information:	Widget Corp. was founded in 1964. The company annually spends time working on Habitat for Humanity homes. The company also donates to the United Way. The company mission statement talks about the value it places on employees and community.
Top Competitors:	ACME Auto Parts, Beijing Automotive
Top Customers:	Ford Motors, General Motors
Industry and Market Data and Projections:	Automotive industry is growing 12% annually; 87% of all new cars have air conditioning as a standard feature. Analysts predict that by 2010, the majority of all automobile parts manufacturing will be done via robotics.
Company Executive Biographies:	Harold Smith (Joe's father) started the company in 1964 after holding executive positions at General Motors. Joe and his sister Laurie will take over the company in the next five years.
Customer Personal Information:	Joe is a graduate of Princeton University where he played varsity hockey. Joe's degree is in Art History. Joe has one daughter, age 8, who has won local youth competitions for skiing. Joe is Jewish (he's on the board of his synagogue) and donates to the American Cancer society.
Key Business Issues:	Widget Corporation manufactures most of their products using manual labor. Not only will the industry be shifting to robotics, but the majority of automotive parts manufacturing is shifting to Asia. Widget Corp. is looking for partners in Asia while simultaneously looking to invest in new equipment that will allow them to focus on creating higher-end automotive parts with tight specifications.
Benefits and Value We Do or Could Provide Customer:	Public relations counsel. We aid Widget in strategic planning. Our connections in the Asia market have provided Widget great benefit. We want to help Widget craft a marketing program for their higher-end product division. Data that we have provided our contacts related to the Asian market, changes in the automotive industry, and new robotic manufacturing technologies have been appreciated.

likely to get invited to the next step in the sales process—presenting a proposal—and that if you continue practicing the "Fourth R," your proposals will be more effective. In addition, by practicing the "Fourth R" after you land a new client, you're more likely to keep that client happy by providing value over the long term, and you're also more likely to keep your margins with your existing clients.

As I mentioned in the opening to this book, *Take the Cold Out of Cold Calling* is not designed to teach you the intricacies of a sales call or how to present to prospects and existing clients. There are many books at your local bookstore that touch on this subject, and many training seminars you can take on how to be a more effective salesperson.

However, over the years in my own business development career, even though I've never had the official title "salesman" on my business card, I have learned through failure and success that if I can show my prospects that I understand their business issues and that my firm can help them solve their business problems, my sales close ratios dramatically improve. To employ a certain degree of consistency in my presentations, I created a series of informal "scripts," or a process, that I follow when I'm making a cold call of any type.

By following a consistent process in the way I present myself to prospects, and how I introduce the information I gathered via the "Fourth R" techniques described in this book, I am able to establish my credibility and my organization's relevance. Using this process and a consistent way in delivering my message, I am invited to the next step—a future meeting or sometimes even the proposal state—a high percentage of the time. When I can have my first prospect meeting in person via a referral, well over 75 percent of the time do I get invited to the next step.

Although the process and "scripts" I used are in my head, as I've worked on *Take the Cold Out of Cold Calling* over the past few years, I started tracking what I said during phone calls, e-mails, letters, and in-person meetings so I could create a series of scripts that I could share with you. Again, these scripts are my own interpretations of how to apply information in a cold call. There are other sales training programs that offer versions of scripts, many tested with tens of thousands of salespeople over many years.

However, I have tested the scripts with numerous salespeople that I respect to ensure that they would work in just about any industry, with just about any product or service. These sales experts did a lot of editing to my scripts mainly to shorten them, but what you'll find in the next few pages represent a simple yet powerful process that if followed will deliver results.

Know that I don't follow these scripts word for word every time; as I've mentioned, my scripts are usually longer because the products and services I sell are relatively complex. However, the following scripts are a guide that you can adapt for your company and sometimes for each prospect.

Review them and modify them for your needs and comfort level. Use them as a guide to help you quickly determine what types of information you need from your CRMT and how to insert that information to make your different types of cold calling more relevant, personal, credible, and effective. Customize them to your company's offering, to the types of prospects you call on, and to your own comfort level and sales style.

One final note: remember that the objective is getting your prospect to say, "Yes, I'd like to learn more." For most, it is NOT closing the deal. Your goal with a cold call prospect is to invite a meeting or, in rare instances, a proposal.

With help from some world-class sales experts, I've designed the following scripts to get you to that next level of customer interaction.

Telephone Script

Staring at a list of names and phone numbers figuring out how you're going to convince each prospect that you have something he or she cares about can be daunting. In addition, you know that more than likely when you make the telephone call, you're going to get a voicemail message, meaning that you probably have about 10-20 seconds to make your pitch in a credible, relevant manner.

The following scripts will help guide you in making your 10-20 second pitch, whether it's on a voicemail or in the rare instance you do get a prospect on the phone. Choose one and modify it based on whether you or your organization has a previous relationship with the client, and obviously shorten it if you have to leave a voicemail. Try to keep to the basic format to ensure you create relevance and generate your own credibility quickly and effectively.

Practice the script often before you make any phone calls. You want to make sure that you don't sound like you're reading a script. Keep your conversation "conversational" in nature: you know something about the person on the other end of the phone and you and your company want to help them achieve a specific objective.

Take the Cold Out of Cold Calling Telephone Script – Industry Info

Use the following script as a guideline if you are cold calling a number of companies in the same industry:

> "Hi _____. This is _____ and I'm calling from _____. We've never met nor were you expecting this call. I would like to take 90 seconds to explain why I called, and then you decide if we should continue the conversation. Is that OK with you? (Pause)
>
> I saw a recent article in _____ [1] about _____ [2] and I thought of your company. Our organization has helped several companies like yours solve similar issues. I'd like to meet with you and take 45 minutes of your time to get some feedback on how your company deals with these issues, and share with you some ideas on how we might be able to assist you.

Follow next with your contact information if you're leaving a voicemail, or if you get a live person, continue with more detail.

If you're leaving a voicemail, skip the "We've never met ..." and instead of "I'd like to meet with you and take 45 minutes ..." mention a day and time when you're going to call back.

[1] Reference the name of a respected publication in the prospect's industry.

[2] Reference an industry trend or issue you're fairly certain your prospect is facing.

Take the Cold Out of Cold Calling Telephone Script – Company Info

Use the following script as a guideline if you are cold calling a single company:

> "Hi _____. This is _____ and I'm calling from _____. We've never met nor were you expecting this call. I would like to take 90 seconds to explain why I called, and then you decide if we should continue the conversation. Is that OK with you? (Pause)
>
> I read the recent article in _____ [1] where _____ [2] was quoted as saying _____ [3] I found that comment really interesting because my firm has _____ [4] I'd like to meet with you and take 45 minutes of your time to discuss _____ [5] and to share with you how we help companies with similar issues.

Follow next with your contact information if you're leaving a voicemail, or if you get a live person, continue with more detail.

If you're leaving a voicemail, skip the "We've never met ..." and instead of "I'd like to meet with you and take 45 minutes ..." mention a day and time when you're going to call back.

[1] Conduct your research using a news, magazine, or industry journal search. In your research, locate a story about the company where an executive is quoted discussing issues the industry or company is facing.

[2] In your script, reference the name of the person who was quoted. Hopefully it's the person you're calling on but if not, use the person's name and title, e.g., "your CEO, Phil Smith was quoted ..."

[3] Summarize the quote you pulled from the article.

[4] Share a brief, relevant story about your company that relates to the quote. For example, let's say that the quote was about a large piece of business your prospect just landed. You could say something like, "I found that comment really interesting because our company has successfully helped our clients launch large new client initiatives quickly and cost-effectively."

[5] Summarize the issue discussed in the quote.

E-mail Script

Many sales calls today start with an e-mail to your prospect, letting them know about your company and your product or service offerings. All too often, however, these e-mail introductions are actually treated as unwelcome spam by your prospect, meaning they end up being deleted without ever being read.

The following script works quite well in breaking through the e-mail clutter. Note that it only works if you or your company has permission to e-mail your prospect. Permission comes in many forms including but not limited to someone giving you a business card at a networking event or trade show, a prospect filling out a form on your Web site requesting data, or someone calling your firm asking for additional information. When a prospect is "asking" for more information, variations on the following e-mail script work well in moving the prospect to requesting a meeting or further information:

Take the Cold Out of Cold Calling E-mail Script

SUBJECT LINE: (please note that the subject line of an e-mail is very important and thus, if you can customize it and make it relevant, the likelihood that your e-mail will get read increases exponentially)

SUBJECT: Did you see that recent article about _____*?*[1]

E-MAIL COPY:

Dear _____ *,*

I enjoyed meeting you or seeing you at _____ *. (Or, if you have not met the prospect, use: Thanks for requesting additional information about ...) I was doing some research this morning and read an article from* _____ [2] *and immediately thought of you.*

In particular, the article discussed _____ _____.[3]

I'm guessing that this could be an issue your company is facing and I would like to have some of your time to share with you how my company, _____ *, helps our clients deal with this issue.*

Following (or attached) is some introductory information about my company that I thought you might find relevant. When would be a good time for me to call you?

Sincerely, _____

[1] Make a brief reference to an article you found relevant to your prospect; try to make it an "issue" that you think your prospect is facing. For example, if you found an article about

how outsourcing is influencing your prospect's business, the subject line might read: "Interesting article about outsourcing in the window industry."

[2] Name the source where you found the information. Make sure it's a source that is credible for your prospect's industry.

[3] Summarize the key elements in the article that you think are relevant to your prospect's business.

Business Letter Script

Because most of us are bombarded by e-mail on a daily basis, and voicemail is the preferred method of avoiding contact with just about anyone, especially salespeople, a personal letter may be an effective way of getting your message across to a prospect. The key to a professional sales letter is to customize it, ensuring it is relevant to your prospects and their businesses.

The following scripts work well as the opening couple of paragraphs for a business letter. You can follow with the standard information about your company:

Take the Cold Out of Cold Calling Letter Script –
Industry Information

Use the following script as a guideline if you are sending letters to a number of companies in the same industry:

Dear _____,

Recently, I came across some information I thought was very relevant to your business and I wanted to share it with you. I saw an article in _____ [1] and in particular, I took note of the following:

"_____
_____."[2]

As my company _____ has quite a bit of experience working with organizations like yours, I would like to have a few minutes of your time to discuss how we help other companies including _____ achieve their business objectives, and how we could do the same for you.

Please find enclosed....

[1] Reference the name of a respected publication in the prospect's industry.

[2] Locate information in a respected trade journal or newspaper that discusses a key issue or trend that your prospect's industry is facing. Then in your business letter, summarize the article and/or pull some key information directly from the article that you know your prospect will care about. NOTE: Do not include a copy of the article with your letter, as this is a violation of copyright law.

Take the Cold Out of Cold Calling Letter Script – Company Information

Use the following script as a guideline if you are sending a letter to a specific company:

Dear _____,

I was doing some reading this morning and came across the article in _____ [1] featuring your company. I was particularly interested in _____ [2] and _____'s[3] take on the issue. I especially liked this quote:

"_____
_____."[4]

As my company _____ has quite a bit of experience working with organizations

like yours, I would like to have a few minutes of your time to discuss how we help other companies including _____ achieve their business objectives, and how we could do the same for you.

Enclosed, please find....

[1] Conduct research using your prospect's company name. Reference the source where you found the information.

[2] Mention in a few words what interested you most about the article.

[3] Reference the name of the person who was quoted. Hopefully it's the person you're calling on but if not, use the quoted person's name and title.

[4] Summarize a portion of the article or pull a quote directly from the article.

In-Person Meeting – Where You Can Really Win with Sales Intelligence

Follow the techniques in this book, and you can use the information you've found almost like a "crystal ball." You'll be able to ask outstanding questions because you already have a good idea of what your prospect's answers might be. Then you can follow up with comments that are spot on to what your prospects want to hear, because you'll be sharing information that is relevant to the issues that they are facing.

I believe that the more information you have about your prospect and the issues he or she is facing, the more relaxed you'll be in your first meeting, the more confident you'll feel, and frankly the more fun you'll have. As someone involved in sales, business development, and/or account management, you are probably a "people person." You like to engage with others, and you feel important and just "good" when you know that what you have to offer provides great value to others.

When you practice the "Fourth R" and the techniques discussed in this book, you'll know the value you can provide the person you're meeting with *before* you walk in the room. With this confidence, you'll engage in a value-based conversation with your prospect, as opposed to a "sales call." Or to put it another way, your first meeting—your cold call—will actually be a warm one.

Following is an outline of how an in-person conversation at a first meeting might go, and how you can use the "Fourth R" to establish your credibility and keep the conversation focused on ways your company can help your prospect achieve his or her company objectives.

I.   **Introduction:** The introduction is a perfect way to establish your credibility right from the get go. Remember: people buy from people they like. People also like to talk about themselves. Therefore, in the first few minutes, try to reference something that you know your prospect cares about.

   a.   **Small-Talk Introduction:** If your prospect greets you with a big smile and starts the conversation with a bit of small talk, for example, "nice weather out today" or "did you watch the ball game last night," assume you have permission to reciprocate. However, after answering any questions asked of you, instead of you then saying something generic, make your small talk specific to your prospect.

   For example, after you answer a few questions, you could say something like: "In preparing for today's meeting, I did a little homework (see the chapter on "Researching a Person") and found that you were on the winning team at the local United Way golf tournament. You must be a great golfer; with your busy schedule, do you get to play often?" (You already know the answer is "yes" because you've looked up your prospect's golf handicap.)

   Immediately your prospect will be impressed that you did your homework prior to your meeting. As important, within the first five minutes of your meeting, you got your prospect talking about something he or she passionately cares about: him or herself.

Note: be careful to quickly steer your prospect back towards discussing business, as you don't want your entire allotted time spent talking about your prospect's hobby.

b. **Down to Business Introduction:** Sometimes when you meet prospects for the first time, it's clear that they want to get down to business. For example, if the first thing out of your prospect's mouth is "So … what have you got to show me today?" you should probably skip the small talk and get right to your meeting agenda.

II. **Meeting Agenda:** Don't waste your prospect's time. Re-affirm how much time you've been given for the meeting. For example, say something like "I know we have forty-five minutes together today, and this is what I'd like to discuss." Then either hand out an agenda or discuss it. Make sure that one of your first agenda items is "background information."

III. **Background Information:** Here's where you can make a great impression with your prospect. Using the "Research a Company" skills you learned in this book, spend a few minutes prior to your meeting learning about your prospect's company, its products and services, competitors, and other relevant details. Then in two to three minutes, summarize what you learned.

For example, you can say something like: "I spent some time researching Widget Corporation and it looks like you're doing quite well. Some of the articles I read showed that you're growing at almost 28 percent annually, and the new products you're coming out with sure look impressive. I also noted how one of your biggest competitors was just acquired by ACME, Inc. How do you think that will impact you?"

What you've also done in these first few minutes is make a great impression and established your credibility by demonstrating that you care about what your prospect cares about. You've most likely separated yourself from 95 percent of the others salespeople your prospect has met with and you've established yourself as one of the best. In addition, your prospect will most likely correct you if any of the information you gave is incorrect (e.g., "we're actually growing at 35 percent per year"), so you have also set yourself up to learn even more about the company.

IV. **Sharing of Information:** This isn't you sharing information about your company yet. Rather, it's important early on in your meeting to get your prospect to share information about his or her company, and in particular, the key issues the company is facing in achieving its objectives.

Even more powerful is soliciting information regarding your prospect's role in achieving those company objectives. Knowing the role your prospect plays is important because when you start talking about your company and the solutions you hope to provide, you can make your pitch very personal.

Imagine giving this introduction to your company: "I'm really excited to show you our new Widget manufacturing process because I know it can resolve your company's issue of having to rely on overseas labor. In addition, I'm committed to working with you to ensure you hit your personal objective of a 25-percent increase in throughput."

How do you learn what a company's key issues are? How do you know what business issues your prospect is facing? *You ask.* But if you just blindly ask without having established your credibility, your questions will most likely seem contrived and your concern for your prospect's welfare might come off as phony.

Instead, use what you've learned in this book about researching a company or an industry to seed the conversation, establish your credibility, and open the door for relevant questions.

Read a few industry articles prior to your meeting and then reference them during the questioning period of the "Sharing of Information Stage." For example, you will encourage your prospect to engage in sharing information if you say something like: "I was reading in *Manufacturing Digest* about how in the last five years alone, more than 40 percent of the manual labor jobs related to manufacturing in your industry have been going overseas. How is that impacting your company? In particular, how is it impacting your ability to hit your company's and even your personal revenue objectives?"

V. **Your Company Introduction:** Now that you've spent the first part of your meeting establishing your credibility and getting your prospect comfortable talking about his or her company, it's time to spend a couple of minutes talking about your company.

Make sure to sprinkle some "Fourth R" material into your introduction when appropriate. For example, during your company introduction, it's very appropriate to say things like: "We've been providing products and services to the Widget industry for more than twenty years. In fact, I saw in an article that one of your customers is XYZ Corp and we've been doing business with Ralph Smith at XYZ for the last five years."

VI. **Your Offering:** Once you've introduced your company and engaged your prospect about what your company does, it's now time to "make the pitch" and specifically discuss what your company can do to help your prospect. Now is the time to impress!

Instead of taking out a product catalog or using a standard PowerPoint presentation, praying that there is something in your pitch that your prospect will care about, use this time to solidify your credibility and relevance. For example, imagine how powerful your presentation could be if you said something like: "My company has clients of all kinds and sizes in many different industries, but I wanted to share with you today a story about how we helped a client just like you overcome [an issue that you've already told me you're facing]. When I researched your company and industry, I found that a key issue to growth seems to be ..."

Continue this line of conversation by referencing articles and data you've read and experiences your company has where you've truly helped clients overcome similar issues to your prospect. Spend time sharing results you've accomplished for others, with companies and/or in industries highly relevant to your prospect. Talk about what you can do for your prospect in a way that resolves his/her issues. As much as you can, use relevant examples, stories, and analogies that show how you can address your prospect's problems, as opposed to talking about your company alone.

VII. **Questions/Discussion:** Hopefully you've been engaging your prospect in conversation all along. If you practiced the "Fourth R" and truly have information about your prospect and his or her industry, it's highly likely that you've been in a great conversation, and your prospect has been sharing information and opinions.

Make sure to set aside time in your agenda for your prospect to ask additional questions. If you've done your job well and shared relevant experiences, it's very likely that during this part of your conversation your prospect will be the one discussing how your company can help meet your prospect's objectives. Your prospect will be "coaching" you on the next steps you need to take to get the order.

VIII. **The Close:** By this point in your meeting the close may be obvious. It's unlikely in today's business environment that you're going to walk away from the meeting with an order. It is likely, however, that by doing your homework and practicing the "Fourth R," you've impressed your prospect enough that he or she is willing to discuss with you the next steps.

Those next steps typically will include another meeting with additional people, a proposal, or both. Regardless, make sure you continue to practice the "Fourth R" during each step in the process to ensure your presentations and proposals establish your credibility, are always customized to your prospect's needs, and are relevant to how you can help your prospect resolve business issues and achieve objectives.

IX. **The Follow-Up:** This is a VERY IMPORTANT step and one where you can make a great impression. Make sure to follow up your meeting with a well-written and relevant e-mail or letter. Obviously, reference your meeting in your follow-up note and summarize any next action steps you've agreed to take. Also, note that the follow-up is a perfect time to practice the "Fourth R" again and further differentiate you and your company.

Your follow-up e-mail or letter is the perfect place to reference something that was discussed in your meeting and include some information you dug up immediately following your sales call. For example, think how powerful this would be in a follow-up note:

> *"Mr. Smith, during our meeting you referenced a new product your competitor, Widget Corporation, is coming out with and you shared with me that you're concerned they might steal some of your market share. I've taken the liberty of doing some research and I'm enclosing a copy of Widget's current pending patent application. Below I've summarized what an analyst thinks about the new product and I believe overall, that you are correct, the product has a chance to steal some of your customers. The good news is that my company has helped firms just like yours...."*

Do you think you've got your prospect's attention? Remember, it's highly likely that your prospect is meeting with a number of companies in your industry, all promising to deliver products and services that will help your prospect solve problems. By practicing the "Fourth R" and showing your prospect that you understand his or her industry, understand his or her business issues, and have relevant experience solving similar issues for similar companies, you will go a long way in differentiating your company from the competition. You will go an exceptionally long way in differentiating yourself from the 99 percent of other salespeople that your prospect will meet with.

CHAPTER NINETEEN

Sales Intelligence Exercise: It's Easy!

"To discover the customer's needs and objectives requires work. But doing this work will get your customer's attention. The fastest and best way to establish credibility and trust is to invest the time needed to prepare – period. No shortcuts here. It requires hours and hours of preparation, including researching the company, its business model, its financial structure, and its issues and objectives."

– Barbara Gerahaughty, *Visionary Selling*,
New York: Simon and Schuster, 1998.

When I am giving a presentation on finding and using information to succeed in business, by the end, attendees are often overwhelmed. Besides the fact that I talk fast, the amount of information I share can make one feel like they've been hit by a tornado, with a ton of data and ideas now running through the brain at warp speed.

Relax! *Taking the Cold Out of Cold Calling* is really nothing more than common sense. Turning a cold call into a warm one is nothing more than spending a few moments finding information, organizing that information using a tool like a CRMT, and then applying that information in a way that is relevant to your prospect.

Locating credible, objective, and relevant information does not have to be difficult or time consuming. Practicing Sales Intelligence and the "Fourth R" is fun and easy!

If you use the resources highlighted in this book and at the Warm Call Center (www.warmcallcenter.com), you can literally practice the "Fourth R" in minutes. You can quickly locate information that will help warm up virtually any cold sales call. Sometimes it only takes seconds to find a nugget of data you can use to make your cold call relevant to your prospect.

In fact, I recommend no more than 10-15 minutes of research prior to making a traditional cold call. Any more and it's likely you're spending too much time researching and not enough time calling on prospects. It's only when you are invited for that first in-person meeting or asked to provide a proposal that you need to spend an hour or more thoroughly researching and understanding your prospects and their needs.

Sales Intelligence "Fourth R" Exercise

To prove my point about how easy the practicing the "Fourth R" can be, I selected a number of privately held companies of varying sizes (publicly held companies are too easy to research for this type of an exercise) and, using the techniques outlined in this book, researched each firm. Then I began to fill out the CRMT that I created on each company using the information that I found. Finally, I took the information from the CRMT and using the sample scripts, conducted a "mock warm call."

You'll notice that I chose Minnesota-based firms for my research. I'm not trying to be provincial. Rather, because I am in Minnesota I knew it would be easy to contact these companies, get permission to research them in a public forum, and avoid any potential contact with lawyers. Obviously, however, the techniques I'm using can be applied for any company in the United States and, for that matter, the world.

Now you'll have to take my word for it, but I promise that I did not spend more than fifteen minutes locating and reading information on a company, industry, and/or person. In fact I spent less than ten minutes on research for most.

So here's your mission (should you choose to accept it):

1. Think about your company and the products and services you sell.

2. Use the information I found on the following companies and, using the scripts provided in the previous chapter, construct phone, e-mail, and letter scripts that are customized and relevant to each company.

3. Finally, pick one of the companies I researched and, using the ideas from this book, spend thirty minutes to see what you can find in addition to what I dug up, and then craft a relevant first-meeting agenda with talking points.

Good luck and I hope you find this exercise valuable. After you've completed this exercise, pick a few of your actual prospects and practice the "Fourth R" on them. Then pick up the phone or fire up your e-mail and put what you've learned into action.

You too will now join the ranks of the top salespeople who understand what it means to Take the Cold Out of Cold Calling and turn any sales call into an enjoyable, warm experience. You too will start achieving your business dreams.

Exercise #1 – New Boundary Technologies

Source 1: Google Site-Colon (Site:) Search

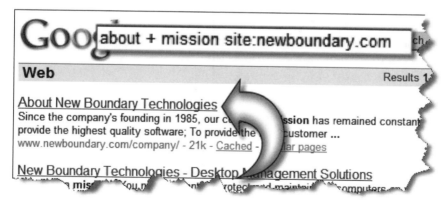

Knowledge Gained: By doing a "Site:" search using the terms "about" and "mission," we go directly to the page on New Boundary's Web site where we learn about the company and its product offerings. We learn that the company was founded in 1985, and is now a global provider of IT management and remote monitoring and control solutions. The company offers a full line of packaged software applications that serve the needs of small to mid-size businesses *and the large enterprise*, as well as custom software solutions that fulfill the unique requirements of our customers. They sell through direct sales and distribution partners in North America, Latin America, Europe, Asia, Africa, and Australia.

Source 2: Manta.com Search

New Boundary Technologies Inc

1300 Godward St Ne # 3100, Minneapolis, MN, United States

Phone: (612) 379-3805

URL: www.pearsontech.com, www.radiem.com, www.newboundary.com

Trade Style Names: Lanovation; Pearson Technical Software

SIC: Computer Programming Services

Line of business: Prepackaged Software Computer Software Developme

Year Started: 1985

State of Incorporation: N/A

URL: www.pearsontech.com, www.radiem.com, www.newboundary.com

Location type: Single Location

Stock Symbol: N/A

Stock Exchange: N/A

Trade Style Names: Lanovation; Pearson Technical Software

NAICS: Custom Computer Programming Services

Est. Annual Sales: $4,252,753

Est. Employees: 34

Est. Employees at Location: N/A

Contact Name: James Hove

Contact Title: Vice President

Knowledge Gained: Searching "New Boundary Technologies" in Manta.com showed us that the company did about $4.2 million last year, and has 34 employees. A key company contact is its vice president, James Hove.

Source 3: Public Library – Trade Journal Database

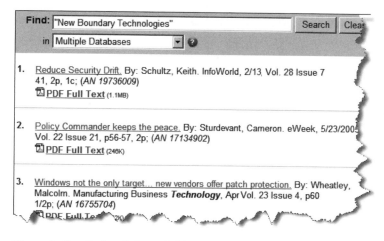

Knowledge Gained: By quickly scanning a few trade journal articles, we learn that New Boundary is one of the leaders in helping companies with multiple office locations keep security software current. New Boundary is certainly an industry leader in issues related to PC security.

Source 4: Industry Articles – FindArticles.com Search

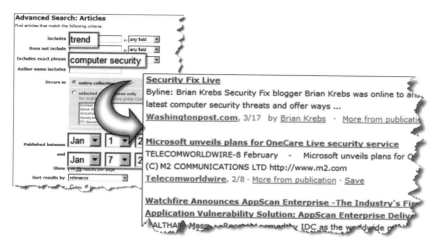

Knowledge Gained: In any meeting with the folks at New Boundary, we want to make sure that we understand the latest issues and trends related to PC security. In FindArticles.com, I used the Advanced Search feature looking for the phrase *computer security* and the word *trend* in articles that have appeared in the last year. After reading the articles, I can reference the statistics and information during my phone call and meeting with New Boundary. In particular, I might discuss the Microsoft OneCare product and what impact, if any, it has had on New Boundary's sales.

New Boundary Technologies CRMT (Client Research Management Tool)

Company Name:	New Boundary Technologies
Customer Name:	James Hove
Address:	1300 Godward Street NE, Suite 3100 Minneapolis, MN 55413
Phone:	612-379-3805
Company Web Site:	www.newboundary.com
Core Products/Services:	A global provider of IT management and remote monitoring and control solutions. Offer products for PC security.
Annual Company Revenue:	$4.2 million
Number of Employees:	34
Additional Company Information:	Founded in 1985. The company offers a full line of packaged software applications that serve the needs of small to mid-size businesses and the large enterprise, as well as custom software solutions that fulfill the unique requirements of our customers. They sell through direct sales and distribution partners in North America, Latin America, Europe, Asia, Africa, and Australia.
Top Competitors:	Microsoft
Key Business Issues:	New Boundary Technologies is certainly in a "hot market" as the need for PC security is important to virtually every company on every continent. Because they are in a virtually limitless market, there are many Fortune 100 competitors. New Boundary is probably a candidate to be purchased, and/or needs to have a niche market for its products.
Benefits and Value We Do or Could Provide Customer:	We have significant experience helping smaller technology companies compete in a global marketplace against large competitors. In particular, we help companies identify niche markets. With one firm, we increased profits by 24 percent.

New Boundary Technologies Sample Warm Phone Call

Following is a sample phone call to New Boundary Technologies. Note how I've modified the script to fit my needs and this particular prospect, just as you should use the recommended scripts as general guidelines that you modify as you like.

> *"Hi James. This is Sam Richter and I'm calling from ACME Marketing. We've never met nor were you expecting this call but I was hoping take 90 seconds to explain why I called, and then you decide if we should continue. Is that OK with you?*
>
> *I was reading Infoworld where your CEO, Kim Pearson, was quoted as saying that PC security issues are one of the greatest threats facing global businesses. I found that comment really interesting because my firm has more than 10 years of experience helping companies like New Boundary market and sell PC-related products to companies across the globe, and in particular in Europe and Asia. I also know that companies like Microsoft are coming out with security products that will embed in operating systems, and I would imagine that they could be a competitive threat to you.*
>
> *I'd like to meet with you and take forty-five minutes of your time to show you how we've helped smaller companies like you defend markets and create global vertical niches when faced with larger competitors. In fact, we have one company we've worked with and they've seen a 24% increase in profits since we've launched our campaign.*
>
> *I'll be in your area next week. Can I stop by and discuss your goals?*

Exercise #2 – Research Harvey Vogel Manufacturing

Source 1: Company Information – ThomasNet.com Search

Knowledge Gained:

With a simple company search in ThomasNet, we learn that Harvey Vogel is a metal stamping company located in Woodbury, Minnesota. They have around 300 employees (according to Thomas-Net) and do approximately $18 million in annual revenue. The company was founded in 1942 and does business around the globe.

Source 2: Global Industry – InformationExport.gov Search

Knowledge Gained: The federal government has a couple of great reports on the metal stamping industry. In particular, we learn that one of the issues most likely facing Harvey Vogel is the continued outsourcing of metal stamping production to countries like China, while simultaneously, Vogel's customers are also building manufacturing plants in Mexico and Asia.

Source 3: Google Filetype-Colon (Filetype:) Search

Knowledge Gained: In looking for PDF files using Google, we found a case study on Harvey Vogel from a company called Epicor. Epicor used its technology to help increase efficiencies at Harvey Vogel. We learn a lot by reading the report, including that Harvey Vogel actually employs 130 people (vs. the approximately 300 that ThomasNet said. Remember, when searching for information on private companies, it is important to use multiple information sources), and that Todd Caughey is Harvey Vogel's Director of Information Technology.

Source 4: People – ZoomInfo.com Search

Knowledge Gained: Conducting a ZoomInfo search on Todd

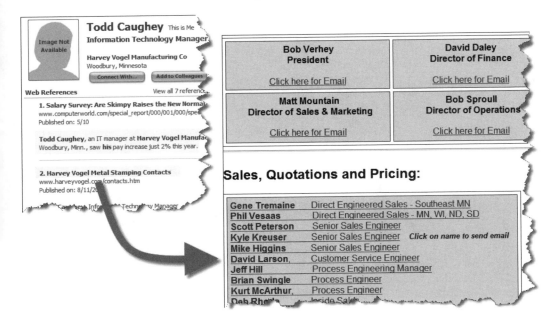

Caughey delivered some interesting results. For one, we learn that there was an IT Salary Survey article written and Todd was one of the examples used. We learn that he only received a 2 percent raise this past year, and although he really enjoys working at Harvey Vogel, he was hoping for a higher increase. The second source identified by ZoomInfo was a Company Contacts that when clicked, opened up a full page of key Harvey Vogel contacts.

Harvey Vogel Manufacturing CRMT (Client Research
Management Tool)

Company Name:	Harvey Vogel Manufacturing
Customer Name:	Todd Caughey, director of information technology Bob Verhey, president Matt Mountain, director of sales and marketing David Daley, director of finance Bob Sproull, director of operations
Address:	425 Weir Dr. Woodbury, MN 55125
Phone:	612-345-6789
Company Web Site:	www.harveyvogel.com
Core Products/ Services:	Metal stamping company
Annual Company Revenue:	Approximately $18 million
Number of Employees:	130
Additional Company Information:	Harvey Vogel was founded in 1942. They export products to Asia, Europe, Canada, and Mexico. They are ISO 9001:2000 certified, thus quality manufacturing is something that is important. They recently underwent software/technology upgrades implementing the Vantage system by Epicor, which increased manufacturing efficiencies.
Customer Personal Information:	Todd Caughey's salary increased 2 percent last year. He is happy at Harvey Vogel, but was hoping for a larger increase.
Key Business Issues:	There is continued outsourcing of metal stamping production to countries like China. Harvey Vogel's customers are also building manufacturing plants in Mexico and Asia.
Benefits and Value We Do or Could Provide Customer:	We're one of the top marketing firms in the region when it comes to working with manufacturing firms. We enjoy working with companies focused on quality and have experience helping firms differentiate their U.S. manufacturing capabilities. Our work consistently helps firms increase bottom line profit.

Harvey Vogel Manufacturing Sample Warm E-mail

Following is a sample e-mail to Harvey Vogel Manufacturing.
Note how I've modified the script to fit my needs and this
particular prospect, just as you should use the recommended
scripts as general guidelines that you modify as you like. Also
note that I reference a personal communication I had with
Todd, as it's important that you only e-mail prospects when

you have "permission," such as having met them at a trade show or networking event.

SUBJECT:

Did you see the recent government report on overseas metal stamping?

E-MAIL COPY:

Dear Todd,

It was great meeting you at the Minnesota Manufacturing event last night. I was doing some research this morning, found a recent government report on overseas metal stamping firms, and immediately thought of you.

In particular, the article discusses how companies that have outsourced manufacturing overseas are seeing quality issues. Knowing your focus on quality and efficiency, I thought the report might provide you material for a marketing campaign that differentiates Harvey Vogel from the competition.

As you know, my firm is one of the best when it comes to helping manufacturing companies market unique value propositions. In particular, our work has helped drive bottom line profits.

I'll give you a call this afternoon to discuss the report and how we might be able to help you achieve your objectives.

Exercise #3 – Research Tastefully Simple

Source 1: Company Information – Dun & Bradstreet

☐ 2: Tastefully Simple Inc

D-U-N-S® Number:	88-428-8457	**Location Type:**	Single Location
Company Name:	Tastefully Simple Inc	**Subsidiary Status:**	Non Subsidiary
		Plant/Facility Size:	200,000 Sq Ft
Mail Address:	PO Box 3006	**Owns/Rents:**	Owns
	Alexandria, MN, 56308-3006	**Year Established:**	1995
County:	Douglas	**Ownership:**	Private, Woman-Owned
		Bank:	Bremmer Bank
Street Address:	1920 Turning Leaf Ln SW	**Prescreen Score:**	Low Risk
	Alexandria, MN, 56308-4505		
	View Map		
County:	Douglas		
Phone:	320-763-0695		
Fax:	320-763-2458		
Web Address:	www.tastefullysimple.com		

Employee Count: *(All Sites)*	310	**Sales:** *(All Sites)*	$6,600,000 US (Estimated/Modeled)
Employment: *(Individual Site)*	Current Year: 310 1 Yr Prior: 310 | Trend: 0.00 2 Yr Prior: 225 | Trend: 37.78	**Sales:** *(Individual Sites)*	$6,600,000 US (Estimated/Modeled)

Executives:	Ms Jill Blashack - Founder and CEO Ms Joani Nielson - Founding Partner and COO
Executive Biographies:	Ms Jill Blashack YEAR OF BIRTH: 1958 INDUSTRY EXPERIENCE: PREVIOUSLY OWNED CARE GIFTS AND GIFT BASKETS MN. DISCONTINUED FAVORABLY. OTHER BUSINESSES: NONE. Ms Joani Nielson YEAR OF BIRTH: 1967 INDUSTRY EXPERIENCE: PREVIOUSLY OWNED SALON ALEXIS, ALEXANDRIA, MN FOR 5 YEARS.
SIC Code(s):	59630000 - Direct selling establishments (Primary) 58120000 - Eating places
Line of Business:	DIRECT SALES
Product(s):	DIRECT SELLING ESTABLISHMENTS, NEC EATING PLACES

Knowledge Gained: We learn a ton about Tastefully Simple by conducting a Dun & Bradstreet search via the public library. The company is a direct food sales firm located in Alexandria, Minnesota. According to D&B, they do about $6.6 million in revenue and have 310 employees. Two years ago, they supposedly had 225 employees, so the company is growing. They are a private, women-owned firm started in 1995. They are a good credit risk, and bank with Bremer Bank. The company's founder and CEO is Jill Blashack; co-founder and COO is Joani Nielson. Jill was born in 1958 and previously owned Care with Flair Gifts and Gift Baskets. Joani was born in 1967 and previously owned Salon Alexis. We can assume that both have an entrepreneurial spirit.

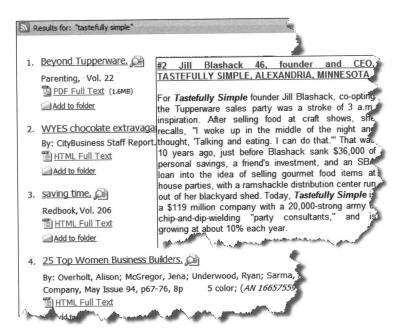

Results for: "tastefully simple"

1. Beyond Tupperware.
   Parenting, · Vol. 22
   PDF Full Text (1.6MB)
   Add to folder

2. WYES chocolate extravaga
   By: CityBusiness Staff Report.
   HTML Full Text
   Add to folder

3. saving time.
   Redbook, Vol. 206
   HTML Full Text
   Add to folder

4. 25 Top Women Business Builders.
   By: Overholt, Alison; McGregor, Jena; Underwood, Ryan; Sarma,
   Company, May Issue 94, p67-76, 8p   5 color; (AN 16657559
   HTML Full Text
   dd to

#2 Jill Blashack 46, founder and CEO, TASTEFULLY SIMPLE, ALEXANDRIA, MINNESOTA

For *Tastefully Simple* founder Jill Blashack, co-opting the Tupperware sales party was a stroke of 3 a.m. inspiration. After selling food at craft shows, she recalls, "I woke up in the middle of the night and thought, 'Talking and eating. I can do that.'" That was 10 years ago, just before Blashack sank $36,000 of personal savings, a friend's investment, and an SBA loan into the idea of selling gourmet food items at house parties, with a ramshackle distribution center run out of her blackyard shed. Today, *Tastefully Simple* is a $119 million company with a 20,000-strong army of chip-and-dip-wielding "party consultants," and is growing at about 10% each year.

Knowledge Gained: WOW! I found an incredible number of magazine articles about Tastefully Simple and after reading a few, it was easy to see why. One article talked about how the company was founded and is similar to Tupperware home parties, except Tastefully Simple sells easy-to-prepare great tasting food products. We also have a perfect example of why it's important to look at multiple sources of information, especially when it comes to private companies. D&B reported that Tastefully Simple does around $6.6 million in annual revenue with 310 independent sales consultants, when in reality, the company earned more than $119 million last year, it has more than 20,000 independent sales consultants, and is growing at about 10 percent each year!

Source 3: Blogs – Google Blog Search

Knowledge Gained: Seeing that Tastefully Simple has more than 20,000 independent sales consultants, I guessed that there had to be some Blog buzz about the company. I was right and in fact, there were more than 7,400 Blog entries related to the company. By viewing a few entries, we learn that people are passionate about Tastefully Simple. They have great tasting products and a wonderful reputation. Many of the Blogs are created by Tastefully Simple independent sales consultants who also sell the company's products via their own Web sites. In visiting the Blogs and sites, one thing that is clear is Tastefully Simple really cares about its brand and image, and the individual consultants share that passion. They obviously have a loyal fan base.

Source 4: Public Library – Trade Journal Database Search

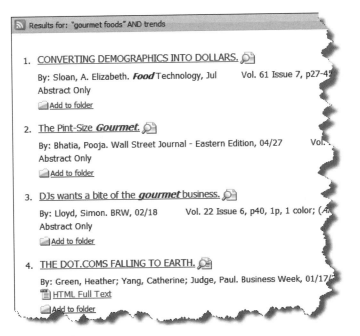

Knowledge Gained: Using a trade journal database available via my public library, I searched for trends in the gourmet food industry ("gourmet foods" AND trends). A number of very relevant articles appeared, including several discussing how it is important that in today's fast-paced world gourmet foods be easy to prepare. In particular, there was a great article about packaged gourmet foods and how more families want healthy meals that are easy to make and affordable. Tastefully Simple is certainly in the right place at the right time. Other articles discussed ethnic foods and other industry trends.

Source 5: Local News – Newslink.org Search

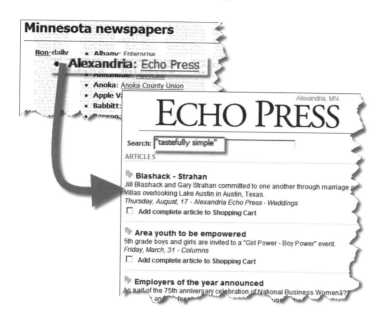

Knowledge Gained: Knowing that Alexandria, Minnesota is a smaller town, I conducted a Newslink.org search to see if any articles had been written about the company, but in particular on any company executives. A number of articles shared some great information about the firm's involvement in the local community and awards won. In addition, there was an article about the company's founder and CEO, Jill Blashack, and her recent wedding.

Company Name:	Tastefully Simple, Inc.
Customer Name:	Jill Blashack, founder and CEO Joani Nielson, co-founder and COO
Address:	1920 Turning Leaf Lane SW PO Box 3006 Alexandria, MN, 56308-3006
Phone:	320-763-0695
Company Web Site:	www.tastefullysimple.com
Core Products/ Services:	Easy to prepare, gourmet foods sold through home parties
Annual Company Revenue:	$119 million
Number of Employees:	300+ at the corporate headquarters 20,000+ independent sales representatives/consultants
Additional Company Information:	Privately held women-owned business. Founded in 1995. Good credit and banks with Bremer Bank.
Industry and Market Data and Projections:	The industry is moving towards easy-to-prepare, packaged gourmet foods. Ethnic foods are also a key trend.
Company Executive Biographies:	Blashack, born in 1958, previously owned Care with Flair Gifts and Gift Baskets. Nielson, born in 1967, previously owned Salon Alexis. Both are successful entrepreneurs.
Customer Personal Information:	Blashack recently got married.
Key Business Issues:	Tastefully Simple has consultants and customers who are passionate about the company and its products. If done thoughtfully, Tastefully Simple can leverage that passion and introduce line extensions, product up-sells, and cross-sells.
Benefits and Value We Do or Could Provide Customer:	Our firm has experience working with companies with loyal customers, and helping them leverage that loyalty to create brand advocacy leading product line extensions and growth.

Tastefully Simple Sample Warm Business Letter

Following is a sample business letter to Tastefully Simple. I've modified the script to fit my needs and this particular prospect, just as you should use the recommended scripts as general guidelines that you modify as you like. Also note how I tactfully introduced personal information into postscript.

Dear Jill,

I was doing some reading this morning and came across an article in Gourmet Retailer. The article summarized a recent survey and in particular, I thought the following was relevant to Tastefully Simple:

"Sixty-one percent of respondents predict Snack Products sales will increase, while 66% expect Confections to do so. Sauces, Salsas & Dips, as well as Cookies & Crackers are expected to increase according to 65% and 68% of respondents, respectively."

Your rapidly growing independent sales force and your customers are passionate about Tastefully Simple products. Based on the survey referenced above, I can only imagine that a marketing program that helped your consultants promote your new line of snack, sauces, and cookie products could really help improve your bottom line.

My firm has quite a bit of experience creating comprehensive marketing programs for consumer food product companies. We have also helped numerous clients implement annual marketing programs that position new products in a way that leverages the loyalty customers have for existing brands. Our introduction campaigns typically see results 25% greater than the industry average for both sales and brand recognition and I'd like to discuss with you how we might help Tastefully Simple achieve similar results.

I am hoping I can have a few minutes of your time to discuss how my firm can help you grow your business. I'll give you a call next week and look forward to speaking with you soon.

Sincerely,

Sam Richter

P.S. In doing my research on Tastefully Simple, I came across an article in the Alexandria Echo Press announcing your recent wedding. Congratulations!

Access the Warm Call Resource Center

A s a reader and I hope now a practitioner of *Take the Cold Out of Cold Calling*, I'd like to make a deal with you. I recognize that this book is filled with online information sources, many of them with Web addresses that are difficult to remember and type into a Web browser. So I'm going to provide you with the only Web address that you will really need to remember to practice what you've learned:

www.warmcallcenter.com

At the Warm Call Resource Center, you'll have access to all of the tips and tricks you've discovered in this book. You can download sample Warm Call Scripts and have easy access to the Invisible Business Web. You'll also find a slew of other resources, updated on a regular basis, to make practicing Sales Intelligence and the "Fourth R" easy.

You can register to receive the ***Warm Call Newsletter*** and each month I'll send you an e-mail with business search techniques, sales success tips, and new and/or updated Web sites. I'll also let you know when I'm in your city for a presentation, or when I'm conducting a Webinar.

PLUS, when you're on the Warm Call Center, make sure to download the Warm Call Toolbar. The Toolbar bolts onto your Web browser, giving you easy access to the best Invisible Business Web sites, plus one-click access to some of the resources shared in this book. I and thousands of others use the Warm Call Toolbar multiple times every day, and I'm confident you'll count on it as one of your most valued "Fourth R" Sales Intelligence resources.

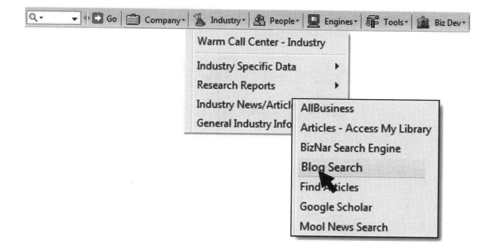

The Warm Call Center and the Warm Call Toolbar are free to you as a reader of this book. In return, I ask two favors:

1. Please let me know what you think of the book and provide me success stories about how you used *Take the Cold Out of Cold Calling* to help you make better sales calls (hey … you might be profiled in the next book).

2. Please let me know if any of the sites I've profiled have changed or if you know of others I should add.

Access the *Warm Call Resource Center* Web site at –
www.warmcallcenter.com

Again, make sure to register for the Warm Call Newsletter. As you know, the Web is constantly changing. Search engines are always coming up with new ways to search, new Web sites appear daily, and some valuable sites unfortunately disappear. We take the guesswork out of your searching and give you the tips, ideas, and tools you can use to practice Sales Intelligence, the "Fourth R" and warm call selling.

Send me a note. I want to learn how you use this book and the Warm Call Resource Center and Toolbar. Most importantly, I want to hear your warm call success stories!

E-mail: sam@sbrworldwide.com

Sales Intelligence
Quick Reference Guides

Use the following Warm Calling Sales Intelligence Quick Reference Guides for search tips and Web sites that will help you quickly find information on companies, industries, and people. Research prospects prior to sales calls, business development opportunities, and existing account meetings. Make a great first impression, boost your credibility, guarantee that your product/service offerings are relevant, and get the information you need to live the Platinum Rule.

Quick Reference Guide ~ **General Search Tips**

SAM TIP	WHAT TO DO	EXAMPLE
+ or AND	Use + or AND (most engines use +) between words in a search. Most search engines assume you mean + when entering multiple words.	**Plastics + manufacturing** delivers results where both words appear somewhere on the page, but in no order.
OR	Use OR to expand your search results. OR is good if you want to expand your search.	**Plastics OR manufacturing** delivers results in which one or both of the words appear on the Web page.
- or NOT	Use - (minus sign) or NOT (most engines use -) to remove search results. The - must be "touching" the word you want to remove.	**Plastics -manufacturing** delivers results with the word **plastics**, but removes all results with the word **manufacturing**.
"Quotation Marks"	Use "quotation marks" around a group of words if you want your results to show those words, in that exact order. Important if searching for a company or a name.	**"Plastics manufacturing"** delivers results with only the exact phrase "plastics manufacturing," in that exact order.
Combo Search	Combine +, OR, -, (AND, OR, NOT) and/or quotation marks for better results.	**"Plastics manufacturing" + Minnesota OR Wisconsin -Iowa** delivers the exact phrase "plastics manufacturing" with the word **Minnesota** or the word **Wisconsin** in the results, with none of the results containing the word **Iowa**.
Word Order	Search engines read left to right, so put your most important words first. If you don't get the results you want, try switching the order.	**Plastics + manufacturing + Minnesota** will deliver results ranked differently than **Minnesota + manufacturing + plastics.**
Cached	Find Web pages that no longer appear (no more "sorry, page cannot be found" errors). When a results page does not appear, click the **"Back"** button. Find your result, and click the **"Cached"** link. A picture of what the site used to look like will appear.	Search terms are also highlighted, making finding words and phrases easy. Therefore, even if the Web site does appear but it's a long page of text, click the **"Back"** button, then the **"Cached"** link, and now the words that you're searching for will be highlighted.
Database or List Of Links search	When you're looking for a list of companies, names, or industry sources, enter **"database"** or **"list of links"** or **"membership list"** along with the rest of your search information.	**Database OR "list of links" OR "membership list" + "plastics manufacturing"** will return results, some of which feature a database of names or lists related to the plastics manufacturing industry.
Advanced or Power Search	Click on a search engine's **Advanced** or **Power Search** link or button to refine your search, producing better results. Spend a few minutes filling out the online form and you'll start to get exactly what you want in the first few result listings.	It takes about five seconds to type words into a popular search engine, but you might get millions of search results. Spend 60 seconds identifying what's important, and what's not, using the **Advanced** or **Power Search** feature, and you'll get the results you want.

Quick Reference Guide ~ **Google Search Tips**

SAM TIP	WHAT TO DO	EXAMPLE
Search Within Results	Scroll to the bottom of a Google search result page and locate **Search Within Results**. Click the link and enter a new term into the search form. Instead of searching the Web, you'll only search for that term within your original results.	**"Medical device industry"** delivers hundreds of thousands results. By adding the term "diabetes" in the Search Within Results form, the number of results declines to a few thousand.
Search a Date or Number Range	Enter the terms you're searching for, and then enter a date range **separated by two periods** (e.g., 1999..2002). Google will deliver results featuring your term(s) but only with pages that also include that date range. Works for number ranges too: e.g., $100..$300.	**"IBM network security"** **1997..2002** delivers only results featuring the phrase "IBM network security," and only from Web pages that also feature dates between 1997 and the year 2002.
Google Amnesia Assistance – let Google fill in the blanks	If you can't remember part of your search, use an **asterisk*** and Google will fill in the blanks. Great for name searches, job titles, even e-mail addresses (e.g. "*@acme.com").	**"Anderson * * Associates"** delivers results with the first word being Anderson, the last word being Associates, and Google will fill in two words in the middle (because there are two asterisks).
Search a Specific Site	Use **Site:** and limit your search to a specific site. Great for quickly finding information on a specific company.	**"Marketing manager" site:generalmills. com** will search for the phrase "marketing manager" but it will limit its search to only the General Mills Web site.
Search for Files	Find files that are posted online using a **Filetype:** (filetype colon) search followed by the specific file type extension. Popular extensions include **doc** (Word document), **xls** (Excel spreadsheet), **ppt** (PowerPoint document), **pdf** (Adobe PDF file). Remember that Office 2007 adds an X after each file extension, e.g. pptx.	**"Lawson software" filetype:ppt (or filetype:pptx)** will find PowerPoint documents residing in cyberspace that contain Lawson Software. Documents you might find online using different extensions could include sales presentations, annual reports, company lists, research papers, RFP responses, budgets, forecasts, membership lists, and more.
Local Business Search	Choose the **Maps** link (above the Google logo). Enter a business type or company name and search for locations. Click the Satellite tab to see images of your chosen location. Click, hold and drag the "person icon" to the map for a street level view (if available).	Enter **"advertising agency"** + **St. Paul, MN** in the search field to see a map of St. Paul showing ad agency locations. Click the link on the left side for more information about your chosen company. Or, choose a location on the map itself, click on it, and get details about that firm.

(continued)

SAM TIP	WHAT TO DO	EXAMPLE
Telephone/Address Search	Enter the name of a person and the area where he or she lives and Google will often provide the person's contact info. Type in a phone number (include the area code and dashes) for a reverse phone directory.	Enter **"Joe Smith" + Minnesota** and you'll receive a list of phone numbers and addresses for Joe Smiths who live in Minnesota. For best results, remember to use quotation marks around the name.
E-mail New Results	Go to Google Alert (**www.googlealert.com**) or Alerts from Google (**www.google.com/alerts**). Enter search terms, and Google will e-mail you when it finds new information.	For best results, set up your search alerts using Boolean logic. You choose how often you want to receive e-mails. All new sites that Google finds are sent in one e-mail versus separate e-mails for each site.
Google Advanced	Click the **Advanced Search** link directly next to the Google search button. Enter information in the various fields and make use of the different options to start getting the results you want in the first few listings. Watch carefully as Google automatically builds the complex Boolean search query. Notice how Google uses Boolean and in a short time, you'll have the concept of Boolean searching mastered.	The more information you can enter into the Google Advanced Search resource, the better and more relevant your search results will be. As you watch Google automatically build complex Boolean search queries, you'll learn how Google works and you'll start searching like a professional.
Google Options	Google lets you to sort results in numerous ways, which makes finding the information you want easier. Conduct a regular Google search and on the results page, click the "Show Options" link under the Google logo/search form. Then click on any of the options to sort your results. Click "Related Searches" for results similar to your search. Click "Wonder Wheel" for a graphical representation of your results list and related searches. And click "Timeline" for a historical timeline of events related to your search. After choosing a results sort option, you can click on additional options to further refine your Google results list.	Conduct a Google search on a company name or person's name and on the results list, click "Show Options." The various options allow you to quickly see if there are videos about the company or person, product reviews, and/or if people are talking about the company or person in online forums. Click on "Timeline" to see results related to events in the company's history. Type an industry name in Google (e.g., "plastics industry") and you will see the most recent news, what people are saying about the industry, other related industry topics, and more.
Google Search Assistant	As you type in a search, Google will automatically make suggestions. Click on any of the suggestions to find relevant results.	As you type in a search like **"automotive industry"** by the time you get to the letter "o," Google has made some highly relevant suggestions.

Quick Reference Guide ~ **Yahoo Search Tips**

SAM TIP	WHAT TO DO	EXAMPLE
Yahoo Search Assistant	At **http://search.yahoo.com**, as you type in your search, Yahoo will automatically make suggestions. Click on any of the suggestions to find relevant results. On the results page, click the inverted triangle under the search form to see additional terms and concepts related to your search.	As you type in a search like **"Lawson software"** by the time you get to the letter "f," Yahoo has made some highly relevant suggestions. On the results page, when clicking the inverted triangle under the search form, you'll find some great suggestions related to customers, financials, products, and more.
Company Friend Search – who's linking?	In Yahoo, type in **Link:** (link colon) and enter a Web site address into the main search form. On the search results page, click the **Inlinks** tab. Use the pull-down menu and select "Only From This Domain" to limit your results to only external Web sites. Choose the "Only This URL" pull-down menu to limit your results to only a specific Web page, or choose "Entire Site" to see links to an entire Web site. As an alternative to Yahoo, try the link tool at **www.altavista.com/web/webmaster.** Make sure to click the "Don't return pages within this site" check box to limit your search to external Web pages.	Vendors, customers, associations, and related sites often link to each other. A good way to learn a company's "friends" is to find other sites linking to your chosen company's Web site. A **link:www.takethecold.com** search finds more than 121 sites linking to the Take the Cold Web site. By looking at the list of results, you can find relationships with third parties. In addition, having relevant external sites linking to your Web site is one of the best ways to enhance your natural search engine ranking.
Free-To-Use Articles	Go to **http://search.yahoo.com/cc** and conduct a search using a broader industry topic. Choose either or both of the check boxes, allowing you to limit your search to articles you can modify, and/or articles you can use for commercial purposes. The results will show content you may use for your company's marketing/sales material.	Finding content online is easy. Finding content that you can use for your own commercial purposes can be a challenge. Yahoo Creative Commons lets you search for content that you can revise and use for your own marketing and sales purposes, without violating copyright law.

Quick Reference Guide ~ **Other Search Engines**

SAM TIP	WHERE TO GO, WHAT TO DO
GoogleGuy Compare Google and Yahoo search results.	**www.googleguy.de/google-yahoo** Enter a search term and compare side-by-side Google and Yahoo results. Note how one search engine typically has indexed more Web sites, and the result ranking can be dramatically different.
Mamma **Dogpile** Search multiple search engines simultaneously.	**www.mamma.com** **www.dogpile.com** A meta-search engine searches the results in multiple search engines simultaneously. A good choice if you're searching a very broad term, and you'd like to see the largest number of varied results.
MSN Industry-related topic search.	**www.msn.com** 1. Enter a broad industry search term. 2. On the results page right-hand side, look at the Related Searches links. 3. Click on a link for results related to that category.
Mool Media Search for news from numerous search engine news sources.	**www.mool.com/media** 1. Enter search terms as you would with any search engine. 2. Instead of searching billions of Web sites, Mool limits its search to about 4,500 key news sources.
Clusty Cluster your results to make locating similar sets of information easy.	**www.clusty.com** 1. Conduct a standard search; you'll see your standard results. 2. On the left side, notice how the information is organized into folders and sub-folders. 3. Enter Site: (site colon) followed by a company Web site e.g., site:www.3M.com, and Clusty will sort information from a company's Web site into easy-to-understand folders.
Cuil Increase the relevance of your search results.	**www.cuil.com** 1. Enter a broad search term. 2. On the results page, choose a main category on the top-level menu, or choose a category in the Explore By Category drop-down menu. 3. As you click on sub-categories, notice how the Explore By Category drop-down menu changes. Continue to click through various sub-categories to help you find results relevant to the information you desire.
Exalead Make searching easier with numerous search features all combined into one engine.	**www.exalead.com/search** 1. Conduct a standard search or use Exalead's Advanced Search link, located directly next to the main search button. 2. In Advanced Search, follow the prompts and narrow or expand your search. 3. Click the "preview" button on the results to see what the site looks like. 4. Narrow your search by choosing one of the links on the right side. 5. Make sure to click the More Choices button on the right side for additional narrowing options.

Quick Reference Guide ~ **Company Search**

SAM TIP	WHERE TO GO, WHAT TO DO
Manta Provides basic D&B information on virtually every U.S. public and private company.	**www.manta.com** 1. Register for free or login with your username and password. 2. Enter the company name on the main page search form. 3. Locate the company you want; click on the link to see basic D&B data.
ThomasNet Online version of the Thomas Registry key manufacturing directory.	**www.thomasnet.com** 1. Use the top navigation tabs to choose your search type. 2. Enter your search term(s). 3. Click on the categories for additional information.
Pending Patents See where a company is focusing its R&D, and what products it may introduce.	**http://patft.uspto.gov (choose Patent Applications Quick Search)** 1. Enter a company name, patent author, or product type in the Term 1 field Enter additional information (if any) in the Term 2 field. 2. Click on any of the patent applications to see if the company owns the patent or is just mentioned in it. 3. On the patent page, click the Image tab (upper navigation) and download the patent application including drawings. Note: special software required.
Google Patents A quick and easy way to locate existing patents.	**www.google.com/patents** 1. Enter the name of a company in the search box. 2. On the results page, click on any patent that appears. 3. Click Abstract, Drawing, etc. for additional information about the patent. 4. Use the Advanced Patent Search feature to search using other criteria.
Touchgraph Get an animated graphical representation of Web site relationships. Knowing these relationships can provide a snapshot of a company's customers and business partners.	**www.TouchGraph.com/TGGoogleBrowser.html** (case sensitive) 1. Or go to www.touchgraph.com; choose the "TouchGraph Google." 2. Enter a Web site address and click the "Graph It" button. 3. Sites that appear either directly or indirectly link to, or have related content to, your chosen site. 4. Click on any of the images to move the graph around. 5. Click any of the listed sites on the left side to see additional information.
Hoovers Find very good information on publicly-held and larger private companies.	**www.hoovers.com** 1. Enter a company name in the main search form. 2. After results appear, if Hoovers offers free information, you'll see it when you click on the company name; if not, you'll be asked to subscribe to see the data. 3. Click the various resource and tool links to see what free information Hoovers provides. 4. See if the company detail page offers a Competition field, with the option to click on a Competitive Landscape link; click on it to see a nice industry overview, forecast, and recent developments.

(continued)

SAM TIP	WHERE TO GO, WHAT TO DO
GuideStar Get detailed financial information on non-profit organizations.	**www.guidestar.com** 1. Enter an organization's name and a city/state into the main search form. 2. Click on a result, and then on the organization's overview page. Click the tabs for detailed data; Form 990 is the organization's tax returns. 3. You will need to register to access information.
Business Journals Located in more than 40 markets across the U.S.; archives include articles on local companies, many of them private.	**www.bizjournals.com/search** 1. Enter the company or executive name in the form. 2. Make sure to use quotation marks with multiple words. 3. To sort your results, choose the "Sort by Most Recent First" or the "Most Relevant First" link directly above the search result listings.
Newslink Local Newspaper A gateway to local media with searchable archives.	**www.newslink.org/statnews.html** 1. Choose a state. 2. Click on one of the newspaper links. 3. Once on the newspaper's site, find a Search Form or an archive link. 4. Enter a company name and see what appears.
Indeed Job Listings Indeed is a search engine that searches other job listing Web sites.	**www.indeed.com** 1. Enter the name of a company; use quotes for multi-word companies. 2. Use the Advanced Search to limit your results. 3. Look at the results to learn more about the company, if they're looking for specific expertise, if they're expanding, etc. 4. Set up an alert to receive an email every time your desired company posts.
Archive.org Way Back Machine View historical sites, or sites that no longer exist.	**www.archive.org** 1. Enter a Web address in the Way Back Machine search form. 2. On the results listing, click on a link to see what the site looked like on the corresponding date.
Blog Search for Company Information Blogs, or Web logs, are created and updated by people who are passionate about a particular topic.	**http://blogsearch.google.com** 1. Enter a company or person's name in the main search engine. 2. Use Google's Advanced Blog Search link for better searching. 3. Use the Google Alerts button (envelope icon on the left side) and when Google Blog Search finds new information, you'll receive an email.
Twitter Search Find out what people, including employees, are saying right now about a company.	**http://search.twitter.com (no www)** 1. Enter a company name, a person's name, or a general search 2. Click on a person to read their bio; see what they're saying about a topic. 3. Use the Boolean minus sign to remove results with words you don't want.
Samepoint Meta-Search A meta-search tool that finds everything from blog postings to the news to employee networks and more.	**www.samepoint.com** 1. Enter the name of a company; for multi-word names, put within quotation marks. 2. On the results page, click on the various category links so you can see all that Samepoint found.

Quick Reference Guide ~ **Industry Search**

SAM TIP	WHERE TO GO, WHAT TO DO

Association of Associations

If you're interested in an industry, locate the industry association and see what's available on its Web site, and what it might be willing send you.

www.asaecenter.org/Directories/AssociationSearch.cfm (case sensitive)

1. Go to the Web address or go to www.asaecenter.org, click "People and Groups" then choose "Directories," and then click the "Gateway to Associations" link.
2. Enter an industry name (e.g., plastics) in "Association Name Contains" search box.
3. Click on a result listing.
4. Visit the selected association's Web site.
5. Contact the association to see what kind of information they will send you. You may need to consider becoming a member of the association to access all available information.

Industry Data Gateway – Valuation Resources

Features links to information on more than 250 industries including trend reports, valuations, and more.

www.valuationresources.com/IndustryReport.htm

1. Or go to www.valuationresources.com and click on the "Industry Research" tab. Use your browser's Find function (simultaneously select the Ctrl and F keys).
2. Enter the name of the industry in the search box and click the Next button. Continue to click Next until the industry that you want appears.
3. Click the link to the Vortal page about that industry.
4. Choose any of the links on the page for information about the industry.

Encyclopedia of American Industries

A one-stop-overview-shop of just about every U.S. industry.

www.referenceforbusiness.com/industries

1. Go to the Web address, or go to www.referenceforbusiness.com, and click on the Encyclopedia for American Industries link; take note of the other links on the page as they also provide valuable business information.
2. Click on a category.
3. Click on a sub-category or SIC code.
4. Use the search engine at the top of each page to locate reports and terms within various reports.

FindArticles

Search for articles from industry publications, magazines, and newswires.

www.findarticles.com

1. Enter your search terms into the main search box.
2. Choose "Free Articles Only" to restrict your search to the free content.

Access My Library

Find articles from databases and publications that big companies pay big money to access.

www.accessmylibrary.com

1. Conduct a search using the main search engine or search individual publications.
2. Click on a search result. You'll need to register and select a local library during your first visit.
3. For the next 30 days, use the site with no restrictions.
4. Following 30 days, you'll need to pay for the articles, or enter a library card number, or just re-register.

(continued)

SAM TIP	WHERE TO GO, WHAT TO DO
Blog Search for Industry Information A Blog Search engine is a great way to find industry information, written by people who are passionate about their subjects.	**http://blogsearch.google.com** 1. Click Google's Advanced Blog Search link (next to the Search button). 2. Look for the "In Blogs" section, and then enter in an industry name in the "with these words in the Blog title" field. 3. If you wish, enter additional keyword(s) or phrase(s) in the appropriate fields. 4. Instead of searching for information from millions of Blogs, you limit your search to only Blogs specifically about your chosen industry.
MarketResearch.com and Google Great industry information can be found in a professional market research report. Unfortunately, the best reports are expensive. Using MarketResearch.com together with Google can sometimes help you identify reports and access portions of them for free.	**www.marketresearch.com** and **www.google.com** 1. Go to www.marketresearch.com 2. Enter terms into the search box using Boolean, (e.g., wireless AND "hospital industry") or use the Advanced Search feature. 3. Locate a report that you want and copy the full title. 4. Go to www.google.com. 5. Enter the full name of the title within quotation marks so the title is treated as a phrase. Consider adding "press release" or "article" to your search query to limit the number of results. 6. Locate a result that does not say "sale" or "buy" in the abstract; you may need to go to later listings. 7. Click on a result to see if it is an article referencing the report or even the report itself.
Google Filetype Search There are millions of research reports online, many of them meant for a "private" audience. You can sometimes locate these reports by using a Google filetype: (colon) search.	**www.google.com** 1. Enter an industry name followed by the word *industry*, into Google, using quotation marks (e.g., "paper industry"). 2. Add additional words that might appear in a report, such as issues, trends, etc. 3. Add filetype: and then pdf (e.g., "paper industry" + trends filetype:pdf). 4. Try other filetypes including doc (Word document), ppt (PowerPoint file) and/or even xls (Excel).
Third Wave Research Market Research Tools Free research tools that provide great information for sales calls and proposals, particularly if your clients sell directly to consumers.	**www.thirdwaveresearch.com/mrttwr** 1. Choose one of the report options. 2. In each report, follow the prompts and use the pull-down menus and geographic selection to create your report. 3. You will be asked for a username and password. 4. You can choose to register, or just click the "To Continue…" link to immediately access your report.
Publist – Industry Media Lists Find which industry journals and magazines cover your and your clients' industries.	**www.publist.com** 1. Type in a broad industry search term (e.g., plastics). 2. Free registration is required to access the list. 3. Use the Advanced Search feature if you want to get more specific and narrow your search. It is located under the search form on the main page.

(continued)

SAM TIP	WHERE TO GO, WHAT TO DO
Small Business Trends Free Industry Journals Get free publications covering dozens of industries.	**http://smallbiztrends.tradepub.com** 1. On the left side navigation, search by industry or click the "Publications by Name" link to search by title. 2. Click any publication. 3. Click the "Subscribe Free" or the "Request Now" button, and fill out the form to receive your free journal.
Government Research Reports – Foreign Industries The government produces tens of thousands of research reports each year, many of them dealing with selling and/or buying goods from other countries.	**www.export.gov** 1. Click on the Market Research link on the left side navigation, and then the Market Research Library link. 2. You may need to register to access the Research Library. 3. Limit your search by choosing a variable from the pull-down menus. 4. Enter your search term(s) in the Keyword field. 5. Make sure to click the "Search the Document Body" check box. 6. Check the "Include Archived Records" check box to include older reports.
Biznar Business Meta-Search Engine Simultaneously search business Web sites, business sites on the Invisible Web, government sites, business blogs and more.	**www.biznar.com** 1. Use the Advance Search option. 2. Enter the name of an industry; keep your search fairly broad (e.g. enter a term like "plastics industry" instead of a detailed Boolean search). 3. Choose a date range to limit your results to a specific time period. 4. Wait a few seconds while Biznar searches its various sources. 5. Notice the star ratings underneath the results, telling you how relevant the result is to your search query. 6. Review the categories on the left side and sort results by topic, sources, author, date, and more. 7. Click the box in front of any result and save it for later access, which you can do by clicking on the "My Selections" link.
BLS Compensation Survey Salary Calculator Knowing someone's approximate salary is helpful if you're selling to them, or need to figure out a company's cost structure.	**http://data.bls.gov/PDQ/outside.jsp?survey=nc** (case sensitive) 1. You will need Java installed on your computer. You can download it at www.java.com. 2. Step 1: Select geography. 3. Step 2: Select an occupation. If it's not listed, find one that is "close enough." 4. Step 3: Select a work level, or approximate experience level, using the pull-down menu. Choose multiple levels by selecting a level, clicking on the "Add to Selection" button and then going back and choosing another level. 5. Step 4: When you've loaded your levels, click the "Get Data" button and view your results. 6. Increase by 2 to 3 percent per year from the listed year and multiply the hourly rate by 2,080 to get an annual figure.

Quick Reference Guide ~ **People Search**

SAM TIP	**WHERE TO GO, WHAT TO DO**
411.com Just like the phone information system, 411.com helps you locate phone numbers and addresses.	**www.411.com** 1. Enter a person's name and choose a geographic location. 2. Conduct reverse phone directory and reverse address searches. 3. The more information you know and enter, the greater the likelihood of success. If you get no results, try a last name only as sometimes first names are listed using initials.
ZabaSearch Locate contact information, including birthdates and even unlisted phone numbers.	**www.zabasearch.com** 1. Enter a person's name into the search form; do NOT use quotation marks. 2. Choose a state. 3. If you receive too many results, use Advanced Search. 4. Click the Map It tab for a Google Map of the person's address. 5. Click the ZabaSearch/Google link to see Google results for the person. 6. Use ZabaAlerts to receive an email anytime the site finds new or updated information.
Newslink See if your prospect has appeared in the local newspaper (e.g., wedding announcement, charitable donation, etc.).	**www.newslink.org/statnews.html** 1. Choose a state. 2. Click on one of the newspaper links. 3. Once on the newspaper's site, find a Search Form or an archive link; it's usually on the top or left-side navigation. 4. You may need to click the Advanced Search link to get older articles. 5. Enter the person's name and see what appears.
CensusScope An easy way to find census data. You can instantly produce graphs that can be copy/pasted into documents.	**www.censusscope.org** 1. Choose one of the four report tabs on the top navigation. 2. Choose a report from the left side navigation. 3. Using the pull-down menus on the lower-left side navigation, limit your report to a specific geographic area. 4. Right mouse click, Copy, and Paste graphs into your document. 5. Scroll down and locate the data. Left mouse click and highlight the data. Right mouse click and Copy. 6. Open an Excel spreadsheet and select one region. Right mouse click and choose Paste to input the data into your spreadsheet.
Claritas Psychographic Reports Psychographic data are attitude, lifestyle, and behavior information about people in a particular area.	**www.claritas.com/MyBestSegments/Default.jsp** (case sensitive) 1. On the site, click the "Zip Code Look-Up" tab on the main navigation. 2. Enter a zip code. 3. Enter the provided security code. Click the Submit button. 4. Click any of the links to learn about the people who live in your selected zip code.

(continued)

SAM TIP	WHERE TO GO, WHAT TO DO

Tweepz

Find people who use Twitter to share what's going on inside their companies.

www.tweepz.com

1. Enter "bio:" (bio colon) and the company name. There is no space after the colon. If it's a multi-word company, put between parentheses e.g., "bio:(Best Buy)".
2. To find other terms within a person's Twitter biography, enter "bio:" and then the term e.g., "bio:marketing".
3. To search a specific geographic area, enter "loc:" and then the area e.g., "loc:minneapolis".
4. Click Tweepz's Advanced Search link for additional search tips.
5. On the results page, if you find someone of interest, click the person's Twitter name to learn more.
6. Sign up for a Twitter account if you don't have one, and then follow the person. You will receive instant updates on your Twitter account every time the person posts a new "Tweet."
7. Use a service like Tweetdeck (**www.tweetdeck.com**) to organize "Tweets" you receive.
8. Consider setting up a Twitter account just for Sales Intelligence and use it to follow prospects, clients, and your competition.

Spoke

Find employee lists and executives.

www.spoke.com

1. Click the Join link in the upper right corner; become a member (it's free), then log in.
2. On the search form, choose "Find: a company" or, click the Advanced Search link.
3. Enter the company name (and other variables if using Advanced) and click on a company in the result list.
4. Your result list will include up to five executives and up to five employees.

ZoomInfo

Imagine a search engine that scours the Web but only looks for pages that contain information about people.

www.zoominfo.com

1. Click the People tab.
2. Choose the "Person Name" tab.
3. Enter the first and last name of the person you're interested in finding.
4. Click Search and find the result. Click on the name of the result to learn more about that person.
5. If the name is a common name (e.g., Pat Smith), use Advanced Search when on the People section.
6. Enter the company name, or a portion of the company name, where the person works.
7. The last field on the Advanced People search form is the name field; enter the person's name.

(continued)

SAM TIP	WHERE TO GO, WHAT TO DO
LinkedIn Networking Build a virtual network of contacts, build your credibility, and help facilitate introductions. Search for detailed information on prospects.	**www.linkedin.com** 1. Register to become a member and complete your profile. 2. Start inviting people to join your network. 3. Enter a company name in the search box to see if someone in your network knows a person at the company. 4. If there is a LinkedIn relationship, request an introduction. 5. Complete the introduction forms and your request will be sent to your contact who can then forward and make the introduction. 6. Don't forget to make recommendations; people usually reciprocate and thus you can use LinkedIn to build your credibility.
OpenSecrets Political Contributions A gateway to U.S. political contributions by individuals and companies.	**www.opensecrets.org/indivs** 1. On the top navigation, choose the "Who Gives" tab. 2. Enter the name of the company or an individual then choose a location. 3. Choose the years you'd like to search by clicking on the corresponding check boxes, or choose Search All Cycles. 4. Enter the given security key.
Golf Handicap Golfers are passionate about their game. If your prospects play golf, you can find their handicaps at the USGA's Handicap Network.	**www.ghin.com** 1. Click the "Handicap Lookup" tab on the upper navigation. 2. Choose the "Lookup by Name and State" section under the Handicap Lookup header. 3. Enter the person's name and state to look for handicap information. 4. Click the name for handicap history.
Pipl Meta-Search Pipl is a meta-search engine for people information, and it's very comprehensive as it searches the "Deep" or "Invisible Web."	**www.pipl.com** 1. Search by name, email address, username, or phone number. 2. For names, enter the person's name and state; click "search." 3. If the person you're interested in has a common name, make sure to view other people-search sources first so you have a good understanding of the person, (e.g., what he or she does for a living). 4. Results will include Web pages, social networks, documents, public records, news stories, blog entries, images, and more.
Zillow Real Estate Values Locate the value of a personal residence, annual taxes, and more.	**www.zillow.com** 1. Enter an address plus a city, state, or zip. If you need to locate an address, try www.411.com or www.zabasearch.com. 2. On the address result page, click the address link to find price information and in some markets, a "birds-eye" view of the home and area. 3. Scroll down to locate detailed information about the home, including sales data. 4. Enter the security ID code and get property tax information.

Quick Reference Guide ~ **Premium Information Sources**

SAM TIP	WHERE TO GO
Dun and Bradstreet Build company lists and research companies using numerous variables.	www.dnb.com/us/dbproducts/sales_marketing
Info USA (Reference USA) Build company lists and research companies using numerous variables.	www.infousa.com
Hoovers Detailed information on public and larger private companies.	www.hoovers.com
Zoom Info Premium Service Detailed information on company executives. Search by company, title, geography, and more.	www.zoominfo.com
Lexis Nexis Research companies and industries using news and industry journals.	www.lexisnexis.com/busdev/
Dialog Research companies and industries using news and industry journals.	www.dialog.com/products/openaccess
Business and Company Resource Center Research companies and industries using news and industry journals.	www.gale.com/BusinessRC
Factiva Research companies, industries, and people using various search tools.	www.factiva.com/segment/sales.asp
Standard & Poor's NetAdvantage Research companies and receive industry overviews and forecasts.	www.netadvantage.standardandpoor.com